THE
INFORMATION
EDGE

The Institute of Management (IM) is at the forefront of management development and best management practice. The Institute embraces all levels of management from students to chief executives. It provides a unique portfolio of services for all managers, enabling them to develop skills and achieve management excellence.

If you would like to hear more about the benefits of membership, please write to Department P, Institute of Management, Cottingham Road, Corby NN17 1TT.

This series is commissioned by the Institute of Management Foundation.

THE
INFORMATION
EDGE

Successful Management Using Information Technology

MARTIN WILSON

the Institute
of Management
FOUNDATION

PITMAN
PUBLISHING

London · Hong Kong · Johannesburg
Melbourne · Singapore · Washington DC

To my parents, Joyce and Peter,
for giving me a continuing desire to learn,
and the skills to do so.

PITMAN PUBLISHING
128 Long Acre, London WC2E 9AN
Tel: +44 (0)171 447 2000
Fax: +44 (0)171 240 5771

A Division of Pearson Professional Limited

First published in Great Britain 1997

© Pearson Professional Limited 1997

The right of Martin Wilson to be identified as author
of this work has been asserted by him in accordance
with the Copyright, Designs and Patents Act 1988.

ISBN 0 273 62584 5

British Library Cataloguing in Publication Data
A CIP catalogue record for this book can be obtained from the British Library

10 9 8 7 6 5 4 3 2 1

Typeset by Pantek Arts, Maidstone, Kent.
Printed and bound in Great Britain by Bell and Bain Ltd, Glasgow

The Publishers' policy is to use paper manufactured from sustainable forests.

ABOUT THE AUTHOR

Martin Wilson combines a passionate interest in business and management with a strong technical background in information systems and technology. Martin is an interpreter. He uses his management understanding and his technical background to build bridges between functional specialists and their senior management colleagues.

Martin now runs Solidus, a multi-disciplinary management consultancy that works with leading clients to enable change to succeed by adopting a people-led approach. Clients come from all sectors including the public, voluntary and private sectors.

Early in the technical stages of his career, Martin came to realise that few, if any, projects involving change or the application of technology failed for technical reasons. The big challenge was handling the people issues around such programmes and handling this became his new role. As a result, much of his recent work has been in bridging the understanding gap between business leaders and their technical specialists.

This book, *The Information Edge*, is part of that ongoing process. Martin will continue to write on critical aspects of management as they are still not handled well by most organisations.

ACKNOWLEDGEMENTS

Although only the author's name appears on the jacket, the fact is that the production of a book is a team effort. I acknowledge the help of all those people, including my commissioning editor, Victoria Siddle, who helped me structure the contents of this book.

I am also grateful to all those other friends, colleagues, clients and other people who gave me ideas, made comments or generally provided snippets of useful material. Due to shortage of space and the need for client confidentiality, many must remain unseen and unsung, but I acknowledge their contribution; without them this book would never have been written. In particular I would like to thank Barrington Hill of American Express, Keiron Snow of North Nottinghamshire Training and Enterprise Council, and Tim Stretton, a friend and colleague, for their time and comments.

All that said, I have to take the responsibility for the material in this book. I have taken their comments, combined them and used them as I felt appropriate to illustrate the ideas. I have had a lot of help, but if this book has errors, they are all mine.

Finally, I have to thank my wife, Alison, and my children, David and Alexandra, for tolerating my absence as I struggled to get the words on to paper. Alexandra in particular has been especially interested, and it is her enthusiasm that has encouraged me when the going has been difficult.

Nottingham
February, 1997

CONTENTS

THE SEVEN LEVELS OF INFORMATION MANAGEMENT

Level 1: **Compliance –**
what are the basic recording requirements of the organisation?

Level 2: **Operational management support –**
presenting data in a way that can be used to assist the
management of the day-to-day operations of the organisation.

Level 3: **Added customer value and personal productivity –**
using information to add value to products, services or client
relationships.

Level 4: **Competitive advantage –**
achieving competitive advantage and sustaining it.

Level 5: **Strategic insight –**
producing a vision and change of thinking.

Level 6: **Transformation –**
a fundamental revision of the business, its organisation,
partnerships, products and even markets.

Level 7: **The Knowledge Net –**
the challenge for the new Millennium.

FOREWORD

The Institute of Management's study *Management Development to the Millennium* confirmed that the demands on managers today are very different from those of ten, or even five, years ago. The demands of the new century will be even more different.

However managers should welcome the pressures that today's dynamic marketplace puts upon them – managing change to achieve something better is a principal, probably on-going task of management.

As the management world has become very much more complicated, a key skill is to be prepared for, and wherever possible predict, the changes that will occur in future. New technology, changing markets and changing organisational cultures are all crucially important influences on managers' behaviour and activities.

Technology is the key to combining the advantages of a very large organisation with the advantages of a very small one, while the competitive nature of the national and global marketplace means that total quality is becoming the minimum standard required to compete. Cultural changes however can never be forced. In a learning organisation there has to be a shift from dominant attention to short-term success towards creating a context that stimulates managers to experiment with opportunities in favour of long-term growth. Organisations must be dynamic – they have to change, both out of necessity and by choice. The manager's job of today therefore focuses more on action and less on analysis, with more emphasis on intervention than on planning. These changes are happening in almost all organisations, both large and small, in both the private and public sectors. So whether you work for a giant multinational or a small local company, it is likely that you will have to change your way of working to keep up with the shifts in your market and benefit from the new opportunities of the new century.

I therefore unreservedly commend *The Millennium Manager* series both for its forward-looking approach and for continuing the debate around the direction of management and management development for UK plc.

Roger Young
Director General, Institute of Management

THE
MILLENNIUM
MANAGER

PRIORITY SKILLS FOR THE MANAGER OF 2001

In July 1995, the Institute of Mangement published a report, *Management Development to the Millennium*, based on interviews with opinion formers at the most senior managerial level of industry and commerce – all who had high expectation of their managers in their ability to lead and grow their organisations.

Managers are expected to have the ability to operate across a broad range of skills and competencies. The *Management Development to the Millennium* report identified those skills and competencies that senior managers felt were essential for management and organisational success into the new millennium.

The following table from the report shows a list of the priority skills selected by respondents. Three-quarters of the managers surveyed indicated a clear focus on the 'harder' skills of strategic thinking and change management. Nevertheless, over four in ten endorsed the importance of facilitating others to contribute, in other words a classic 'softer' skill.

Skills for the manager in the next millennium

Base: 1,241 respondents	%
Strategic thinking, eg longer term, broader perspective, anticpating	78
Responding to and managing change	75
An orientation towards total quality/customer satisfaction	67
Financial management, eg role and impact of key financial indicators	46
Facilitating others to contribute	44
✓ Understanding the role of information and IT	42
Verbal communication, eg coherent, persuasive	38
Organisational sensitivity, eg cross-functional understanding	37
Risk assessment in decision-making	35

This book addresses the indicated skill – *understanding the role of information and IT*. Other books in the **Pitman/IM Millennium Manager** series concentrate on some of the other skills listed above.

INTRODUCTION

All managers need to manage information. Yet few seem comfortable doing so.

● ● ●

It is clear that the 21st century worker will need to be adaptable and knowledgeable, rather than merely task-trained. . . Valuable transferable skills could include improved computer literacy, proficiency in at least one other language and communication techniques.

James Watson, Institute of Management, *Management Development to the Millennium*

● ● ●

All managers need to manage information. Yet few seem comfortable doing so. Many see information management as the responsibility of others, and frequently those others are the technicians in the computer department. I hope this book will make managers realise two things.

First that information management should be one of their key competences to support their decision-making. Secondly, and perhaps most importantly, that information management is not a specialist, technical skill that should be left to technicians. They should understand that it is primarily about the business, not technology. They can and should take responsibility for the information they use, and should ensure that appropriate technology is used to give them, as managers, what they need to do their job. They do not need to become information technologists, but they do need to be able to state their information requirements clearly and accurately.

This book sets out to develop the information management skills of the active reader. With the support of other reference material, it will equip such readers with the skills to define how best to use information to assist them in their own work. It will also allow them to 'buy' appropriate technology to support those clearly defined information needs from technicians. *The Information Edge* does not seek to turn managers into technicians; that is neither desirable nor possible in the space and time available.

The need for this book is highlighted in the Institute of Management's report, *Management Development to the Millennium*, chaired by Professor Tom Cannon and Geoffrey Taylor. During their research, 42 per cent of respondents to a survey felt that information management and the understanding of information technology (IT) was, and would continue to be, one of a manager's most important skills. This made information the sixth most important skill for a manager as we go into the new Millennium; just behind financial management which was third with 46 per cent.

By a clear margin, strategic thinking and coping with change were first and second with over 70 per cent. As *The Information Edge* will show information management and the use of appropriate technology are inextricably linked with these and most other aspects of management. In the 21st century managers and many of their staff will need to be competent in the management and use of information, both quantitative and qualitative. Their organisations will be relying on and using information as never before.

TARGET READERS

This book is intended to be an accessible introduction for readers with any level of general management responsibility. It does not assume that the reader has any information management or information technology knowledge. It will be appropriate reading for:

- directors and senior managers;
- middle managers;
- all those who are just starting out with management responsibility or aspire to a management role.

Furthermore it should be valuable reading for information technologists and other specialists who appreciate that they need to understand the business implications of their work. This book will help them understand the business requirements for information management, and thereby help them to work with general managers. The most successful managers of technical disciplines, including information technology, need to genuinely understand the business role of their work. To be successful, they need to be able explain the technical possibilities in the language of business, and avoid the jargon of their specialist fields. This book should help them.

This book is intended to be an accessible introduction for readers with any level of general management responsibility.

Finally, there is one other group who will benefit from reading this book. Business studies and information technology students will, from an early point in their careers, need to take responsibility for information management and to make decisions on the best knowledge available to them. They, too, need to understand the business framework for making the most of information.

OBJECTIVES

The objectives the book seeks to address are to enable the reader to:

1 understand the role information plays in modern management;
2 appreciate the importance of effective strategic and business planning processes to produce practical information management;
3 identify the information needs of their organisation or department;
4 have a feel for how appropriate technology can support their information management strategy;
5 procure suitable technology support from third parties either within their own organisation or from external suppliers;
6 manage the implementation of their information strategy and its supporting systems.

STRUCTURE

The book as a whole guides the reader from an initial explanation of information management and its place in an organisation's planning processes and management systems through the steps that are needed to determine the information needs of a department or the organisation as a whole. It will stress the need for such requirements to be determined within the context of the corporate strategy and the objectives in the business plan. Once the needs are defined, the alternative strategies need to be assessed and costed. Guidance is then given on carrying out a cost-benefit analysis or investment appraisal to ensure that the costs are justified. Then the reader is shown how that work should produce both clear and measurable benefits as well as a suitably detailed specification.

Once the needs are defined, the book explains the procurement process and gives guidance on how to deal with specialist technical suppliers.

Finally *The Information Edge* takes the reader through the implementation process. This will cover both the implementation of the technology and preparing staff for the new systems.

Except for the last four, each chapter has broadly the same structure. After the Summary, the last three chapters are intended to provide ideas to encourage readers to find creative solutions to their own business needs.

Introduction

This will give an outline of the topics to be covered and how they should be approached.

Objectives

All good managers set out the objectives for any series of actions, and this book is the same. The objectives will state what the chapter is intended to achieve, and what the reader should get from working through the chapter.

Questionnaire

As a starting point, most chapters will start with a self-assessment questionnaire. This is intended to give the reader a feel for their existing understanding of the matters to be covered in the chapter.

The reader should answer the questionnaire again to test understanding once he or she has worked through the background and practical implementation of the theory.

Background

This section is the substance of the chapter. It will cover the background theory of some aspects of information management and its practical application. It will be supported with real case studies, tips and personal views from practising managers.

Analysis of questionnaire

The questionnaire will be explained in terms of the background in the previous section, helping the reader to reinforce what he or she has learnt.

Action list

This section will be of particular value to readers who are using this book to support their running of an information-planning project. It will set out the steps with reference to the background that should be undertaken in a real project.

This, then, is the practical application of the background theory, and even for experienced managers it should provide a valuable reminder of the tasks that need to be undertaken.

Further reading

Information is an enormous subject, and thinking is always changing. This book cannot hope to cover it all in detail. The *Further reading* section will be carefully chosen to enhance the work already covered in the chapter, and readers should seek to extend their understanding by reading at least some of this recommended material.

Checklist

All books with a practical intent need checklists as memory joggers. We all use them when we are starting out on a new project, even if it is similar to one previously undertaken. This then will include the key points that need to be remembered.

Summary

Finally, the chapter will summarise the objectives and how they have been achieved. It will also provide a summary of the key points and some suggestions for the way forward.

HOW TO USE THIS BOOK

It is intended that this book will work in two ways. First, it should be a structured approach to the issues and challenges of information management. This can be worked through as a self-paced study programme, by the end of which the manager should be able to undertake their first information project from start to finish.

Secondly, this book should be treated as a resource whenever the manager is running an information project. The checklists, sample documents and so on can be used to refresh readers' understanding as they reach each stage in their own work. Or they can be used as the starting point for preparing project plans or other documentation such as Invitations to Tender. Each manager should tailor the examples to meet their own need, but they should form a useful starting point – they cannot be definitive, as each project is always unique in some way.

WHAT IS INFORMATION MANAGEMENT?

We will explore how information management has been handled in the past and what we are doing now.

INTRODUCTION

Information management predates the computer. It is not a product of the so-called information age, although technology has accelerated its development and produced new capabilities; and new challenges. Information management is a necessary function of social, industrial and commercial enterprise.

We will explore how information management has been handled in the past and what we are doing now. We will introduce a framework to allow us to try and look forward, not far because the future is unpredictable, to the changes that are actually taking place. We will try and understand how such developments will alter the way we use information and share knowledge in the new Millennium.

The objectives of this chapter are to:

1 give an insight into what information management is all about;

2 make clear where information management fits into an organisation's strategy;

3 enable the reader to understand how information use develops within an organisation;

4 show where information and knowledge management can take an organisation which is serious about exploiting the possibilities;

5 suggest some possibilities for where effective use of corporate information and knowledge might take an organisation in the future.

QUESTIONNAIRE 1

What is information management?

1 Information management requires a strong technical background especially with computers?
   a Yes
   b No

2 Is information incidental to business strategy?
   a Yes
   b No

3 Are data, information and knowledge the same thing?
   a No
   b Yes

4 All management information is numeric.
   a Yes?
   b No?

5 All management information originates within the organisation.
   a No?
   b Yes?

6 Is information management the responsibility of the IT or Computer department?
   a Yes
   b No

HISTORY

As the human race organised into larger communities and started working collaboratively, so the need to use and share information became essential. The great empires were masterpieces of communication and administration – and they had no computers, radio, telephone or even motor vehicles. They had to rely on runners and riders on horseback to stay in touch with their outposts. Genghis Khan built the largest-ever empire, and it was run centrally from his capital in Mongolia. Despite not having modern communications, he could still get messages to and from the far reaches of Europe and the Pacific coast in days. His bureaucrats in Mongolia were thereby able to manage a vast enterprise.

Even the British Empire, on which the sun never set, had to rely on such apparently crude communications. The telephone and radio were not in common use until well into the current century, especially over the great distances to India and Australia. It is only since the advent of satellite communications in the 1970s that mass communication around the world has become possible, and indeed economically viable.

So new possibilities are opened up by new technology, but information management has always existed. It has constantly been refined to make use of new opportunities created usually, but not always, by technological development. There have been other important developments such as written language, number systems, systems of weights and measures, printing; all of which have contributed to the sharing of knowledge which is at the heart of information management.

At the end of the 20th century we are in a period of rapid technological, social and economic change. These all have a major impact on how information is used – both at work and at home. The information systems that are used at home are changing. Only ten years ago, most people who needed information for educational or leisure purpose used words printed on paper. Now the words are increasingly likely to come through a computer, either from a CD-ROM or from some form of on-line network such as the Internet or CompuServe. Ten years ago, only a few, often in academic institutions, had ready access to an on-line community. At the same time, a few business users might have been experimenting with electronic mail, and using expensive databases for literature and other information search purposes.

BACKGROUND

● ● ●

'When I use a word,' Humpty Dumpty said in a rather scornful tone, *'it means just what I choose it to mean, – neither more nor less.'*
Lewis Carroll, *Through the Looking Glass*

● ● ●

Information or knowledge management is rather like that. As a concept it has been hijacked, as so often happens with any ideas at all related to the computer industry. It then means whatever a supplier wants it to mean. There does not appear to be a single definition of information management, so we need a definition that we can use for the purposes of this book. Indeed, I would like to clarify what I mean by information management, information systems and information technology.

Information management

The idea of information management as a management concept appears to be relatively new. Even James Martin and Adrian Norman in their 1970s classic book *The Computerized Society* do not talk about information. Most other books until the 1990s focused on data-processing and information technology with lip-service paid to the management of these functions. Little recognition was given by most managers to the cost, or the value, of the data held in corporate systems.

Data

Data is the raw material of information. It is expensive to collect, maintain and store, yet it is of little intrinsic value. Its value comes when it is processed into information. Hence it tends to be a seriously undervalued corporate resource which tends to be only used properly for compliance purposes.

Bear in mind why data is collected:

● compliance – accounts, health and safety records, payroll etc;
● operational purposes – production activity, sales orders etc;
● management control;
● 'might be useful';
● commentary.

Consider then these reasons and the value of the data provided. Compliance has to be undertaken, and should be performed as effectively and efficiently as possible. Operational data needs to be collected to ensure that the organisation is doing what it should; even so, in many organisations it is collected inefficiently, and even poorer use is made of it. Management and control data collection is an extension of operational data collection to be used to support decisions, or more often, to know who or what to blame for mistakes!

Data is the raw material of information

So many organisations collect data because it 'might be useful' or because they think they ought. From my experience in many organisations, large and small, public and private sector, very little of value is done with such data. It is usually not collected efficiently or processed effectively. It just disappears into a black hole never to reappear. Consequently, the people responsible for its provision lose faith and become careless with the accuracy of the data they provide; it then becomes unusable for analysis, so nobody bothers. But it is still collected, and memorandums fly around between managers when it is not produced on time.

Finally, much data is collected simply to record what happened the month before last. All I ask at this stage is: why?

That covers most data collection for most organisations. Yet there is an enormous amount of other information, both within the organisation and outside it. Everybody who works for a business has knowledge that would be of value to colleagues if only they could get at it. They have knowledge about how the organisation works, its processes, its technology, its customer and its suppliers. Similarly, there is vast amount of data outside the organisation that would be of value if it could be collected, processed and presented as information or even better made part of the corporate knowledge. To expose just the tip of the iceberg, what shared use does your organisation make of:

- market intelligence: who is buying what and why, market trends, who is moving from customer A to customer B, who is buying whom?
- technology: trends, new developments, future thinking, technology substitution. The technology round your product and to support its production, distribution, administration, etc.?
- management thinking: on human resources, information management, benchmarking, TQM, etc.?
- economic: economic trends, export opportunities, rising competition etc.?

- political: forthcoming elections in prime markets, proposed legislation etc.?
- public opinion: on the environment, your products and those of your competitors and suppliers?
- staff: morale, opinions and ideas, etc.?

That is only a taste; the scope of the available data is enormous. It also highlights the fact that there are two types of data. Most people are comfortable with the idea of quantitative data – the numbers if you will. They are simply counts or measurements, and are readily handled both by people and computers. They are readily recognised as 'facts'. However most of the knowledge of an organisation originates with qualitative data – this is much more subjective or at least textual in form. Some of it can be recognised as facts: a key customer has broken his leg or she has been promoted. But much is opinion or an impression – perhaps a customer 'seems' to be unhappy about our service. This is extremely valuable information, but it is not easily handled on a corporate basis. We all handle it happily on a personal basis, or even jointly in informal ways.

The first problem is how to collect it, the second is how to process it into information. Finally, how is it turned into knowledge by the organisation? That has to be the challenge.

CASE STUDY

Pilkington Glass

Pilkington Glass had a potential problem. It was developing, and becoming more automated. The people with traditional experience of glass-making and processing were leaving the company through retirement and other reasons. Pilkington saw it was going to lose that knowledge built up over decades and expertise, because the new people who were coming through no longer used the traditional methods. It was not known when that knowledge might be needed but it was important background, and possibly a source of new ideas.

So the company methodically set about collecting, collating and storing that knowledge – it was more than data. As a result it was able to formalise the organisation's memory.

Information

Information is data processed into a form where it can be used to support decisions or other action. That processing can take many

Information is data processed into a form where it can be used to support decisions or other action.

forms: aggregation, charting, analysis, ordering, etc. It does not have to use state of the art technology – information was produced before computers. But it does have to make use of the knowledge of people within the business, so that it is processed in an appropriate way. Only by using that expertise will the data really become usable information. The more detail there is in the processed data, the less information is passed on, because the message becomes obscured in the detail.

Consider then that the value of the information is inversely proportional to the amount of data presented in the report or analysis.

Information can vary in precision. At one extreme it can be accurate when, say, number-based; at the other end, it can be opinion, or otherwise subjective. As it tends towards the latter, it becomes much more difficult to manage and use effectively. As already indicated, a lot of business information is of this form – it is handled informally, but there is a growing need to use this information in a more formalised corporate way.

Apart from information created from data collected by the organisation, there is a considerable amount available from outside. Some of it is raw, but much has been pre-processed. Unfortunately that base of information is growing at such a pace that no individual can hope to add it to their own knowledge. Indeed 'experts' have to become increasingly specialised to stay up to date with their own field. They have to specialise either by retaining wide high-level understanding, but not going so deep into the detail, or narrowing the field, but knowing all there is to know about that restricted field.

Knowledge

Storing the corporate knowledge of the organisation is a much bigger challenge. This will include everything from the activity-based numbers, to the impressions of salesmen in the field, personal details about contacts and staff. Consider all the knowledge about the business, its history, its future direction, its technology and all the other aspects that is held in the heads of everyone involved with the organisation. One can then appreciate the challenge (and perhaps the impossibility) of recording and managing that knowledge in a way that can be shared by staff, customers, suppliers and other people in the future.

Storing the corporate knowledge of the organisation is a much bigger challenge.

• • •

The longest march starts with the first step.

Mao Tse-Tung, *Thoughts of Chairman Mao*

• • •

That has to be the vision, even if it is barely possible to begin to address the challenge. People, organisational structure and technology are not yet capable of doing so, but we have to start down the road, otherwise we will never make progress. The potential rewards for those organisations that achieve even a tiny fraction of that vision are enormous.

Information systems

Information systems are the means by which data is turned first into information and then into knowledge. It is also the means by which organisational memory is achieved and shared. All systems have an input, processing and output (see Figure 1.1): see Figure 1.2 for an illustration of what this means with regard to information (and knowledge) systems.

The processes do not have to be technology-based. In the past, businesses used counting houses to perform much of the processing now carried out by computers. Counting houses were essentially teams of clerks performing calculation, analysis and other processing on data to produce information. It relied on the ability to break down the processing to a series of small tasks that an individual could perform reliably, accurately and efficiently. This, and the labour cost, limited the amount of processing that could be achieved or justified.

Indeed the word 'computer' was originally used to mean an individual who performed calculations or computations – not a piece of equipment.

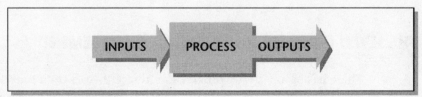

Fig 1.1 BASIC SYSTEM

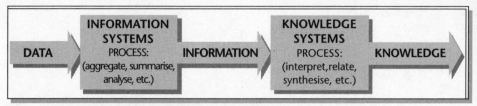

Fig 1.2 INFORMATION AND KNOWLEDGE SYSTEMS

● ● ●

*Compute (v.) 1631 . . . (1. trans.) To determine by calculation, to reckon, count . . . (2. intr.) To make computation 1634 . . . Hence **Computer**, one who computes; (spec.) one employed to make calculations, etc. **Computist**, one skilled in the computus or calendar; an accountant, a computer.*
Shorter Oxford Dictionary

● ● ●

The words 'compute' and 'computer' have effectively had their current meanings for more than 300 years. The electronic digital computer is around 50 years old and has been in widespread business use since the 1970s. Electronic computing has boomed since the 1980s with the arrival of the personal computer. Unfortunately, the effectiveness of information management has not followed that investment. Many organisations are repeating the mistakes that were being made 20 years or more ago.

Information technology

Information management and information systems do not rely on technology. Technology allows more to be done, but it is only a tool. Indeed it is not even the most important or powerful tool – that falls to the human mind and its ability to be creative. People who innovate effectively will achieve far more than those who simply throw money and technology at the problem. Technology is only as good as the thinking and people behind it.

THE SEVEN LEVELS OF INFORMATION MANAGEMENT

There has been a steady progression in recent years from traditional data-processing into a more information-based approach. Despite all the hype, the actual management use of data, information and knowledge progresses much more slowly than the technology. New technologies, new management thinking develop faster than organisations and their management can adopt them.

I propose a framework for assessment of where an organisation is in its use of information. I describe this as the 'Seven Levels of Information Management'. Bear in mind that different parts of organisation will almost certainly be at different stages in their information management.

Level 1: Compliance

This first level encompasses the basic recording requirements of the organisation. These were the first ones to be automated with the advent of computers. Before computers there was little opportunity to do much more, as it was labour-intensive, and therefore expensive and time-consuming. Typically, these were functions such as accounting and payroll, where there was a statutory requirement for such records. Often it was simply a means of cutting the costs of compliance, and provided little benefit to the organisation beyond those reduced costs.

Surprisingly, considering this automation started in earnest in the 1960s, many organisations are still at this first age of information management. Indeed, I suspect most organisations will still have substantial parts of their operations which have never moved beyond this stage. Small and medium-sized organisations particularly tend to still be locked in this first age. This is not surprising as they do not usually have the technical expertise and the breadth of management expertise. They record what has happened, but do little with the data. This is still mainly a data-processing process – little useful information is produced.

The whole process is seen as a necessary evil – the alternative ways of complying with the regulations are perceived as even worse. But it is merely commentating on what has happened in the past.

Level 2: Operational management support

The next step is to present that commentary data in a way that can be used to assist the management of the day-to-day operations of the organisation. It still tends to be retrospective and is frequently bureaucratic. The data is still not seen as a valuable resource that should earn a return on investment just as any other capital expenditure of similar value would.

There are few organisations that have genuinely moved much beyond this stage after more than 30 years of information technology. Even fewer actually perform this level of information management very effectively. As a consequence a considerable proportion of the investment in information technology is made largely for technology's sake.

CASE STUDY

A Training and Enterprise Council

A Training and Enterprise Council (TEC) has teams of specialist advisers working with clients in most areas from training and education to specialist business support. Even with many advisers sharing the same office, they were still having occasional visits where they met colleagues leaving the same client. The problem was compounded by each adviser, and their colleagues, collecting the same information from clients several times.

This clearly gave a less than professional image which was not acceptable for a TEC which rightly prides itself on its reputation for high quality services. Furthermore there was a waste of resources in the duplicated effort. Something had to be done.

The solution, initially for the team of business advisers, was to provide a centralised client and contact management system. This gave them access to centralised diaries, and a single source of information (size, number of employees, industry, membership and client status, etc.) for all organisations in their patch, and others outside with whom they have dealings.

This system ensured that they could see who else had visited, or was about to do so, when they were booking their calls. They already had a paper-based system of visit reports held in a central file, but this was not always convenient. So when they marked a visit in the central diary as completed, they were required to enter their visit report. This meant that someone arranging a visit could see what had been discussed by the client at previous meetings with their TEC colleagues. This creates several advantages.

First, it makes the incoming adviser look better informed, and more 'on the ball'. It also enables the adviser to avoid irritating the client by going over old ground. And it stops the client from wasting advisers' time trying to get grants and other support for which they have already been turned down, by using a different adviser.

Finally, it also reduces the clerical workload on advisers and their administrative support as many of their monthly returns can be produced automatically. They no longer have to plough through their diaries to fill out forms. As the system is developed it will provide a lot more valuable information for marketing, planning and administrative purposes.

It is now being rolled out across the whole TEC in stages, and there are plans to implement a full-blown corporate information system (see Chapter 12) with the aim of taking a leap forward to Level 4 and perhaps 5 in the next two years or so.

Many organisations at this stage are investing in the latest technology because of technological push, rather than being management-led. This is a failure of management – all managers who leave the development of information-systems strategy to information technologists. Even worse is to leave the information needs of the organisation in the hands of enthusiasts for the technology. All managers need to take a grip of their own information needs if their organisations are going to progress to the next level and beyond.

Level 3: Added customer value

The next step, the third level is to use information to add value to your products, services or client relationships. At this stage the emphasis is moving away from cost reduction and improved productivity to using information to support the product offering.

Initially, it is usually an extension of the second level, but shared with customers. For example, a computer maintenance company might share its call analysis information with its clients to allow those customers to make informed choices about which equipment to buy. Similarly fleet maintenance and fuel card companies provide feedback on service history or fuel consumption. Their clients can therefore use that to identify vehicle users who are mistreating vehicles, and who require training or increased supervision.

At this level, the organisation will also have moved the operational systems into a more active support role for those dealing directly with the customer. Computerised proposal production, for instance, belongs in Level 2, until the salesperson can produce and revise it whilst with the client. For example many financial services 'advisers' use portable computers to do just this and more.

When the organisation is providing a technical product or service, then the added value often takes a different form, in that customers can be given technical support. This is a sharing of know-how, rather than activity-based numbers. Typical organisations that offer this type of added value include those selling agricultural chemicals, who provide guidance on usage and on safe handling, software companies with problem-solving help desks, or engineering plastics companies who advise which of their products are suitable for a particular customer application. There are many other examples.

This is moving away from simple number-based information and starting to use knowledge in the broadest sense.

Level 4: Competitive advantage

To some extent, all use of information is about giving competitive advantage (or should be), but Level 4 is about achieving a leap in advantage and then sustaining it, rather than refining existing competitive strategies through the use of information.

Michael Porter author of *Competitive Strategy* identified three key aspects of competitive advantage: cost reduction, differentiation and focus. We will explore these in more detail in Chapter 4. Basically they are about being the lowest-cost supplier in your industries, having products with special attributes, or being a niche player rather than attempting to have wide coverage of either (or both) products or industries. In the last case of a focus strategy, you need then within your narrower scope to adopt either a cost reduction or a differentiation strategy.

So to be at Level 4, a business needs to have used information and information management to gain or support a significant advantage over its competitors.

CASE STUDY

Direct Line Insurance

Direct Line Insurance revolutionised motor vehicle insurance by providing a direct quote over the telephone, cutting out the middleman – the broker. This allowed it to become a cost leader in the field, and it rapidly stole market share from other traditional insurers.

The new strategy could not work without the efficiency of good informations systems. These were needed to handle transactions efficiently, and to provide market intelligence to allow them to identify and manage the risk.

Level 5: Strategic insight

The next step is for information to support a strategic insight and new form for the organisation.

At this stage, the organisation's approach moves on from a position of relatively simplistic and incremental improvements to its competitive position. Instead it has new, big ideas which, once they are worked through, will produce a vision that is completely different. It may well require new information systems to support that change of thinking and move it on to the next stage.

A simple and straightforward example is the case study below. But it is not the only form that the insight can take.

CASE STUDY

CCN Group

In the 1970s, the IT department of Midland Household Stores (MHS – part of the Great Universal Stores group) developed a major credit-referencing system with the aim of improving the bad debt performance of the credit business in its furniture stores. It was very successful, and the service was taken up more widely by other businesses within the group – perhaps most notably the mail-order catalogue businesses (Great Universal, Kays, etc.).

As it became involved more closely with more of the group, businesses, MHS developed expertise in direct mail, management of credit agreements, and later store credit cards and other areas, using much of the same core data and knowledge.

Eventually as a business with a leading-edge expertise in this field, it began to be asked to provide its services to non-group companies. As it eventually became clear that here was a business in its own right it developed the additional expertise and systems that it needed. When it and the market were ready, CCN was born. It has since gone from strength to strength, and become a major supplier of credit-referencing services and demographic information. But it required both a strategic insight and a clear vision to succeed: many other IT departments have tried to become businesses independent of their parent, but only a small proportion have flourished.

Strategic insights can take many forms, and most will not involve making information management a separate entity. Instead the insight will change the parent organisation in a substantial way.

21

Level 6: Transformation

This is more than business process re-engineering by another name, and it requires Level 5. No organisation can go successfully from Level 4 to Level 6 without Level 5 and achieving real strategic insight. It may mean taking the organisation into completely new areas of operation. It is more than merely changing the way existing services and products are provided.

This is a fundamental revision of the business, its organisation, partnerships, products and even markets.

Level 7: The Knowledge Net

This is a largely hypothetical stage as no organisation has really gone this far. There is much discussion going on about 'virtual corporations' – businesses that do not exist or at least do not have any permanent staff. They are formed to undertake particular work, and when the work is completed the organisation ceases to exist. It is much like a project team within an organisation but on a larger scale.

Such organisations and other similar structures will develop as we move into the new Millennium, and will create opportunities and new ways of doing business. They may well use 'employees' or 'stakeholders' who may be based anywhere in the world, but sharing information and knowledge to give value to their customer – who may itself be a virtual corporation.

But the Knowledge Net could go much further and link in customers and suppliers. It may make the difference between in-house departments and external bodies all but invisible. So the picture may be of value in products or services and information flowing around, but with no real division into separate bodies.

It is doubtful whether any organisation has yet reached Level 7. Much of the technology is probably available, but the organisational and management structures lag a long way behind. Achieving Level 7 will be the challenge for the new Millennium, and it will require the development of imaginative long-term strategies. But without a clear business and information management strategy it will simply not be possible.

Where information management goes after Level 7 is anybody's guess. As few, if any, organisations have achieved the Knowledge Net, this is a challenge for future generations of managers, both general managers and information specialists, working together.

PURPOSE OF INFORMATION MANAGEMENT

So, information management is the efficient and effective exploitation of the data, information and knowledge resources available to the organisation. Information should seek to maximise the benefits from those resources in pursuit of corporate objectives.

The purpose of information management is therefore to:

1   ensure that all the data and information needed by the organisation is collected efficiently and effectively;
2   process that collected data into information useful to the organisation in meeting, or defining, its objectives;
3   support decision-making by allowing action to be taken on the basis of timely and sufficiently accurate information;
4   continually improve the quality of the information, increase the knowledge content and reduce irrelevant detail;
5   enable users to make effective use of the information and the knowledge that it represents with training and the provision of suitable tools;
6   improve access to that knowledge by the use of appropriate technology;
7   achieve better corporate memory as staff are able to share the knowledge and learn from expert colleagues, colleagues in other functions, customers, suppliers, external experts, other agencies and even from former colleagues.

The benefits that should accrue from effective information management are:

1   better decisions because they are based on a sound understanding of relevant knowledge;
2   better planning from improved understanding of customers' needs, economic environment, the organisation's operations and so on;
3   less 'fire-fighting' because potential difficulties are identified earlier and corrective action taken before they become problems;
4   provision of greater value to customers, shareholders and other stakeholders through greater awareness of the opportunities and impact of the organisation's activities;
5   new markets from new ways of doing business based on information and its supporting technologies;
6   new products and services – some as yet unimagined;
7   new ways of meeting customers' needs;
8   more effective staff as they learn and develop from the corporate knowledge available to them through information management.

23

But it cannot be achieved by one department working in isolation. To be effective, information management requires a multi-disciplinary team, working within a clearly understood strategic vision and planning framework. That team must be allowed, indeed required, to work across the whole organisation, not in the interests of a single function or other group.

ANALYSIS OF QUESTIONNAIRE 1

1 **No.** Information management, as I hope I have shown, is not simply about computers or technology. It is fundamental to a manager's work, and all managers have a responsibility for using information effectively.

2 **No.** Business strategy can only properly be built on the basis of good information, and it can only be implemented if the information systems are there to support managers in achieving their objectives. Information management therefore has to be integrated into the strategic and business planning process.

3 **No.** Data, information and knowledge are not the same. Information is derived from data by using people's knowledge. From information, further knowledge and understanding can be achieved and from that arise the benefits of effective management of information.

4 **No.** Increasingly managers have to manage and use 'soft' information. Many existing systems are based on numerical data because they are much easier to handle. But in the future, business success will be based on effective use of qualitative data backed up by sound analysis of the numbers.

5 **No.** In the past a large proportion of management information has been concerned with internal performance and activity, and it will continue to serve an important purpose. However market intelligence, competitor analysis and technical know-how are already playing a growing role and will continue to grow in importance.

6 **No.** Information management is often left to the IT department but it is an abrogation of their responsibility by other managers. Information and its use is a corporate issue and therefore is a responsibility of all managers.

1 Audit your organisation's information management against the Seven Levels.

2 Identify existing systems:
   a Computerised
   b Manual or paper-based
   c Informal, local or departmental systems.

2 Ensure that the strategic vision is:
   a Up to date
   b Clear
   c Shared widely and fully understood.

FURTHER READING

N Caroline Daniels, *Information Technology, The Management Challenge*, Economist Intelligence Unit/Addison-Wesley, 1994
This is a readable book that will give another insight into the role of information technology in support of management objectives. It is not technologically specific and should be understandable by managers who are not IT specialists.

It makes particular points about the global aspects of business competition and how it can be enabled by the appropriate use of information technology.

It adds a different viewpoint to the same issues as this book and will provide a useful adjunct to it. In places, it is slightly academic in tone, but the material is oriented towards practical application.

Peter Drucker, *Managing for Results*, William Heinemann, 1964
Peter Drucker, *The Effective Executive*, William Heinemann, 1967
Although these books are 30 years old, they are still highly relevant to the 21st century manager. They probably ought to be required reading before anyone is promoted into a management or executive position – Drucker makes the point that they are not necessarily the same.

They are not turgid academic treatises, and should be accessible by any person who aspires to management or executive roles. They should have them on their bookshelf a long time before they are promoted!

Alvin Toffler, *The Third Wave*, Collins, 1980
Toffler developed the early ideas for the knowledge worker working from wherever they wanted to live. It provides an insight into thinking on the future of work and leisure, and the blurring of the distinctions between the two. It is an interesting starting point for how an information- and knowledge-based society could work. It could spark ideas in many people's minds although it has perhaps been slightly overtaken by technological developments.

SUMMARY

Many organisations are already highly dependent on good information, and the importance of effective information management will continue to grow rapidly over the next few years, into the new Millennium and beyond. Information has always been a key management tool from the earliest days of community working.

Yet information management as a topic is relatively new, and postdates the introduction of computers. Even so the importance and value of the information held within an organisation and its people is surprisingly under-valued. This is probably in part due to managers' – at all levels – lack of confidence in using it. If any asset of similar value was so consistently under-utilised as data is, there would be serious repercussions for managers' careers.

Data is valuable only when it is processed into information using the combined knowledge of individuals. It is only when data is turned into information that it can be used effectively to make informed decisions and to improve the performance of management.

With much greater effort, that information can be further processed into knowledge, and then the organisation begins to develop a corporate 'memory'. That knowledge can then be used to take the organisation forward, and to build on what has gone before. In most organisations, the same mistakes are repeated by each new generation of staff, even though such performance would not be tolerated of individuals. Why is it tolerated of organisations?

We considered the **Seven Levels of Information Management**, and it is clear that few organisations have moved beyond Level 2. The opportunities for improved performance by better use of information is therefore enormous. Indeed the higher levels offer much greater benefits than those achievable by Level 1 and 2 organisations.

The higher levels need managers to understand their industry and their customers, understand their business, understand the opportunities and challenges that they face. All of those require managers to use and understand information, and then be creative in using information to create new strategies supported by information to achieve the benefits that are possible. It needs imaginative and information-literate managers.

By using information as a tool and an opportunity, managers should be able to transform their businesses. They need the will and the understanding.

Above all they need a clear vision for their organisation and its future.

CHAPTER

VITAL SIGNS MONITORING

Plans should be a management tool, and should be action-oriented.

INTRODUCTION

All managers grumble about the amount of paper they have to shuffle, returns they have to make, and not having time to get on with their real job. Much is made of the importance of using their time effectively. But, often part of the problem is not so much poor time management but bad information management, throughout the organisation.

Often managers spend too much time trying to get hold of reliable information to support routine decisions, yet are provided with vast amounts of apparently irrelevant data. They have neither the time, inclination, nor often the skills to make use of the latter, because they are spending their time sorting out problems that could have been foreseen and prevented.

There is an approach that facilitates the management process. It reduces administration, and by reducing the time spent fire-fighting, increases the time a manager has for opportunity-seeking and improving the contribution their team or department makes to the organisation's objectives. I call it 'Vital Signs Monitoring'.

The objectives of this chapter are to:

1 provide an approach to minimising the amount of time spent on basic, routine management;

2 show ways of getting early warning of potential problems;

3 develop a way of working that is applicable across all levels within the organisation;

4 provide a method that gives managers time to think about ways of improving business performance;

5 free other staff to give more time to meet customers' needs and growing expectations;

6 eliminate much bureaucracy and many non-productive meetings.

QUESTIONNAIRE 2

Making better use of your time

1 Do you receive regular reports on performance, activity, market share, production or whatever?
   a Yes
   b No

2 Are they always on time?
   a Yes
   b No

3 How old is the information in the important reports?
   a More than three months
   b More than a month
   c A month
   d A week
   e A day
   f less than a day

4 How long are the reports?
   a One page
   b Five pages
   c Ten pages
   d More than ten pages

5 Do the reports use:
   a Just numbers?
   b Numbers and some comments?
   c Just text?
   d Numbers and charts or graphs?
   e Numbers, charts and text?

6 Are the reports useful in your day-to-day decision-making?
   a Yes
   b No

047 by 047

---

7 Can you get ad-hoc information readily; for instance when you are trying to track down a problem?
a Yes
b No

8 Do you have clearly defined performance targets?
a Yes
b No

9 Does the information in the reports match those targets?
a Yes
b No

10 If your targets are not being met, or indeed you are over-achieving, do you have to report how your are going to respond to your manager?
a Yes
b No

11 Do you have to produce performance or activity returns (not basic timesheets or expense claims)?
a Yes
b No

12 How long do such returns take to prepare, on average, each week?
a Ten minutes or less
b About an hour
c Around half a day
d A full day
e More than a day

13 Where do you get the figures for the returns?
a From your own systems – computer or paper-based (such as your diary)
b From the performance reports
c From other centrally produced reports
d From copies of forms I sent in for other purposes.
e All of these and perhaps more.

Make a note of your results and we will examine what they mean later, when we have considered the background.

BACKGROUND

Cycle of Control

First we need to understand the Cycle of Control. In practice, many managers work in this way without even being aware of it. The cycle is often not explicit in the procedures of the organisation, but it is implicit in the way they work.

The Cycle of Control is straightforward, but in one way or another it takes up a lot of all managers' time. So we need to understand the process, so that we can make it work effectively whilst using as little resources as possible.

The Cycle of Control is illustrated in its simplest form in Figure 2.1 – we will develop it in later chapters. It is a never-ending loop; perhaps even a treadmill for many people! It has four elements which are essential to the management of any venture, although they may be skimped or handled informally.

Plan

Most organisations are familiar with the need to plan, even if it is only to set budgets for the new financial year. The more enlightened will have an annual business-planning round and produce a glossy business plan. After two or three months' work, all the managers breathe a big sigh of relief, and put the plan in their drawer and forget it about until the next planning round.

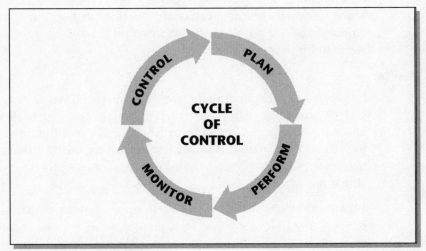

Fig 2.1 CYCLE OF CONTROL

Plans should be a management tool, and should be action-oriented. Business planning should be a continuous process with the annual document, if it is needed at all, being a snapshot of the current plan. Plans should set out what is to be achieved, what is to be done, who is to do it, when it is to be done by and how success is to be measured. It does not need lots of textual justification. Ideally it should be built into the management information and personal appraisal systems, whether computerised or not.

Plans should be a management tool, and should be action-oriented.

All managers and their staff should have their own performance targets in their own departmental extract of the plan. As will be seen later, this is fundamental to the Vital Signs Monitoring approach.

Perform

Once the plan has been agreed, everyone has to perform their part in making it work. They have to take the actions set out in the plan, with the intention of achieving their objectives.

● ● ●

The best laid schemes o' mice an' men
Gang aft a-gley
Robert Burns, *To a Mouse*

● ● ●

As Robert Burns rightly points out, plans never go entirely smoothly. This is due to a variety of reasons. They can be based on false assumptions so that reality intrudes as soon as the plan is actioned. The external environment can change so that the plan is no longer entirely valid. Or people in the organisation fail to deliver their part of the plan for whatever reason.

Monitor

It is therefore necessary to monitor the results achieved against the plan, so that action can be taken to respond. Unfortunately this part of the control cycle is often poorly handled. The monitoring is often too late to allow managers to respond effectively, or the information needed to guide decisions is buried in a mass of inappropriately structured data.

Whatever the reason for ineffective monitoring, it leaves management fighting fires that could have been put out before they had time to become established. The result is that managers spend too much time on problem-solving rather than improving performance.

Action

If the Cycle of Control is going to work effectively, there has to be feedback applied to the plan and thereby to the performance to put everything back on track. In some cases the plan is wrong, and the plan has to be changed to reflect the new situation. Alternatively, corrections have to be applied to the way the existing plan is being executed.

Care has to be taken in deciding on the response. It is the lazy manager's way out to simply change the plan to reflect what is actually being achieved. That should be a last resort and only for very good business reasons. More likely there will need to be changes to the way the plan is being performed. Ideally, individuals should be monitoring their own contribution to the plan and taking the necessary remedial action themselves. This requires individuals, at all levels within the organisation, to have both a clear understanding of the overall plan and their part in it. But most importantly, it requires them to have clear targets that allow them to monitor their contribution effectively.

Feedback or control

The plan will need to be re-examined to check whether assumptions were correct, whether the external or internal environment has changed in a way that requires targets to be redefined. Any changes made to the plan in the light of experience should be fed back into the performance of the plan and in the targets by which it is monitored. Hence business-planning should be seen as an on-going process – the annual production of the business plan document should simply be a snapshot of a continuous process, just like the balance sheet.

Objectives and performance measures

Any plan should have clear objectives with associated performance measures. Such performance measures should be able to assessed objectively. Not simply 'improved', 'better', 'fewer' or 'quicker': but 'improved to 120 per cent of last year's sales', or production or whatever. Similarly for the other subjective descriptions.

Performance measures should be defined for the organisation as a whole, and used to create targets for business units, departments and individuals. Such targets should be SMART:

- Specific
- Measurable
- Agreed or Accepted
- Realistic
- Timed

Although this will be familiar to most readers, I believe it is important enough to be stressed again. In my work as a management consultant, I frequently see organisations which (at best) pay lip-service to this idea. They have targets but do not monitor them, or even worse do not take action as a result of their performance monitoring – what a waste of everybody's time!

Any plan should have clear objectives with associated performance measures.

Targets need to be specific to the person who can achieve them. It is no good setting a figure for sales, and then expecting the performance of the order-processing clerk to be assessed on the basis of that target. The clerk can have no real impact on the sales figure, and therefore it is not sufficiently specific to them. It would be appropriate to the performance of the sales manager or sales director – in that case it would be specific.

It has already been stressed that targets should be objective, there should be no doubt whether they have been achieved or not. Targets should be measurable, or expressed in terms of measurable indicators. Woolly targets expressed in subjective terms are a complete waste of time – who is to say whether they have been achieved?

Different people say that targets should be 'Agreed' or 'Accepted'. Essentially the principle is the same: the individual (or team) with responsibility for achieving a target should accept or agree to that responsibility. They ultimately have to accept that it is their responsibility – even if they do not necessarily like the implications. It is no good setting someone a target, and not ensuring that they understand their responsibility for achieving it. Unfortunately, it is all too often the case.

Targets should be achievable, but only just! They should not be too easy, but they should be realistic. People will strive to reach something that is just out of reach, but if it is too far away they will not try. So a difficult but possible target will achieve better results from most people than one that is clearly impossible.

Finally, all targets should have a clear timetable. Part of the target should be to achieve the required performance by a particular date. It may be desirable in many cases to state the performance measure as a series of staged targets. Even if the overall performance is a single target, say, sales for the year, good managers will turn that into a series of, perhaps, monthly targets. In that way they can monitor their performance and take action at an early stage if they are under-performing.

The aim must be to detect under-performance as early as possible, and take the necessary corrective action. Small adjustments are relatively easy, compared to trying to pull the plan round in the last quarter.

Decision-making

In management, it is usually more important to take a good-enough decision at the right time than to take the perfect decision too late. Unfortunately managers are people, and they seek to avoid making mistakes. As a result, many managers will analyse the data to death, seek additional information and by the time they are comfortable (if ever) with taking the decision, the action is too late.

As we will see later the problem of late decision-making is compounded by the systems that many organisations use.

Commentary

The majority of reports produced regularly have no relevance to the management of the organisation. A strong statement but unfortunately true. Most reports are simply commentary on matters that have long since been consigned to history. If the contents were at all relevant, they have ceased to have any useful management function because their time has past. Decisions should have been taken without those reports which make the reports of no use as guide to future action. They are an expensive waste of time and are there simply to create an illusion of management activity. They create a false role for middle management in particular.

Why? Apart from the information in them having been overtaken by subsequent events, they are not sufficiently timely. Two-month old activity figures are of no use to making a decision on what is happening now. It is commentary on what has happened, not even what is happening and even less a forecast of what is likely to happen. Much of internal corporate reporting, even if timely, is quite simply irrelevant in content or it is in an inappropriate form and cannot be understood by the staff who receive it. The reports are simply not designed to support management actions.

Information overload

Most experienced managers who have worked in large corporate bodies during their career will be familiar with the reports produced by traditional computer systems. They will have been the recipients of weekly or monthly reports that were two inches thick. At best they would have glanced at the last line, and unless there was something unusual, filed the report in the wastepaper bin. Many reports would never have been read, but they would still keep coming. Unfortunately, there is still a surprising amount of such reporting around in all sizes of organisation.

But there is a hint at the answer in the way the reports are used. Users look at the totals line or their department's sub-total to get a feel for their performance. So why not just give them that totals line? Nine times out of ten they never use the rest, so why bother producing it? 'Ah', I hear readers saying, 'but I need it when the bottom line is out of line with my expectations. I need to find where the problem is and then I need the detail so I have to have the report'.

This thinking is the cause of information overload and gets in the way of using information effectively. The detail does not need, and should not, be produced routinely as it clouds the real issues which are encapsulated in the summary. However the detail does need to be available quickly and easily when possible problems are identified. How it is provided is relatively unimportant compared to making it available speedily. If a manager can get at the detail by examining a master report held centrally, by requesting or running a paper-based report, or even better through a terminal or personal computer, than they should be happy not to be inundated with irrelevant detail.

If the reports are concise, they will be more easily understood and therefore used to support decisions and management action. On the other hand, if there is too much data, then the information contained therein will not be appreciated by the reader – if they even bother to try.

Bureaucracy

A senior manager at a public-sector client was asked by the staff in one section for a new cupboard as their existing ones were all full. As he could not understand why they had so much filing, he asked them to show him how they were using their existing three cupboards. They were full of reports and the forms from which they had been created going back several years. When he asked why they were kept, he was told, 'just in case' somebody needed to examine them. Digging further, he was told that no one had asked to see them for at least three years. What is more no one else knew they had them!

'Ah', I hear all those private sector managers saying, 'it is not like that in the real world'. Oh yes it is. At a large car company, there was a small group whose sole role was to get data from various departments and produce reports: which they did assiduously every month for years. They then put them in the drawer of their desks. They did absolutely nothing with them! At one time they had sent them on to another team, but when that team was disbanded, no-one told the reporting group to stop or to send their reports elsewhere. So they just blindly carried on producing them to no purpose. At least in the public-sector example, the reports were produced as a by-product of other necessary processing.

There is a lot of time wasted producing reports about what has been done. But that is history and cannot be changed, so change your emphasis to look at what is happening now and what is likely to happen in the near future. From that, you can make informed management decisions.

If you focus on what is important in the operational management of the organisation, and avoid simply commenting on what is past, then you will be able to avoid the worst of the bureaucracy.

I am sure many readers will have experienced 'Information Ping-Pong'. A department asks you and other colleagues for data. You spend time extracting it from various reports and perhaps from your own local systems (such as your diary) and pass it over. Two weeks later you get a report from the requesting department, feeding your own data back to you in a consolidated or at least different form. It can get even worse where you are using data from one edition of the report to enable the next edition to be produced. The next step up is for the teams simply to spend their time passing data backwards and forwards, and not actually doing anything that adds value to the products or services delivered by the organisation. That is for the real élite of Information Ping-Pong, but there are plenty of people playing this pointless game in organisations all over the world.

So avoid commentary for the sake of it. Ensure that the data you process has a real purpose, and is not simply to create work in the administration sections or an administrative burden in the operational areas.

Measures and indicators

You need to choose suitable measures or indicators appropriate to your work.

Measures

Measures are just that. They can be quantified and show performance directly. They would include sales revenue, production quantities, scrap rates or machine utilisation and could have clear targets set against them. Most areas of business management lend them to setting targets based on clearly defined measures of performance.

Indicators

However, there are areas where direct measures are more difficult. For example how does one measure staff morale or outcomes in a mental health unit? They are intangible, and there are no obvious direct measures. On the other hand, there are factors that can be measured to give a guide to performance. These are not absolute and can only give a clue to possible under-performance, but they are objective and lends themselves to measurement.

Possible indicators for the staff morale question include staff turnover rate, absence rates and grievance rates. These may well constitute departmental targets in their own right. But they are not unequivocal. A sudden increase in turnover rate may not be due to a problem with increased job dissatisfaction, it may be that a new employer has been recruiting in the area. So it will require further investigation – hence the need to be able to get at the underlying detail and to genuinely understand what is happening.

On the other hand it would suggest a change in the external environment, and therefore the possible need to take some action to get back on plan or to revise the plan. The response may be a need to increase wage rates to retain valuable staff and that will have an impact in other aspects of the plan and other managers' targets. Hence the need for a continuous cycle of control.

Budgets, targets and trends

Budgets and other targets are essential. Many organisations already have budgets for financial measures, but targets should be set for all other key management measures and indicators. Some, indicators especially, may not lend themselves to absolute target values. This may be because the changes are small or swing around between high and low values. In such cases trends should be watched, and other techniques to smooth the swings should be used. All managers need to become familiar with basic techniques such as moving averages to show trends of widely varying measures.

Early warning

By watching trends and understanding what is happening, managers should get an early warning of potential problems. Indeed the measures and indicators and their associated targets should be chosen for the assistance they give to the prediction of problems.

Using measures and then projecting them forward to their likely consequence as part of the reporting process will help provide the required early warning.

Some years ago I did some work for the treasurer of a Scottish Health Board. He had a very simple approach. If the forecast for his spending for the whole year was within his budget, he slept at night and did not need to worry about the detail. He could leave that to his staff and he could concentrate on the Board's strategy and the high level financial planning. I know other directors and managers who work in a similar way. They have understood the Vital Signs Monitoring approach and used it effectively to the advantage of their organisation. Interestingly those who operate the approach fully and effectively all seem to be successful in their careers – I wonder if there is any link?

Understand the implied message

However the numbers are not the whole story, especially when they diverge from the plan. It does not matter whether they vary above or below the plan the implications need to be understood.

A colleague who is working with a rapidly growing manufacturing company faced just such a problem. The client was well ahead of the target sales, but the figures seemed to be showing a growing bank balance – a rather unusual circumstance. Most growing businesses using typical terms of business are in need of more working capital, rather than generating cash. He was concerned about this apparently strange behaviour, and was concerned that there was a problem with the way the management accounts were being prepared. We have both met this problem before where businesses use rather optimistic treatments in the preparation of figures. Or it was possible that the business had missed or not received invoices from a major supplier, or that it had received payments on account that had not been treated correctly?

Fortunately, after investigation, it turned out that the management figures were correct. What had happened was that the company's debt collection on their 30 day terms was extremely effective, and they had payment terms of 60 days with several of their major suppliers. Hence they were paying in 60 days, and getting paid in around 40 days – hence the growing cash and no need for increased working capital. The suppliers were providing the additional working capital to fund the extra expansion.

The important point is that a situation that looked good was not masking a different problem. In the Vital Signs Monitoring approach, it is essential that the figures are prepared properly, and that any unplanned figures are investigated and the implications understood.

In another case, the company was very careful to monitor the gross profit margin on each sale. Staff could not accept an order that did not achieve the required margin without authorisation from a director. Turnover was growing, profits were growing, they had a good order book and the directors were happy. They were happy until they ran out of cash and the bank called in their overdraft. The directors did not understand the implications of what was happening and they were not using appropriate indicators. By all means monitor the profit margin, but also ensure that the cash flow is being managed at least as tightly. More businesses fail for lack of cash, than for lack of short-term profits. Long-term lack of profitability will of course lead to a lack of cash. Both should be picked up by monitoring cash flow and understanding the implications of and reasons for divergence from target.

Appropriate in content, form, timing and accuracy

Reports and other forms of information presentation frequently are not designed by the users, but by other managers and technicians. So often the content is another person's view of the readers' needs and is often inaccurate, incomplete or more than is required. It is important, as we have explored, that information intended for management use should be concise and to the point so that the message is not buried in spurious detail.

Even if the content is correct, then the message may still be lost if the form of presentation is inappropriate. This is frequently a problem for finance reports amongst others. Accountants are comfortable with numbers and formal accounts formats, but most other managers are not. So financial reports designed by accountants for their own use are not usually suitable for other managers and staff. If they are number-based, they often need simplification to not much more than budget amounts, actual amounts and amount left to spend/earn. In many cases it would be even better to use non-numeric forms of presentation so that the information can be assimilated visually. Adding a *little* colour can also help. Some form of traffic-lights-based, colour scheme is well-accepted, red for under performance, green for on-plan or over-performance and orange for warning of marginal under-performance.

A few words of caution. The aim is to make the information as clear as possible so avoid using three-dimensional charts, they are pretty, but they are not as clear in communicating the information. Two-dimensional graphs have been developed over the centuries to make complex information clear and are elegantly simple. Also because colour is available does not mean you have to use it – restrict yourself to the absolute minimum. Sometimes less is more.

Accuracy vs timeliness

Tremendous accuracy is rarely required if one is using information to take decisions. What one is looking for is major differences rather than minor nuances . . . In itself, management is a pretty coarse activity and has to be applied on a substantial scale if it is to make any real impact.
Sir John Harvey-Jones, *Managing to Survive*

● ● ●

All too often, organisations seek to make their working reports completely accurate. Apart from being impossibly elusive, perfect accuracy is expensive and unnecessary. Remember what Sir John Harvey-Jones said – management is a crude art that has to be applied in big chunks. Remember we are talking about information for management purposes, not accounts that have to be audited. So only make the accuracy good enough for its purpose and no more. (By the way, even audited accounts constitute only one of several possible views – auditing and account preparation is not an exact science.)

Even worse problems are caused by chasing spurious accuracy, in that the information becomes too late to be useful to support management decisions. So many organisations produce masses of 'management information' that is completely useless for management use. It gives a false sense of doing the right things, but managers are still managing by instinct. The reason it is useless is because it is simply too late. Typically the figures for January are processed during February and are usually published towards the end of February (at best), by which time it is on average six weeks out of date. That means a problem highlighted by such figures has probably continued for over a month with no action being taken. Such organisations have to rely on managers picking up problems in other ways, by instinct, by their own local record keeping or from customer complaints. As a result, managers are wasting time sorting out problems that are more serious than they should be, simply because they were not spotted early enough: the information was accurate but too late.

CASE STUDY

Auditable management accounts

The financial account at a voluntary sector client was proud of his management accounts. His proud boast was that they were auditable! His and his team's commitment to quality work was (and still is) to be applauded.

Unfortunately, accurate as the management accounts were, they were always late, despite key people having to work late to get them out. Unfortunately, by the time any of the other departmental managers got them, they were too late to use to support action. Decisions had to be taken intuitively or, as often happened, were avoided.

As an example, they have always been conscientious in accounting for payments that span accounting periods to give a true figure. They spend hours working these out each month, yet because of the nature of their business, they could ignore all but the odd exceptional item. The routine figures are not significant in the overall scheme of things, and give a spurious accuracy that is not justified in accounts whose primary role is as an aid to management decision-making.

What is more, they could let these figures take care of themselves by changing how they post them into the computerised accounting system. The problem was compounded by the fact that because the finance staff were always under pressure, they did not make time to automate the process or even to review their priorities. They have a powerful accounting system which could facilitate much of the production of their management information if they could find time to plan and implement it.

They are starting to change, but it will take some time before they are comfortable with accepting that quality is a compromise between accuracy and timeliness. They accept in their heads that for management accounts, 'good enough at the right time' is just as much an indication of high quality as being auditable, but it will not happen until their hearts have accepted that view.

As an aside, they also have the problem that information is presented in a style favoured by accountants which is not readily understood by other functional managers. Again, the lack of time prevents finance staff talking to their internal customers and developing forms of presentation suitable to such managers' needs. They have the computer-based tools to provide information that is appropriate in content, form, timing and accuracy. They have yet come to terms with information management as a cross-functional tool – we will get them there.

Access to underlying detail/analysis

I used to have a rule of thumb that said no routine management report should be longer in pages than the number of working days between each edition. I now believe that to be far too many. As a general rule a page or a screen on a terminal or a personal computer is enough, and for most management roles, contains sufficient information to highlight whether there are any problems developing.

Sometimes, if problems arise, then it may be necessary to analyse the underlying detail and that should be readily available. These days, that may well be through a personal computer linked to the main corporate information systems with tools designed for the casual user.

A management tool across all levels

Vital Signs Monitoring is an approach that can and should be used by everyone from the top to bottom of the organisational chart.

Take the overall corporate objectives – sales, profit, number of patients treated or whatever – and break them down for each tier of the chart. What do they mean for individual divisions, departments, teams or whatever organisational structure you have? What can they control and deliver that is a measurable contribution to the overall objectives. Turn them into departmental objectives, with the department manager having responsibility to achieve them, and the authority to take the decisions necessary to do so.

Vital Signs Monitoring is an approach that can and should be used by everyone from the top to bottom of the organisational chart.

Repeat this at each level with the appropriate manager and her team. Eventually, it will reach the vital signs for an individual who will have responsibility and authority to achieve those results. All Vital Signs should be SMART as discussed earlier (see page 36). At this level the salesman knows what sales they have to achieve, the production worker knows what volumes they have to make and to what quality and so on for all jobs in the organisation.

These Vital Signs are clear, and are derived *directly* from the overall objectives of the organisation. They are measures of a each individual's contribution to the business's success. If every person keeps their Vital Signs on course, the organisation will automatically achieve its objectives.

Using Vital Signs Monitoring

So how does it work in practice? Each person has responsibility to achieve their targets and are monitored by their immediate manager. However their targets should not be managed by their manager.

Each individual will from time to time check their performance. In a traditional environment, they will receive a weekly or monthly report, highlighting their targets, what has actually been achieved against those targets and the gap, good or bad from target. Similarly, their manager will receive a copy for all the individuals for whom they have responsibility, and a copy of their own performance report.

The manager takes no action immediately – however good or bad an individual's performance. Remember the individual has responsibility for their own performance and the authority to take any necessary action. The individual examines the performance, does further more detailed analysis if needed and decides on a course of action. The course of action should aim to bring the performance back into line with the plan. The individual then lets their manager know why there is a problem, what action they have taken and their expected outcome from that action. This may result in amended targets over subsequent months as the plan is revised in the light of experience – back to the Cycle of Control (see pages 33–35). In such circumstances, the manager may well act as a mentor to help the individual achieve the best possible response, but they do not take control.

The only time a manager should need to take action on an individual's performance is if the person concerned does not act promptly or the response is inadequate or badly flawed in some other way. Then they take appropriate action either to coach the individual, arrange training or otherwise enable the person to take on the responsibilities asked of them. If they are unable to do so, then other action to replace or discipline them may be necessary.

It works exactly the same for managers. They take action on the information in their performance report and pass their action and consequences on to their own managers. So it works up the organisational tree, until the board monitors corporate performance as whole.

At each level, the performance reports will be an aggregate of the group's individual targets, with the addition of additional Vital Signs appropriate to the manager's particular responsibility.

If the organisation has set achievable targets, and people are working properly, then most Vital Signs will be on or close to target. So there will be little remedial action or more detailed information required. The manager or individual can look at the report, satisfy themselves that the basics are right. The bureaucracy is then out of the way in minutes, and they can get on with doing the job or seeking to improve performance beyond target. People have become freed to be opportunity seekers not problem solvers.

CASE STUDY

Arm's length management

An engineer friend runs a successful medium-sized engineering company that manufactures its own range of products and customised versions for special purposes. He has a good team, and leaves them to get on with it. He receives a regular brief management report with the key performance figures. The management report generally keeps them focused on the important issues, and therefore everything runs smoothly.

Due to diversification, he has another business that is growing rapidly. It produces specialised one-off equipment, and needs a considerable amount of his time for management, to do the very technical design work and to liaise with customers. This leaves little time for the older manufacturing business.

Instead, he manages the production company at arm's length. He has delegated the responsibility and authority to the existing staff, and he just watches the performance report. From time to time, there will be some divergence, and he will go and spend a few hours at the factory walking the job. With the little bit of information from the report, some discreet questions and by using his eyes, and experience, he can usually identify the problems and steer his management team back on track. But because this Vital Signs approach is so effective, he rarely needs to do so.

Indeed he is considering retiring to the US to play golf and continue to 'run' the production business (he will probably sell the other, or move it to the States). His argument is that the need to get into detail is so rare, he could afford to fly over on Concorde if needed. The rest of the time he can run it as now, using the fax and telephone.

Encourages delegation

As will be appreciated, Vital Signs Monitoring encourages delegation, and that buzz word of the 1980s, 'empowerment'. People are expected to manage their own performance, and are given the tools to do so.

It must be stressed that the approach works if delegation is done properly. That means that whilst an individual has the responsibility for meeting targets, they have sufficient authority to take the actions needed to achieve that target. The whole purpose of Vital Signs Monitoring is to minimise routine bureaucracy: it is undermined if an individual has to go back to their manager for permission to take action to meet their targets. In that case the manager might as well manage the individual's performance directly – an old-fashioned waste of talent both of the individual and the manager. Good people with properly defined responsibilities and authority are the secret of a successful enterprise.

Role of technology

Technology is not strictly essential. But in this day and age where most administrative systems are computer-based, it makes sense to use it as far as appropriate. Indeed, most of the routine management information ought to drop out of the administrative and operational systems; and to be available at any time not just the end of the month or week. Similarly, much of the underlying detail from which the targets' report is derived will be in such systems.

The challenge, then, is to give managers the capability of getting at that data and using their knowledge, turn it into the information they need, when they need it. This is something we will return to in more detail in Chapter 12, when we will explore a concept, corporate information systems, for developing such a facility.

Technology can deliver the information to an individual at his or her desk, at a client or on the road, or even at home. It need not depend on someone being at the other end. It can also automate most of the essential analysis, aggregation and other processing, and do so in ways that are tailored to each user's current need. In many cases, it can do so even if that particular form was not originally built into the system. Current technology can support flexible needs, but it needs people who think flexibly and do not simplify the solutions to make it easy to meet limited, stated needs. The technology needs to be exploited in open-minded ways. It needs people who can accept and manage the complexity that such an approach needs. Organisations need general managers, information managers and information technologists who can cope with such creative and intellectually demanding roles. It will be exciting and challenging for those people who can, and their skills will be in great demand in the new Millennium.

Well-proven

Vital Signs Monitoring is not an entirely new concept, as it owes much to the old management by exception approach. It is updated to make use of modern management information systems, and to recognise the changing nature of business and management. But that said, it is essentially well-proven, and many effective managers have used it in some way, and without formalising it with a name through much of their careers.

ANALYSIS OF QUESTIONNAIRE 2

1   **Yes**. All managers should receive performance information on a regular basis. It should be appropriate to their role.

2   **Yes**. Information is only useful as a management tool if it is timely. Accurate and late is no use, almost accurate and in good time is far more useful.

3   **A maximum of a month or less**. Information should be as fresh as possible if it is to support management decisions and prevent problems growing unnecessarily. Ideal information on current performance should be available immediately, so that questions are asked and decisions taken as issues arise. But not many achieve that. Having information that was a maximum of a month old would be a major improvement for most organisations – a week should be a short-term target.

4 **One page**. Routine management information should be brief and to the point. It should be supported by speedy access to the underlying detail when it is needed. The detail should not be produced as a matter of course, as it only serves to cloud the issues.

5 **Not just text**. Management information should be against SMART targets. Use of simple charts and graphs may be more appropriate for less numerate people, and to make the information more readily assimilated by all. Graphs were developed over history to show complex data in a simple and effective way. Use that experience.

6 **Yes**. If the answer is 'no', why is it being produced? It does not have a purpose. If it is for information only, then it is contributing to the problem of information overload. By all means make it available for those who are interested, but do not automatically send it to everyone. If you check, you will find few people bother to read it.

7 **Yes**. Management has a need for answers to questions that can neither be predicted nor planned with regard to their timing. Management information needs to be able to support the analysis needed to answer such questions – the data needs to be held in a way that any manager can access for such purposes. And managers have to have the skills to use it effectively.

8 **Yes**. All staff should have personal targets that they can manage. How else can one be sure whether someone is effective in their work?

9 **Yes**. If performance targets are to be of any use, they need to be backed up by information on what is being achieved. The performance reports, if they exist, should be structured in the same way as the targets and should be specific to each individual. They should not have to dig their performance out of the department figures, or even worse the company results.

10 **Yes**. If people are to be empowered, they need to take responsibility for their own performance. They should be self-managing, and report their actions to their manager, rather than have their manager instruct them as to what action to take.

11 **No**. The performance reports should drop out of the basic administrative recording. It is a waste of time for people to have to collect data for it to be processed and fed back – they could do that themselves. Make the reporting efficient.

12 **Ten minutes or less**. That would be the best answer: ideally, it should be none. But consider your answer, and then gross it up for all the

people in the organisation, and it then probably starts to look very expensive. And it is a cost that can largely be avoided.

13 **None.** None of the suggested answers are correct. They all suggest that there is unnecessary bureaucracy, and people are just passing paper around within the organisation. None of which will be adding value to the delivery of customer services, or contributing to achieving the corporate objectives.

1 Redesign the targets for the people in your team as Vital Signs, and introduce Vital Signs Monitoring.

2 Ensure that your team have properly delegated, clearly defined responsibility and the authority to take all necessary action to deliver their part of the plan.

3 Explain what you expect of them, and leave them to run with it.

4 Monitor the performance of the changes, coach individuals and encourage them to manage their own performance.

5 Do not interfere, show that you really want them to take control of their own performance. Let go!

FURTHER READING

Managing to Survive, **Sir John Harvey-Jones, Heinneman 1993**
A very readable book that is based on Sir John's experience. He has a practical, essentially down to earth approach, that many can learn from. Experienced managers will not always agree with him, but he will make you think.

Whilst he recognises the importance of good information, he stresses the need to avoid over-analysis and to not try to fine-tune management decisions. He does not see management as a particularly subtle art.

SUMMARY

Doctors use vital signs, pulse, respiration temperature, as the basic indicator of a patient's health. So should managers, as it will save them a lot of time on routine 'management' and allow them to take positive action to improve performance.

Using a Vital Signs-based approach will also require individuals to take responsibility for their own performance, and give them encouragement to improve that performance.

Vital Signs Monitoring is applicable to everyone in the organisation, and shows them what their contribution is to the success of the organisation as a whole. If all individuals achieve their target, then the organisation will meet its objectives.

It is well-proven and simple to implement. It should be kept simple and supported with prompt and reliable performance information. The information should be readily available from existing administrative systems, and should not require additional bureaucracy to feed it. If it does, you are doing it wrong!

Computers are useful, but not essential. But in most organisations of a reasonable size, the essential information will be on a computer – it just needs to be unlocked.

It allows everyone to get on with the important function of improving performance, and meeting the needs of customers and clients, rather than managing the performance: an essentially negative role.

CHAPTER

3

UNDERSTANDING
THE BUSINESS

Information management is a business tool, and therefore it requires a complete understanding of the business, its products and its processes.

INTRODUCTION

Information management is a business tool, and therefore it requires a complete understanding of the business, its products and its processes. As already explained, information management is not a synonym for information technology; IT is only there to support the information management objectives, and through them the corporate objectives.

This chapter will seek to describe some of the planning issues and tools that will be useful in determining information and systems needs. It makes no apology for the fact that these have considerable overlap with more general strategic and business planning methods. The two functions are inseparable if they are to be successful.

The objectives for this chapter are to:

1 evaluate how the existing systems meet current expectations of the organisation;

2 understand how planning for information management fits with overall corporate planning;

3 ensure that essential strategic planning can be undertaken;

4 provide an outline of some techniques for determining information management needs;

5 analyse the options available, and decide which projects should be taken forward;

6 provide guidance on where more detailed guidance on specific techniques can be found.

QUESTIONNAIRE 3

Where does information management fit in?

1 Information management is separate from:
   a Strategic planning
   b Business planning
   c Both of them
   d Neither of them

2 Modern management techniques rely on information management.
   a Yes?
   b No?

3 Information is about finding a solution to a problem once it has been defined.
   a Yes?
   b No?

4 Information should happen as part of the strategic and business planning process.
   a Yes?
   b No?

5 Should each department be responsible for its own information management systems?
   a Yes
   b No

6 Can the effectiveness of information management and information technology be measured?
   a Yes
   b No

7 Organisations are better now at information management than they were 20 years ago.
   a No?
   b Yes?

8 Most organisations have aligned their IT strategy to their corporate objectives.
   a Yes?
   b No?

9 Do managers need to understand the IT-based solutions on offer to determine their information management needs?
   a Yes
   b No

CHANGE

Most people find change unwelcome but it is completely unavoidable. All we can do is work to make the change as beneficial as possible. In our working lives as managers we have to make it beneficial to our organisation and the people who have a stake in that business: employees, shareholders, customers and the wider community in which it operates.

● ● ●

Laws of motion. . . Every body continues in its state of rest, or of uniform motion in a right line, unless it is compelled to change that state by forces impressed upon it.
Isaac Newton, *Principia Mathematica* (*Laws of Motion 1*), 1687, trans. Andrew Motte, 1729

● ● ●

Management action is one of the forces needed to move an organisation from its straight line. There are other, external, forces that will change the organisation's direction, often undesirably. Without management applying a corrective force, the business will set off in a new but unwanted direction.

Therefore, all planning, indeed all management actions, should be about producing change. And the change should be desired, and regarded as desirable.

Information management and strategic planning

In many organisations, functional planning, particularly for 'support' functions, is carried out in isolation from the development of an overall corporate strategy. Strategic planning in such organisations, and the associated changes, are passed down from above with little involvement of those in the front line providing direct customer service.

. . . all planning, indeed all management actions, should be about producing change.

It is therefore not surprising that corporate plans are not regarded as realistic by the 'troops'. Similarly, it should not come as a surprise that departmental plans bear little relationship to overall business strategy. Each exercise is largely undertaken in isolation – it is no wonder they do not complement each other.

This is particularly true of information systems. It is seen as a technical function in which few senior managers build their careers, unlike marketing, finance or production. As a result, such leaders do not properly understand the issues around information and undervalue the contribution it can make. Information management will deliver its full capability only if it is treated as an integral part of strategic planning where it can support new ways of doing business.

Other management approaches to change

There are always new management approaches; some are fads, many are merely new frameworks for achieving existing best practice. Rarely are they completely new approaches. But they all have one thing in common – they require the organisation to change; and to manage that change, information is needed.

If we consider some recent management theories and how they use information, we will see how the management of information is intrinsic to the 'new' approaches.

Business process re-engineering

A company that cannot change the way it thinks about information technology cannot reengineer. A company that equates technology with automation cannot engineer. A company that looks for problems first and then seeks technology solutions for them cannot reengineer.
Michael Hammer and James Champy, *Reengineering the Corporation*

● ● ●

Basically, business process re-engineering is about fundamental ways of rethinking working practices. And they require those making the changes to fully understand information issues and opportunities and not simply to think about it as part of the solution. It should be considered as an integral part of the rethinking of ways business is carried out.

Total quality management

In order to be sure of meeting customer requirements, and continuing to meet them, it is clearly necessary to create a quality information system.
John S. Oakland, *Total Quality Management*

● ● ●

All quality management approaches require tracking of customer requirements, production and compliance with those requirements all through the production or service delivery process. Without information this is not possible. Indeed quality management is a clear example of the cycle of control as detailed in Chapter 2.

The learning organisation

A learning organisation seeks to learn from experience. This is because as a body and as individuals within it, it should learn from the corporate experience. To do so, it is essential that there is corporate memory, so that mistakes are not repeated. To build a successful learning organisation, it is essential to build an effective shared corporate-knowledge base. Information management is central to the approach.

Empowerment

As discussed in the previous chapter, information can be used to empower and support staff in improving their performance. *Knowledge is Power*. Employees need information and knowledge to be empowered in any meaningful way.

And others yet to come . . .

It is probable that future thinking will assume effective information management. Increasingly, products are enhanced with information, and with markets changing so rapidly, no business will be able to succeed without having the information to track those changes. Information management will be critical for 21st century organisations.

General and functional managers' roles

The role of the information manager, especially one from a technical background, is to manage the complexity that is needed to produce information systems that are usable. Usable, that is, by non-technical staff who require access to information to support their main functions: in other words, people who are occasional computer users, as opposed to those whose role is essentially computer-based. Such users need:

- a consistent simple approach from all systems;
- appropriate forms of presentation;
- reliability, as they are not equipped to resolve systems problems;
- and, above all, confidence in the information and the system.

As will be appreciated and will become clear as we work through the planning and specification issues, there is a growing conflict between users' needs for wide-ranging information and their need for it to be presented simply and consistently. The complexity that arises in the planning, design, implementation and operation of such systems continues to grow rapidly. Many of the technical tools themselves are becoming easier to use, but their number is increasing, and their use in combination, and of course the needs of the business are growing more demanding. To be successful, an IS/IT manager needs high-level technical skills, coupled with sound general management skills and high-level corporate planning expertise. Such people are rare, and expensive!

Therefore it is essential that general managers and functional managers, including the IS/IT manager, work together as team. They need to agree a joint vision of what is required, to use a common language avoiding their specialist jargon (or at least agreeing what it means) and to communicate. On the latter point, a lot of value will be achieved from informal contact – for example, simply talking shop in the pub or at the coffee machine. We will consider more formal meetings, and the like, later.

PLANNING FRAMEWORKS

It is essential that all planning should take place within a single corporate framework. This should cover all levels and all time periods. It should be designed to encourage action, rather than bureaucracy. The success of such a framework will rely on good communication – not just from the top down, but from the bottom up, and across functions.

All planning should be looking for incremental improvement opportunities, as well as searching for more fundamentally new ways of providing their services and products. Information should be integral with the planning processes.

Indeed, the knowledge sharing that is essential for good planning might make a good early project for the development of information management. Sort that out, and many of the other issues will pale into insignificance.

Strategic

Good information is needed to inform the strategic planning process, but the information systems cannot be defined without understanding the business strategy – something of a Catch-22 position. No organisation starts completely from scratch, so the planning can be refined on each cycle.

Strategic planning and thinking should be a continuous process and is especially the responsibility of senior management, who need time to think strategically. They also need to understand information, what is available (internal and external) and how it can be used for competitive advantage (see Chapter 4).

The strategic vision and its supporting information will need to be fed into the business planning process. Most organisations should do this each year, with a strategy defined for the next three years (longer in some circumstances).

Business planning

Business planning should involve as wide a group as possible, and should concentrate on how the strategic vision should be achieved. It will need information additional to that used to define strategy. Again the business plan is continually being refined as part of the Cycle of Control (see Chapter 2) with a major review annually. It is at this annual review that the new targets are usually set for the forthcoming year.

Information systems planning

Information management planning should take place as an integral part of both strategic and business planning. There may be administrative systems that it is possible to define separately from the higher-level systems, but this should not be used as an excuse for taking the simplistic route. Care should be taken and a more holistic approach to information management should be adopted.

Information technology planning

Information technology planning cannot even start until there is a clear statement of the information management systems strategy. With the 'what' of information systems defined, it is then possible to define 'how' they should be implemented, and what technology would be appropriate. Many organisations put the cart before the horse and try to meet the information needs with previously selected technology.

FUNDAMENTAL THINKING

Business process re-engineering is touted as a panacea, which it is not. It does, however, incorporate a complete approach to improving how business is done within and outside the organisation. That break from a traditional functional thinking creates new opportunities, and a similar approach is essential for effective information management.

Corporate data models of the 1980s suggested a complete enterprise-wide view of data, but it rarely produced new ways of doing things. It failed to do so for a number of reasons:

● it was usually undertaken as a computer department project, not by a cross-functional general management team;
● it tended to record what was happening, rather than what should or could be done;
● the technology was not really ready to support a true enterprise-wide database, with reporting capabilities suitable for occasional users;
● managers and others were not ready for the change in working practices that would have been necessary to exploit a corporate approach to information management.

Now there is a much greater acceptance that organisations have to look at the way they produce and provide their products and services in a much more complete way. It is generally recognised that a multi-disciplinary approach is essential, if the changes are to be made that will be needed to compete in the globalised markets of the 21st century.

Cross-functional

New thinking is increasingly multi-disciplinary and crosses traditional separate functions. For example, in product development it is now increasingly common for research and development, production and marketing to work together, right from the start, all through new product developments.

Traditionally, it would have been research and development who would have passed on a working prototype on to production for the product to be prepared for manufacturing. At some stage along the way, marketing would become involved to prepare for the product launch. The new ways allow products to be brought to market much more quickly as the decision-making process is shortened.

This is now happening with business process re-engineering for other departments to work together. Indeed, completely new organisational structures are based on this new multi-disciplinary approach to doing business.

Thinking 'out of the box'

The successful organisation will increasingly be capable of thinking in completely new ways about their business, customers, products and services. They will see the opportunities before their competitors.

A premium will be placed on organisations that can innovate in all aspects of their operations. They will be able to make major jumps in performance that will leave those evolving companies behind, many will perish. Creative thinking supported by good analysis will be the only way of surviving.

SOME PLANNING TOOLS AND METHODS

SSADM

Structured Systems Analysis and Design Method (SSADM) and related approaches were methodologies for systems analysis that came to a peak in the late 1980s, especially for major corporate systems. It tended to be combined with data modelling and was often supported by a corporate data model.

It was criticised at the time as being bureaucratic, but its main proponents (usually with a commercial interest) suggested that it allowed relatively unskilled staff to do the analysis. The danger was that, as with most formal methods, it stifles creativity and it therefore tended to produce systems that merely fossilised current practice. Strictly applied by technicians and with little imagination, it will not produce the fundamental change that is required to meet the needs of organisations in today's (and especially tomorrow's) fast-changing environment.

However, as with most things, it was not all bad. It incorporated techniques that are useful if used selectively, and with appropriate flexibility and imagination.

PEST, SWOT, COST, etc.

There are many traditional techniques and tools that remain appropriate. They have to be used in a multi-disciplinary way and incorporated into a much more holistic view of the organisation, its purpose and its market.

It is not intended to detail these techniques, as they are an essential part of any manager's armoury. Suffice it to say they explore issues around:

Political, Environment, Social, Technology

Strengths, Weaknesses Opportunities, Threats

Concerns, Opportunities, Strengths, Threats

Value Chain Analysis

This technique was developed by Michael Porter, and has become a major plank of strategic planning. However it only recognises information as a support to the main value chain. In a recent article, Jeffrey Rayport and John Sviokla have developed this further by adding the idea of a Virtual Value Chain in parallel with Porter's Physical Value Chain. This is based on the idea that information can contribute to the business, and that it provides new opportunities all along the Virtual Value Chain. Combined with the Physical Value Chain, there is a matrix of product and service opportunities.

GET THE BASICS RIGHT FIRST

It is important that the organisation addresses any problems with its existing working practices. It must get control of its operations and get them into good shape before embarking on a new round of major change.

Whilst change is necessary, it should be managed so as not to overload staff and managers with too many initiatives in too short a time. There have to be occasional periods of consolidation to allow reflection on what has been achieved, what the new challenges are and what the organisation's strategy should be in response. If it is too unrelenting, then people switch off, and do not work to achieve the objectives.

It is important that the organisation addresses any problems with its existing working practices.

So to summarise:

- managers must be able to get their own functions working as well as possible, using best practice as far as the existing management structure and processes allow;

● senior managers must have a strategic vision which is shared with and understand by all employees.

Once such basics are in place, then the business can start to work on its information-based strategy.

IDENTIFYING INFORMATION NEEDS

Some readers may be surprised that this section is so late. In fact, I nearly left it for another two chapters! As should be realised by now, identifying the information needs is only part of a much wider exercise, and should not be undertaken in isolation. Information management should not be seen as a quick fix; information technology is even less of a panacea.

Existing information systems capability

The first step is to evaluate and document the existing system's capability. This will highlight problems, including many that can be resolved quickly and without using a lot of resources.

Whoever documents the system should not do it from their own desk – they will need to get out and talk to the IT department and to users at all levels. The aim is to get a good picture of all the systems, formal and informal, in use within the organisation.

The easiest way of doing this is to track through all the key processes. At each step, document the data items that are asked for, what is recorded (it may not be the same!), where and how it is recorded and how it is used. This last point will include the production of reports, returns to other departments or to other agencies outside the organisation. Where a report, form or information in whatever form is passed to another person, then that will be a branch that will have to be followed and documented, especially if it is internal.

It is essential to remember we are not concerned just with computer-based systems. We need to identify all key data recording, processing and use, however it is achieved.

Bear in mind that there will be many informal systems in the form of notebooks, diaries, personal organisers and card index systems. It is essential that these are identified and documented, as they are the systems that people really use. They will provide an insight into what is really needed to undertake particular tasks.

A paperchase

Even in organisations that are apparently sophisticated in their use of information and supporting technology, this exercise will be an eye-opener! We undertook such an exercise for a client, a mental health unit, with large centralised patient management systems. For example, we identified seven parallel patient records in addition to the main computer record. These were in manual registers of one sort or another – usually to give quick access to key information. This was only the tip of an iceberg, there were many other such examples.

This highlighted that there were problems with the computer systems not meeting the real needs of users. It also raised important questions about data security and accuracy. These manual records sat on secretaries' or receptionists' desks with little control over access, despite the highly confidential nature of the data. Many patients would be unhappy for even their attendance at the unit to be known, because of the stigma that is still associated with mental illness by many. Medical staff were often reluctant to share patient notes with their colleagues for reasons of patient confidentiality. Yet there was information lying around on desks throughout the organisation, sometimes in public areas, without any control over who had access to it.

Furthermore, there was no validation of the data accuracy. Those seven patient records were all at different stages of update; there was no consistency or control. Yet these were more important to most users than the formal systems.

How this data is recorded is relatively unimportant, as long as it can be readily pictured and shared with colleagues. Various forms of flow-charting are probably the most appropriate. The diagrams used by SSADM techniques are as clear and complete as any, but there is not scope to do it justice here. However *SSADM*, by Geoff Cutts is a straightforward text that explains and illustrates the process well (see page 78).

Evaluation of current practice

The above process will document what actually happens, but will not give any indication of how the systems are perceived or what users see as their needs. For that we need to undertake an evaluation in several areas, and consider both the overall assessment and the specific requirements or problems.

We need to identify key issues under each heading, and understand their relative importance. We then need to score existing practice against those criteria to give a baseline for future reference. We also need to determine the specific problems or needs to use as a basis for action. By resolving many of those specific items, we should be able to improve the existing capability quickly and at minimal cost. The baseline will then give us a reference point for checking how much the systems have been improved.

Bear in mind the questions listed are only an indication of the questions that need to be asked. There are many more, and each organisation will need to develop their own set of questions, which will need amendment from time to time, and from project to project.

Content

This is about the completeness of the data. Some of the issues and questions that need to be asked are:

1 Is the data and information what is required?
2 How complete is the essential information?
3 How much redundant data is there?
4 What data items are missing?
5 Which are never used, no longer relevant or not possible to collect?
6 What reports are never produced or if they are, not actually used?
7 Do any forms match the required data – are they structured correctly, are they clear and easily understood by whoever completes them?

Accuracy and reliability

This section is about the quality of the information. Some of the questions and issues here are:

1 Is the data up to date?
2 Does data go missing or get corrupted?
3 If there are problems are they speedily resolved?
4 Does the data match across systems. Are the results consistent?

Suitability

The issues here are around how useful the systems are in supporting managers and their staff in their work.

1 Does it make your easier or more effective?
2 Could it be achieved in other ways?

Usability

The issues here relate to the level of skill required to use the systems and their performance in day to day use.

1 Is it easy to use?
2 Is the level of skill required commensurate with the job role and the frequency of use of the system?
3 How well does it service ad-hoc needs?
4 Is it fast enough or too fast?
5 Are there easily understood guidance notes?

Flexibility

As already discussed, the nature of work is constantly changing and the pace appears to be quickening. The issues here are about how well the systems accommodate such changes.

1 Has the system been adapted to meet changed needs since its implementation?
2 Is it flexible enough to accommodate necessary changes?
3 Are changes made quickly enough to maintain the system's usefulness?

Importance

This is a measure of the impact that the system has on the work of the organisation and its staff. As part of that, it needs to be considered whether the security is appropriate to the system's criticality.

1 How dependent is the organisation on the system?
2 How dependent are users on the system?
3 What would happen to the business if the system failed for an hour, a day, a week?
4 Is the system sufficiently secure from interference from unauthorised users?
5 Are there procedures in place to allow the organisation to continue to operate if the system is unavailable?
6 Are there appropriate contingency plans for the system being unavailable, for example, because of a fire or flood?

Future

The issues around this require users and other managers to look into the future. Ideally, they should have a clear understanding of the corporate vision and its implications for their work. Most managers will have some understanding of how they expect their work to change over the next one to three years. That timescale is probably as good as is required – few industries can plan further ahead than that in any meaningful way.

Some of the questions that need to be answered are:

1 Will the system meet the future needs as you understand them?
2 What changes will be required for the system to maintain or improve its usefulness in the future?
3 How well does it support the current corporate strategic plan over the lifetime of the plan?
4 Will it support future customer, supplier and regulatory requirements.
5 Does the system provide a suitable basis for future needs, albeit with appropriate modification?
6 Has the system's time past?

There are also two further areas that need to be considered, and as they are essentially technical, they are probably the responsibility of the IT manager or whoever is responsible for the support of the systems and technology.

Note also that the IT manager and IT staff should evaluate the system against the above criteria, but from their own standpoint and understanding of user needs. The difference between the user evaluation and the IT department evaluation will illustrate the understanding gap between the two groups. That gap too will need to be addressed – a closer understanding of each other's needs should be sought.

The gap between user and specialist staff understanding is a major barrier to effective use of information in most organisations. They do not speak the same language. That gap has to be bridged, and as a reader of this book you have recognised that. It is essential that senior management seeks to understand the information and related technology issues, but in business rather than technical terms. On the other hand, it is a responsibility for IM/IS/IT managers (whatever their title) to be able to explain the technology in business terms, or better still, plain English. They need to become business managers with a responsibility for information and its technology, rather than technicians first and foremost. Therefore they need to develop an understanding of business, and then to be involved in the strategic planning from the start. But they need to be helped to that understanding by their colleagues, and especially by senior managers involving them at an early stage of the planning process.

Supportability

The issues and questions around this topic include:

1 How well-supported is the system by its supplier?
2 How well-equipped is the organisation to meet its support obligations for this system?
3 How easy is it for the IT and user staff to support the system?
4 Does it fit with existing anticipated standards for hardware and software?
5 Can it be maintained?

Performance

This is about the performance of the system from a technical viewpoint, and the questions include:

1 Is the system reliable? Bear in mind that modern systems, ought to be available to users 97 per cent or more of normal working hours.
2 Are there any problems with corruption, loss of data, etc.?
3 Is it is as fast as needed?
4 Does it have capacity for growth?

Get the basics right

Once the existing systems have been documented, there will obvious areas of improvement that can be addressed without having to implement new systems.

These will probably require changes to existing processes, and to the information systems that support them. These changes should be treated like any other project: their objectives and benefits should be defined, the resources and timetable planned and project management put in place. They should be actioned before any more fundamental developments are contemplated.

New systems need firm foundations, so it is essential to get the basics right.

Information systems benchmarking

Techniques similar to those described above for establishing a baseline can be used to establish benchmarks from other organisations. Obviously, it will be impossible to have the same knowledge of competitors' systems as of one's own. But a view can be taken and an evaluation made. If the result is the result of an excessively rosy view of the competition's systems, then that can be positive, as it gives you a more demanding target. Meet it, and you have gained an advantage. Better that way than underplaying the capability of rivals.

Actually, there can be quite a lot of information available about systems in similar and competing organisations. Many case studies appear in journals, managers present their systems at user group meetings or conferences as do suppliers. Many organisations are quite open about what they do, especially in the not-for-profit sector where they share information amongst themselves quite freely. Much of the best work will be featured as case studies in magazines and conferences.

The benchmarks do not have to come from competitors or even closely similar organisations. Often it is ideas from completely different businesses that will demonstrate best practice that can be transferred to your own sector. You need to do it before the competition – the information is equally available to them!

Evaluating ideas from the outside is the same as evaluating your own systems; if others are ahead, then you have to look at ways of closing that gap and ideally reversing it, as the competition will not be standing still.

MISTAKES TO AVOID

There is a lot of room for getting any project wrong, but with information systems, there are some obvious mistakes that continue to be made. They are so easily avoided, but I keep coming across them. I suppose I should be grateful as it keeps me in work, but it is disheartening when I see the same mistakes being made that I saw at the beginning of my career 20 years ago.

I do not promise that if you avoid the following mistakes that you will have none, but you should avoid some of the worst difficulties.

Excessive expectations

There is much hype surrounding information technology which raises the expectations of both managers and technicians. Unfortunately it does not explain that the success of any system is dependent on the people who implement and operate it. As a result, they over-estimate what the technology or the systems can really deliver. They also grossly under-estimate the effort required from colleagues and especially from themselves, to achieve any real benefits.

Consequently, most information projects take longer, achieve less and cost more than expected.

Expectations have to be managed at all levels. It is therefore essential that all key interest groups are represented on the project team by influential leaders of those groups. Whilst it is important to create excitement around the new opportunities that a project should create, these have to be realistic and achievable. If they are not, then everyone becomes disappointed and demotivated. This will impact on not just the current work, but on future projects as well.

Not involving users

Managing expectations requires user involvement, but it is not the only reason. Users have the knowledge about what is required to do their job. They may not be aware of the opportunities for doing things differently, but they know what end-results are required of the processes for which they have responsibility.

Not using that knowledge will lead to systems that do not meet users' needs (or expectations). If users feel ignored, they will not feel any responsibility for making the system work – it is not 'their' system. That is the biggest single cause of new systems not delivering benefits.

It should not be left to a single group, as they will have their own parochial agenda and the needs of others will not be given due consideration. This is a particular problem, if technical specialists are left to implement new systems – their view is even more specialised and less business-oriented than most.

Cross-functional teams are essential for corporate information management to be fully effective. Do not let one group dominate.

Mismatch between business and IS/IT

Not involving users is one of the biggest causes of a mismatch between business needs and the proposed IS/IT solution. All new systems should be the result of a true partnership between general managers and appropriate specialists.

However even by involving users, there is scope for such a mismatch. Managers at the highest level need to be involved, as they have the overall view of the corporate strategy. The information systems have to reflect that strategy, but cannot do so if its authors are not properly represented on the project team.

Again a major failing of many change projects, not just information-based, is the lack of commitment and involvement of senior managers. If senior managers do not demonstrate that they believe a project to be important by their involvement, why should anyone else put in the effort?

Being at the leading edge

Whilst it is exciting being at the leading edge of new technology, it is not appropriate for most organisations. New technology is expensive, and by its very nature is unproven, therefore the risks are greater. It is likely to take longer, cost more and deliver less than hoped. Because of the lack of knowledge, planning for problems is more difficult.

Furthermore in a significant proportion of cases, the technology will be a blind alley, and will need to be replaced at an earlier date than originally envisaged. This increases the cost to the organisation.

Arrogance

There is a danger in being arrogant enough to think that you can do it all yourself. As already suggested, information needs a wide set of skills. Management is about judgement and a key judgement for any manager is whether they are competent to take on a particular task. If they are not justifiably confident, then they should seek that expertise from elsewhere – either internal to the organisation or from consultants.

Bear in mind that both technology and the business environment are changing rapidly. It is difficult for specialists to stay up to date with current thinking in their own field, so it is unreasonable to expect a general manager to have the skills necessary to do all the work themselves.

Managers should devote their personnel and other resources to those aspects most vital to the continuing success of the organisation, and where their skills will be best used. Using staff on critical developments for which they are barely equipped is neither fair on the individual, nor good use of resources for the organisation.

It can be downright dangerous – *a little knowledge is a dangerous thing*. I have had to sort out many projects, at premium consultancy rates, where people have got out of their depth or have used students or similar with insufficient experience to see the pitfalls – until they fell into them.

Too much rigidity

As we have already said, information strategy is not a destination, but a journey. One can make a case for starting an information strategy with the words similar to those used by old Sea Captains in their log – 'this is the log of the *such and such* bound, by the Grace of God, for. . .' We know where we want to go but do not really know where we will arrive.

Information strategies, indeed all plans, should recognise that uncertainty and be designed for modification as the need unfolds. Too much rigidity results in achieving a result that is no longer relevant and may be positively harmful. As we discuss in Chapter 8, project management is about managing the risk, not simply achieving the timetable. Too many projects have failed on time. . .

So we need to be flexible within a properly based strategic framework that allows the plan to be updated as more is learned about the directions other journeys are taking. The plan should not be so flexible that any result will be acceptable – that is no plan.

Over-simplification

Information systems are not simple – they are complex multi-disciplinary projects that cross functions and even go outside the organisation.

Like the old joke based on Rudyard Kipling's *If* :

If you can keep your head whilst all about are losing theirs – then you don't understand the problem!

. . . if it looks simple, then you do not understand the problem. Unfortunately, many people see it as straightforward and make it so by simply computerising existing systems. As a result, old thinking is fossilised and the business is in danger of becoming so.

This means that the investment is not taking the business forward – and if it is not taking the business forward, why is it being made?

Not evaluating

This raises a common mistake: lack of evaluation at all stages of the information project definition and planning. The benefits and costs should be evaluated before committing resources to ensure that the investment represents value for money and is going to give measurable benefits. Those benefits must be stated in terms of their contribution to achieving corporate objectives.

Furthermore the costs and benefits should continue to be monitored during implementation, and there should be management decision points where a decision to continue or to kill the project should be made formally. All too often further investment is made to try and keep a project alive because of the investment already made. Such sunk costs are not a justification for further investment. Further investment should only be made if the balance between cost and benefit is still right and there is a realistic prospect of success. Otherwise further investment is the equivalent of a gambler raising his stake in the hope, usually forlorn, of recovering his losses. Unfortunately it is far too common.

Even if the project gets to completion evaluation is still not finished. As will be explained later, there is a need to learn from what has gone before. A formal review is required to make sure that lessons are learned, documented and shared with future project teams. The whole of this book is about knowledge management and this element in particular is about organisational memory after all!

Inadequate resources

All too often, information-related projects are under-resourced. This is partly because senior management does not see the benefits, and partly because the business case is not properly prepared.

As a result, the costs are pared in the plan, so that the project is given the go-ahead. Then, as the work develops (and usually expands to include other things), the additional funds are sought. Because of the investment already made the money is made available. But it becomes a vicious circle – because everyone worries about the costs, the original budget is scaled down in a vain attempt to control the overrun – so it is bound to be over budget.

But it is not just finance; other resources are under-estimated, including time and the number of people to be involved. As a result, everybody is trying to do too much with too little time, too few people and not enough cash. So the project is too expensive, too late and it fails to deliver the anticipated benefits. All largely avoidable.

Defining the problem to fit the solutions

It is all too easy to start with preconceived ideas about the requirements, or even worse, a particular computer system. Once that has happened, it is a straightforward task to force-fit the latest whiz-bang technology, with little reference to business objectives. Worse still, it leaves the business open to being sold a system, rather than buying the solution it needs that meets those corporate objectives.

The result is an expensive white elephant that meets no-one's needs, but absorbs a substantial part of the information management budget for the next few years. As a consequence, the organisation cannot afford to replace the unsuitable system, and loses rather than improves its competitive position.

Avoid salesmen

Many people like to attend demonstrations and look at possible solutions before they examine their own requirements in any detail. It is done to give them 'ideas'. That is a euphemism for accepting a technically led solution and letting external suppliers set your information management strategy. By doing so, they are putting the whole future of their organisation in the hands of sales people whose only concern is their own commission and their employer's success.

I recommend that you do not look at solutions or talk to salesmen until you have written your specification. That way you can be sure that you have not inadvertently defined your problem to favour a particular solution. Your specification should take no account of what is on offer in the market; it should be entirely based on what your organisation needs.

You do not need 'ideas', at least not initially with regard to the information systems. The solution should come from a deep and genuine understanding of the business and what it hopes to achieve. In any organisation of more than a handful of people there will be more than enough ideas to reengineer processes and from there to specify the supporting information systems to make real business gains. That must be the aim and external sales people cannot do that for you.

Also bear in mind that sales people will seek to create FUD – Fear, Uncertainty and Doubt, so that you are not confident of your own judgement. It is a well-established technique used by many – not all –

salesmen in the IT industry, where buyers are often less than comfortable about their own knowledge. I had a case recently where the Finance Director of a client went to an exhibition, and came back worried about their information technology. He asked the IT manager, 'Why aren't we using X, Y and Z?'.

Fortunately, the IT manager knew exactly why they were not using X, Y and Z, and told his boss why. In this case X,Y and Z were reasonable choices, but they were the Number 2 players and commercially aggressive. The systems already in place were the market leaders in their field, and for good reasons. Either would have been safe, but the IT manager and his staff also had considerable expertise with their market-leader-supplied systems and little with the alternatives: therefore had no good reason to change.

A weaker or less confident manager might well have been frightened into making changes for the sake of it – I have had to sort out the aftermath.

So do not talk to salesmen and suppliers until you are preparing your shortlist of those invited to bid. That is plenty early enough, and even then they will absorb more of your time than you would wish.

ANALYSIS OF QUESTIONNAIRE 3

1 **Neither of them.** Information management is required to support all planning processes. The need for information and how it might be used to benefit the organisation, and its customers, also means that the information management strategy should be defined as part of those processes. It is integral to all business thinking and should not be separated. Information is an expensive and valuable corporate resource.

2 **Yes.** Most modern management thinking, such as business process re-engineering, total quality management and learning organisations, relies on good information systems.

3 **No.** Information should be seen as part of the forward thinking, not as a fix to problems. Lack of information is not the problem, it is the lack of a strategy to exploit information in the organisation's operations.

4 **Yes.** Information management should be defined as part of a cross-functional planning process. Too often it is bolted on after the event, and this cannot take advantage of the opportunities information provides for new and better ways of doing business.

5   **No.** Not really. Each department may have particular requirements that it can define, but it should do so as a holistic approach to planning the organisation's operations. All strategic and business planning should cross departmental boundaries, otherwise it will reinforce communication and other problems.

6   **No.** It is possible to find performance measures for any human endeavour. Information management is no different. It just may need some lateral thinking.

7   **No.** It is a personal view, but most organisations are not much better than they were 20 years ago at using information. There may be more of it produced faster. But the understanding and application of information, especially qualitative information, are not really very much better. We continue to repeat many of the same problems. Most organisations are still stuck at Level 1 or 2.

8   **No.** Most organisations pay lip-service to aligning their corporate objectives and their use of information technology. But it is usually superficial. It is bolted on after the event, usually by technical staff who have little genuine understanding, or indeed interest, in business and management issues. There are some notable exceptions.

9   **No.** The issue is your organisation's needs, not the solutions. You understand your business or should do. Do not let the solution lead the requirements. That has been the big failing ever since computers became widely used – the business needs have been fitted to the solution, not the solution to the business needs. You can buy the expertise to produce the solution, but only when you know what you want it to do in business terms.

ACTION PLAN

1   Establish a baseline score for the effectiveness of current information management.

2   Identify the information available to the organisation from existing systems.

3   Track the data flows through all systems, not just those that are computer-based.

4   Understand the informal systems: they reflect genuine needs and use of information.

To avoid assumptions being made, ask people to do it for departments or teams other than their own. Allow, no, encourage them, to challenge why information is collected and how it is used. And do not accept glib answers.

FURTHER READING

G Cutts, *SSADM*,Paradigm, 1987
A practical exposition of structured systems analysis which will be valuable for anyone needing to undertake formal documentation of systems. Before moving into the academic world, Geoff Cutts had an extensive background in the management of software development (I worked for him for several years), and it shows in this textbook. The techniques are described in a way that should be readily understood by any manager.

M E Porter, *Competitive Strategy*, The Free Press, 1980
This is a heavyweight book that provides a complete framework for analysing an organisation's competitive position and developing its strategy. It introduced the Value Chain concept that has become a standard part of strategic planning. It also made clear the generic forms that competitive advantage can take.

Not an easy read, but it rewards study. It provides essential background, and is a valuable reference for anyone having a role in strategic planning. Most later work on planning is built on the foundations laid by Michael Porter in this book.

Mankin, Cohen & Bikson, *Teams and Technology*, Harvard Business School Press, 1996
This book is about creating information systems to allow collaboration and building teams to take advantage of technology and information. It is based on an on-going case study, and builds the thinking along the way. A useful starting point to understanding the possibilities.

Turner, Grude & Thurloway, *The Project Manager as Change Agent*, 1996
This is a practical, but not superficial, book aimed at preparing for change, and it recognises the importance of people in that process. Using information requires change and will cause change. The information manager will therefore need to be a change agent and a project manager – this book will help equip them for that role.

Indeed, the general manager will increasingly work as a project manager (as well as an information manager) leading teams to achieve a particular set of objectives. A manager's life is getting exciting!

SUMMARY

Success in business, whether for profit or not, requires change. Increasingly that change has to be substantial and frequent as the whole business environment accelerates its changes.

Information is a tool of all management thinking and theories. Whether you subscribe to them or not, your planning will be

influenced by them and your need for information will increase. You will need to analyse and understand what is happening in both the marketplace and within your business. It has often been said that knowledge is power – it has never been more true. And knowledge is derived from good information, often gained piecemeal then aggregated, to provide a clearer but still incomplete picture. There is never time to build a complete picture; by the time you have the scene will have changed.

All planning processes need information to produce meaningful plans and strategies. And those strategies need to define the objectives in terms of information that will be available for their management. So information is an integral part of all business processes, and cannot be separated if there is to be a meaningful strategy for information.

Innovation is the key to success in the new world, and it can only come from creative thinking based on a deep, often subconscious, understanding of what is happening and what is possible. That means all managers and others need to have access to information and the skills to make use of it and to understand it and its implications. It is only through that deep understanding that new insights are achieved from which creative opportunities arise.

But there is a need to get the basics right, and to eliminate bureaucracy in the solutions that are currently in use. Management has to be made more effective by being based on timely information about what needs to be achieved, and what is actually being achieved.

So there is a need to identify requirements and establish a baseline for future developments. Without a measure of the effectiveness of current systems, it will not be possible to determine whether any replacements are justified. All investment needs to be properly justified on the basis of the contribution it will make to improved performance.

Finally, it is important to learn from mistakes, so there is a need to manage the knowledge that is learned from each project to ensure that the mistakes that are made are not repeated. Over 20 years in information systems, I see the same mistakes being made by each new generations – there seems to be no organisational or industrial memory. Information management is about giving an organisation that memory, and the expertise to use it.

CHAPTER

COMPETITIVE ADVANTAGE AND ADDED VALUE

Competitive advantage can be achieved in a variety of ways, but at the end of the day it has to be manifest as some added benefit for the customer.

INTRODUCTION

There has to be a business purpose behind information
management. The only advantage that is meaningful is to gain
or maintain competitive advantage in some way. Competitive
advantage can be achieved in a variety of ways, but at the end of
the day it has to be manifest as some added benefit for the
customer. It may be added value, more for the money, or it is the
same, but at lower cost. It may be expressed differently, but the
concept of competitive advantage is equally applicable to not-for-
profit organisations, such as charities. It may not be stated in
terms of profit or market share, but it may well be stated in terms
of funding attracted or alliances made.

The objectives of this chapter are to give the reader some insight
into:

1 the nature of competitive advantage;

2 information's role in achieving and sustaining competitive
   advantage;

3 customer's perception of what constitutes 'value' or 'quality';

4 how information can change the environment in which the
   organisation operates and thereby change the nature of
   competition;

5 the issues surrounding the value of organisational memory.

QUESTIONNAIRE 4

Strategic planning for competitive advantage

1 Do you know what type of strategy your organisation had adopted?
   a Yes
   b No

2 Does your organisation have a clear vision of its purpose?
   a Yes
   b No

3 Does your organisation analyse and refine the processes in its Value Chain?
   a Yes
   b No
   c What is a Value Chain?

4 Do you understand that there is a different Value Chain based on intangible information?
   a Yes
   b No

5 Does your organisation analyse:
   a Internal qualitative data such as customer complaints or customer queries?
   b External qualitative data such as market trends, market research, government policy documents, technological developments, etc.?
   c Internal quantitative data such as product performance, customer purchasing trends, market analysis?
   d External quantitative data such as industry performance statistics, competitors' published accounts?

COMPETITIVE ADVANTAGE: GENERIC STRATEGIES

Introduction

In his two major works (*Competitive Strategy* and *Competitive Advantage*) on business strategy, Michael Porter set out much of the basis for current strategic planning. Porter identifies five competitive forces on an organisation and their source, within those forces there are many factors that influence their relative importance:

- From potential entrants: there is a threat of new entrants into the industry, thereby changing the structure of the competition within that industry. Even if the new entrant is unsuccessful, they will alter the framework within which existing rivals compete.
  - Economies of scale.
  - Entry costs – what does it cost to equip for this market?
  - Distribution issues – how does it work in the industry?
  - Will customers switch, or are they locked into existing suppliers, agreements or technology?
  - Regulation and government policy.
  - Product differences.
  - How strong are existing brands?
  - Response by existing suppliers.

- Buyers clearly provide a competitive force, through both the choices they make and their bargaining power.
  - Brand identity.
  - Customers' ability to switch suppliers.
  - Proprietary technology.
  - Industry and supplier capacity.
  - Support or knowledge requirements.
  - Growth of industry sector.

- Suppliers, too, affect the forces of competition through their pricing and other negotiating strengths.
  - Possibility of substitute products.
  - Licensing, intellectual property and the proprietary nature of the input product.
  - Importance of volume to supplier.
  - Significance of input costs to competitors.
  - Integration within the supplier and industry chain. Are competitors integrating backwards or suppliers forwards?

- The final source of competitive forces is from the threat of product substitution. This may be due to a variety of factors from fashion to changes in technology.
  - Price performance of alternative inputs.
  - Costs of switching to alternative inputs products.
  - Differentiation between alternative inputs.
  - Willingness of buyer to change sources.
  - Environmental pressures.

- Within an industry, there is also the rivalry between existing competitors which have an impact on each other's competitive position and adopted strategies.
  - Sensitivity of market to price or performance changes.
  - Buyer knowledge.
  - Brand identity.
  - Ability of competitors to change products.
  - Relative economies of scale.
  - Ability to offer new products, services or technology.
  - Relative capacity of rivals and market share.

A business has to be aware of these factors in analysing its competitive position and defining strategies. It must be stressed that the relative importance of the above forces will vary from industry to industry and even to different firms within the same industry. The list of influences on the above five competitive forces are only a small sample of the possible factors.

Porter went on to suggest that there are only three generic competitive strategies. The strategies are cost leadership, differentiation and focus. Of these, focus could be broken into two sub-strategies of cost focus and differentiation focus. We need to explore these quickly, so that we can then start to determine what role information management might have to support whichever strategy our organisation has chosen. It will inevitably be very much of a quick overview as Porter took over 1,000 pages to set out his arguments!

Cost leadership

The aim with a cost leadership strategy is to become *the* low cost supplier in your industry. Even though the strategy is based on cost, it is still essential that there is no substantial difference between you and your competitors as regards performance or other determinants of customer value. Buyers will not purchase simply on price: price will, however, be used where products or services are otherwise similar.

Differentiation

Here the purpose is to be different from your competitors in a way that is genuinely valued by customers. By doing so, you can attract a premium price for your products or services. The form that uniqueness might take can vary from high performance to the less tangible value of 'image'. But it must be a genuine uniqueness or perceived to be so by buyers, if it is to maintain a premium over competing products.

Focus

Focus is concerned with limiting the range of a firm's activities. The objective is to be the leader in a market segment, even though it is not possible to be a leader in the industry as a whole. To be a leader being simply focused on a particular niche is not enough: it has to be combined with a cost advantage or unique customer value amongst the players in that segment.

COMPETITIVE ADVANTAGE: VALUE DISCIPLINES

Introduction

Michael Treacy and Fred Wiersema offer a slightly different view of possible competitive strategies. They set this out in *The Discipline of Market Leaders*, where they suggest that successful companies succeed by excelling at providing a single type of value to their customers. Once they have chosen their 'value discipline', such organisations build their entire strategy and operations around it.

Operational excellence

Adopting the value discipline of operational excellence requires an organisation to take control of its costs, and provide the best total cost solution for its customers. It is about control in all aspects of the organisation through standardisation and efficient transactions through automation of administrative and production processes. It requires a team-based rather than an individualist approach.

McDonald's are an example of operational excellence, as are Ford, who probably invented the modern operationally excellent approach.

To sustain operational excellence requires growth through new customers, new products or greater utilisation. Growth leads to economies of scale which helps support the reduction of unit costs.

As can be seen, this is essentially the same as Porter's cost leadership strategy.

Product leadership

To provide product leadership is about innovation and the development and launch of genuinely new products, not merely 'improved' ones. A classic example is Sony, who have consistently led with new ideas such as the *Walkman* portable cassette player, *Betamax* video cassette player, generally regarded as the best technical solution, even though it did not ultimately win the marketing war, and the *Mavica* digital camera.

To sustain operational excellence requires growth through new customers, new products or greater utilisation.

Such innovation needs to be brought to market quickly and effectively: this requires cross-functional working, with research and development, production and marketing working together in parallel to achieve fast times to market for new products.

Customer intimacy

Customer intimacy is about providing a total solution for the customer. It requires the organisation to genuinely understand its customers and their needs; the best often understand customers' needs better than customers themselves. As a provider of a total solution, this strategy will often require customer-intimate organisations to extend into related services to continue to provide a total solution.

However, as can be seen, the 'value discipline' view still owes much to Porter's generic strategies. Operational excellence is similar to cost leadership, product leadership equates to differentiation and customer intimacy owes much to the focus strategies. You make your own decisions as to how your organisation's strategy is expressed. What is important is that as an organisation you have a clearly defined strategy that is understood by everyone and accepted because it is based on shared values.

DEVELOPING A CORPORATE STRATEGY

It is beyond the scope of this book to guide you through the process of developing a corporate strategy. All it can do is give you a feel for some of the issues, and indicate the necessity of having a formal strategy before embarking on any information management developments. If you do not have a strategy, read some of the books listed in *Further reading*, and develop one for your organisation. Then come back to this book to develop a supporting information management strategy.

If you try to build any low-level strategies without a clear and overarching business vision, then you will have the tail wagging the dog. Information management and technology strategies, along with all others, must follow on from a clear strategic direction.

PULLING IT ALL TOGETHER

Sustaining competitive advantage

Competitive advantage has to be maintained over the long run if the desired result of above-average performance is to be achieved. Harvesting (or milking) can apparently give above-average performance, but only in the short-term and often at the expense of sustained competitive advantage

Role of information systems and technology

Cost leadership or operational excellence strategies are about efficiency and effectiveness. If we think back to Chapters 1 and 2, we will recall that information management is about supporting the Cycle of Control and effective decision-making. Good information is essential to provide the high level of control needed for this strategy. The need for efficiency will mean that cost leaders will tend to use automation for both reliability of control and cost reduction.

Competitive advantage has to be maintained over the long run if the desired result of above-average performance is to be achieved.

Product leadership is based on using corporate knowledge, combined with sharing the skills and knowledge of individuals to create innovation and new products. With the move to multi-disciplinary team-working, sharing information and knowledge becomes an important part of the product development process.

Similarly the customer-intimate approach requires excellent market intelligence about the needs of its customer group. Furthermore it also requires knowledge of existing customers and how they use the products and services. Much of that information is qualitative, and although it is more difficult to handle, it still requires effective information management.

So all strategies rely on good information, but will put the emphasis on different aspects of its management. Only you can determine what is important to your organisation, and then only if you have a clear strategy.

American Express

American Express has always been concerned to manage its relationship with both its members and its merchants to mutual benefit. Basically, American Express operates as a 'customer-intimate' supplier to its members and its merchants – it values and seeks to build on its close relationship with both.

Statements were always seen as a useful way of communicating with members. When faced with the need to update its statement production systems American Express did not simply replace them with similar but more modern systems. It went further and re-examined the purpose of the statement and its role in the company's relationship management.

There were two important threads that led to the final innovative approach. First, American Express recognises that its cards are more expensive for merchants to accept than most others. So it has always sought to give extra value by giving merchants access to members, especially those with an international interest. It is always looking for ways of tailoring that access but have done it traditionally by market segmentation of members' interests.

Secondly, there was the need and opportunity to redesign the way statements were produced to take advantage of the new technology. The aim was to make the statement more useable. AmEx wanted to use the statement to reinforce the value of the relationship to the member. The problem was that traditional statements were at best neutral in that respect. It found that members' prime interest was 'How much do they owe?' and 'Was it really my transaction?' AmEx statements give more information about transactions than most other card companies. They also ensure that the location in which the transaction took place is shown – not, as is often the case, the base location of the merchant company. That makes it easier for the member to recognise the transaction as its own. But that was not enough.

American Express has a close relationship with its merchants and handles all phases of the transaction between members, merchants and itself, and therefore was well placed to make an innovative leap. Because of this relationship, AmEx already collected considerable data from the point of sale about the products purchased, site and so on – which it reported back to merchants as part of the value in the relationship. But AmEx also has considerable knowledge about members' buying patterns – not only what they buy but where they buy it and even when.

The innovation in the approach of combining that knowledge with its new statement print formatting capability came by turning the normal approach of segmenting the membership by market sector on its head. Instead of asking 'Which members might be interested in this offer?' the question now is 'What offers are appropriate to this member?' The details of the relevant offers are then printed on the statement, often against similar transactions from the previous period. It now takes account of where the member buys particular types of product. For example, they may buy clothes near where they work but gardening products near their home, and only at weekends. This is reflected in the offers made.

There have been several other benefits from this new approach. Products and offers can be designed which are more effective than can be achieved by segmentation. AmEx is able to turn round such offers in two to three days as opposed to weeks for the traditional shotgun approach – this allows 'perishable' offers to be made. The high level of focus also allows small scale or local offers – based on home or work, depending on where the member tends to make such purchases. This has proved to provide highly cost-effective marketing with better take-up and lower cost to reach each prospect.

Merchants could not achieve this themselves as even if they have the information on their sales they are unlikely to have the detailed knowledge of customer spending patterns. The latter would be particularly expensive to collect. And AmEx monitors the effectiveness of the offer for the merchant. So this approach adds considerably to the value of being an American Express merchant.

For members it means that they only get relevant offers which improves the quality of the service – one does not have to search through masses of irrelevant flyers to find the statement. And it goes without saying that the statement is clear and well presented so it readily answers the members' questions 'How much do I owe?' and 'Is this my transaction?'

But the key point about this case study is summed up by Barrington Hill, Senior Vice-President – Product Development:

'American Express has always had a strategy for managing its relationship with members and merchants for mutual benefit. This allowed us to use the opportunity provided by the redesign of the statement platform to develop this new approach to enhance the value of those relationships. Without that clear strategy it would have just been a technical upgrade of the statement production.'

Clear vision and strategy is the key to success with information just as it is with all other aspects of business management. This case study is only the tip of the iceberg, it required considerable innovation on how matters were handled internally – and there is a lot more innovation to come. American Express is only too aware that it cannot stand still if it wishes to remain a leader.

Changing the environment

The rapid development of technology and equally rapid changes in the business environment mean that there are opportunities for organisations to alter that environment. Those who can combine business opportunities with new technology quickly and effectively will often be able to change the rules of the game: however, the risk of getting it wrong is great. The danger of doing nothing is also dangerous, but the consequences manifest themselves more slowly.

All organisations need to manage those risks and therefore need to understand the costs, the risks and the potential benefits. But first they have to have a clear business strategy and see the opportunities of information management. Combine strategy, opportunity and supporting technology, and it will be possible to weigh the risks and returns.

Inaction is not an option in a rapidly changing world.

ADDING VALUE

Introduction

There are opportunities from information that go beyond cost reduction. Indeed the opportunities for cost reduction from the use of

information and its supporting technology are decreasing, as most of the obvious opportunities have been used.

So to use information for business benefit means adding value to existing products or exploiting the value of the information itself (see the CCN Group case study in Chapter 1, page 21).

The Virtual Value Chain

As we are well aware there is a market place for physical products and a value chain for meeting the needs of that market place. But Rayport and Sviokla in 'Exploiting the Virtual Value Chain', *Harvard Business Review* November–December 1995, argue for a complementary 'marketspace' where value can be created from information.

They argue that whilst managers have refined the links in the physical value chain (see Porter, *Competitive Strategy, Appendix D*), where information has merely been a support for the value-adding process, managers have not considered the Virtual Value Chain. The Virtual Value Chain is the value-adding steps involved in the production of value from raw information. There the value is created through and with information. They set out activities by which information is turned into value:

- gathering;
- organising;
- selecting;
- synthesising;
- distributing.

They also argue that all executives need to consider both value chains, and that they need to recognise that they work in different ways. This all takes place in the 'marketspace' and increasingly leads into the customer's Virtual Value Chain without entering the Physical Value Chain – for example through such means as the Internet or Electronic Mail.

Strategic alliances

Information and technology make new kinds of alliances possible. Some will be based on closer relationships with existing suppliers and customers. Others will be with suppliers of different products and services to the same market segments which will add value to both your products and theirs.

Ford Trucks

This is now a classic case study having been used in several books on business process re-engineering.

In its Transit Van plant near Southampton, and other truck plants around the world, Ford has developed a close relationship with its suppliers. For example the supplier of brake parts to Ford Trucks does not receive purchase orders. Instead it is linked to Ford's production scheduling computer, so that it can see what type of vehicles will be going down the line during the period in which it is interested. The supplier then sends a series of deliveries to arrive just in time to go straight on to the end of the line. There is no goods inward section or inspection.

The parts are used, but the supplier does not invoice Ford. Instead Ford counts the vehicles it has produced, and from that it knows what brakes it has used, so it pays the supplier accordingly. So there is no purchase order section.

The result is efficient and accurate with little scope for mistakes. It satisfies the needs of Ford as an operationally excellent company. It makes for efficient transactions and close control – both central to such a strategy.

In fact, that close liaison extends further back in the whole product life cycle, as there is an exchange of technical and engineering information during the design process. This continues during production through simultaneous engineering, with the aim of continuous improvement of the product: a strategic alliance that relies on modern information technology.

IT'S A BIG WORLD

Globalisation

Markets are becoming increasingly international, and all businesses need to recognise this and act accordingly. New information technology is supporting this trend and creates opportunities for those who are bold enough to accept the challenge.

Communications

The Internet and other on-line service providers give even the smallest organisation access to experts all around the world. I regularly use such services and have developed support and business relationships with people whose nationality, marital status, age, sex or disabilities are not known to me, nor am I bothered. Our relationships are based on common interests and mutual benefits, usually an exchange of ideas and expertise. It is potentially an emancipating technology, at least for those people and organisations that have access to it.

It is also a valuable research tool, because of the amount of expertise that is freely shared, especially if you are prepared to contribute your knowledge.

I also use such services to work with colleagues and clients around the country. Using electronic mail, I can send a document from my word-processor for a colleague to review, edit and return to me. I can then send that on to our client who can then publish it to his colleagues again across his in-house computer network. The document may never appear on paper.

Indeed I have had letters published in magazines, and I know that they never appeared on paper until the magazines were printed. I wrote them straight into my computer and E-mailed them to the magazine editors. They were then edited on-screen, typeset electronically and sent to the printing plate makers. The magazines were then printed – the first time the text of the letters had been printed.

These are simplistic examples, and there are many who have created businesses from the revolution in communications. And not just those who are in the communications business, but those who are simply using high speed electronic communications to do old business in new ways.

ANALYSIS OF QUESTIONNAIRE 4

1 **Yes.** You should know what broad strategic approach your business is taking: otherwise how can you contribute to improved performance. Different strategies need different approaches towards excellence. Making an inappropriate 'improvement' can reduce performance and weaken your strategic strengths.

2 **Yes.** All organisations need to be clear about their specific purpose in measurable terms that are relevant to performance and how they are going to meet the needs of their customers.

3 **Yes.** All businesses take an input and process it through a series of activities to add value and to get it to their customers.

4 **Yes.** If you are aware and use it then you are ahead of the game, especially if you sell physical products rather than knowledge-based services. Few businesses treat information as they treat the raw materials of their more tangible products and services.

5 **All.** You should be using all such information to support your decisions and strategic planning. Few businesses use it all equally effectively, and even fewer formally compare their own performance against industry norms or their rivals (benchmarking). It is a valuable technique, as it shows up your strengths and weaknesses very effectively.

1 Establish which generic strategy your organisation is adopting.

2 Decide which value discipline you are using.

3 Determine what you need to do to focus on your chosen option.

4 Analyse your information systems against those strategies and identify where they do not fit.

5 Clarify your business strategy and the information systems needs that imposes.

6 Compare your performance against industry norms and the published accounts of your competitors.

7 Look for added value by using information.

FURTHER READING

M E Porter, *Competitive Strategy*, The Free Press, 1980

M E Porter, *Competitive Advantage*, The Free Press, 1985

M Treacey & F Wiersema, *The Discipline of Market Leaders*, 1995

This is a book I would recommend to anyone who is interested in business strategy. Like Porter, it suggests a clear and readily understood view of the limited real options in broad business strategies. Unlike Porter, it is an easy read, but it is not trivial.

It provides a framework and case studies around which you can develop your own detailed strategy.

SUMMARY

We explored Porter's generic strategies of:

- cost leadership;
- differentiation;
- focus.

We considered the value discipline approaches of:

- operational excellence;
- product leadership;
- customer intimacy.

We explored the similarities between these approaches, and then briefly examined some of the information system approaches that are required to support these strategies. Both approaches stress that you cannot be all things to everybody, otherwise you undermine your own strengths, and try to compete against rival's strengths – a recipe for failure.

We then identified that to develop a realistic strategy, we need market intelligence and other information, internal and external, to provide an insight into the opportunities.

Added value for the customer can come from information, and it needs to be recognised that more and more products have an information element. Information too, can be a product in itself. Ultimately, information can lead to completely new ways of doing business or indeed completely new business.

The growing globalisation of business and the use of strategic alliances require information to be shared. This sharing needs rapid communication which feeds the on-going globalisation.

COSTS AND BENEFITS

*The true costs of
information systems are
rarely properly assessed.*

INTRODUCTION

The true costs of information systems are rarely properly assessed. They are usually under-estimated at the planning stage and under-recorded during implementation and subsequent operation. In particular, the on-going costs that will be incurred during the lifetime of the system are not properly considered.

On the other hand, the cost reductions and other benefits are over-estimated in planning. But no-one knows, because they are usually not monitored, in any proper sense, during or after implementation. This is a failure of management, at all levels, to exercise due diligence in their work.

So far, this book has stressed the need to identify what has to be achieved for the project to be successful in meeting business needs. Now is the time to formalise that assessment and to monitor its achievement. No project should be allowed to go ahead without a proper cost and benefits assessment that considers the key options, including doing nothing. Only if the project will deliver measurable benefits that contribute to the achievement of the corporate strategy at a justifiable cost, should it be signed off by management and allowed to proceed.

It is also important to monitor and control it during and immediately after implementation. On many projects, especially where there are several phases, it may be wise for there to be management review points during implementation to ensure that the benefits continue to justify the costs – if they do not, then management should be prepared to abort the project.

The systems then have to be managed throughout their life against the budgets as defined at this stage and modified in the light of changing circumstance.

All the experience should then be applied to the projects that come after.

The objectives of this chapter are to enable the reader to:

1   appreciate the true costs of implementing new systems;

2   understand the opportunity costs of change;

3   learn from the experience of the current project so that the lessons can be applied to later work;

4   be able to identify the benefits that are expected to be achieved and evaluate to what extent they have been realised when the work is completed;

5   test whether some of the more subjective aims of the project have been achieved.

QUESTIONNAIRE 5

Dealing with costs

1 Is cost reduction the main justification for the new information management system?
   a Yes
   b No

2 Can all benefits be expressed in quantifiable terms?
   a No
   b Yes

3 Do you only need to worry about the one-off costs, as the new system will replace an old system?
   a Yes
   b No

4 Training is a one-off cost for a new information system.
   a Yes?
   b No?

5 Are all costs incurred and managed by the project team?
   a Yes
   b No

UNDERSTANDING LIFETIME COSTS

Most information systems projects estimate the capital costs and some revenue implications for one to three years. But that estimate is usually superficial in the extreme, as many of the costs do not fall against the sponsoring department's budget or they are lost in general overheads. Thus they become no one person's responsibility, and they are therefore not managed in any meaningful sense.

Rarely then are the running costs monitored against that original estimate, let alone against a realistic estimate of the lifetime costs of the new systems or processes.

There may be a budget for the capital costs, which is managed up to handover of the system, but the many small and not so small costs that are incurred shortly after implementation are again lost in overheads. Few organisations do a thorough post-implementation audit of the project against both cost estimates and expected benefits. Everybody relaxes and starts to think about the exciting new things they are going to be doing. In my view the project is not finished, at least from an internal point of view, until that audit is signed off by senior management.

INITIAL ONE-OFF COSTS

I was going to call this section 'Capital costs', but the costs I intend to discuss may not strictly be capitalised, so to avoid correction from our accounting friends, I have called it 'One-off costs'.

We are concerned here with *all* the costs incurred in setting up the system which will not be recurring items. Any expenses that arise during the operational life of the new systems are treated as on-going costs and are discussed later.

Organisational changes

We have discussed the need for information management to be linked to other fundamental changes in working practices or products. Without such changes full benefit of the investment will not be realised. These will usually result in structural changes to the organisation and there is a cost associated with that.

Those costs may be modest in that they may only be related to rewriting some procedures and relocating a few staff. But they may well be much more substantial involving redeployment, redundancies or regrading, all of which will incur significant costs that will have to be included in the true cost of the project.

Unfortunately many of these costs are carefully forgotten and left to fall on the departments concerned to accommodate as best they can. This means the cost of the project is understated, and therefore cost-benefit appraisal is flawed, and indeed a marginal project may be allowed to go ahead when it would not if the real costs had been known. That is money that could be used in more effective ways and a failure of management's duty of care.

New technology

Clearly new technology in the form of equipment will be built into the budget costs, but how many of the incidental costs of that new equipment will be missed or quietly forgotten? If it is a computer-based system, what about costs such as:

- cables, connectors and other minor works?
- odd items of furniture?
- blinds for windows or changes to the lighting?
- fire certification for altered office layout?
- modifications to new equipment for disabled staff?

Systems

Any new software and many of the costs associated with it will be built into the original estimate but what about:

- supplier support – is the time built into the contract sufficient?
- lost time for the supplier 'because we are not ready' that becomes chargeable when we need extra days at the end of the project?

Identifying requirements

It is all too easy to lose sight of the costs incurred in identifying the need for the project. It may be appropriate for some of the work to be part of the overall planning budget, but once the project moves from the general to the specific, then the costs should be attributed to the project. It is important because these costs can be a significant part of the cost of a project, especially if eventually it is not taken forward

. . . how many of the incidental costs of that new equipment will be missed or quietly forgotten?

for some reason. There are many good reasons why it might not: insufficient benefit, overtaken by events, costs too high, merger and so on. But the costs should be recognised and accounted for – as always, there are lessons that can be learnt. Even aborted, perhaps especially aborted, projects should be reviewed for their lessons to help avoid similar difficulties in the future.

It is all too easy to lose sight of the costs incurred in identifying the need for the project.

The costs incurred are not just a few days of an analyst's time. There are costs for the user teams. The costs will not just be for lost time, but there will also be opportunity costs – what benefits have been missed by staff having to give time to the information project?

Specification

Even the specification preparation and agreement is time- and resource-consuming. Again there will be opportunity costs, because the staff could have been doing other things – would those things have generated more benefits to the organisation?

It is also very easy to under-estimate the amount of work involved in preparing a specification. It is not just a few hours, days or even weeks writing up the results of the requirements study. There is also:

- the time spent evaluating options and priorities;
- management time in overseeing the specification process;
- user and analyst time in walking through and agreeing the specification and the time spent on revision;
- senior management time understanding and giving agreement to the specification and the associated budget.

All this time is expensive and will take a significant elapsed time which has an opportunity cost in itself. The additional costs identified above could easily double the true cost of the specification stage.

Selection process

I recommend elsewhere that the number of bidders for the work should be kept to a sensible minimum. It is often forgotten how much time a selection process takes and how expensive it is to produce and distribute a full set of documents for all but the most trivial of projects.

Time and money is spent on amongst other things:

- producing documentation;
- preparing the list of bidders;
- resolving bidders' queries;
- evaluating bids;
- presentations and demonstrations;
- negotiation;
- legal fees for preparing or reviewing the contract.

It is important to remember that much of this time will be for senior managers and high-level technical staff. This time is both expensive, and tends to be in particularly heavy demand – it needs to be used carefully.

External support

It may well be appropriate to use external support in the form of consultants, project managers or other contract staff to provide the necessary depth of knowledge in particular areas. This could be from initial facilitation of the planning process to advisers undertaking a large part of the analysis, planning, specification and procurement phases with almost full-time project management support during the implementation. Consultants with good skills in the necessary disciplines are expensive, but if used effectively they should be value for money.

Remember that a common mistake is to over-estimate the in-house capability from both an expertise and availability point of view. Availability is a particular problem as the people who form the project team had full-time roles before this new work started, so how are they to be freed now? If members of the team have other priorities, especially in operational areas, then their availability for project work will be compromised. Consequently the success of the project will be at risk.

Other costs

There will be other costs that are unique to your organisation. These must be identified and included in either the one-off costs or the on-going costs. They should on no account be ignored, lumped into general overheads or left for other budgets to carry.

IMPLEMENTATION COSTS

Management time

Again as with the initial costs there is a considerable cost associated with management time during the implementation. This takes the form of oversight by senior management, policy decisions and reviews at key milestones during the project.

There is also a need for the continuing involvement of users, specialist staff and their managers for advice, opinion and to check understanding and to seek agreement of details of the implementation. From time to time on many projects, it will be desirable to present the possible options in the form of a user workshop to seek opinion and agreement on the best way forward.

As has already been stressed, continued user involvement is essential if the new systems are to be implemented and operated smoothly. Take the users with you, and they will make a poor system work – lose their support and you will struggle to make the best systems in the world work!

Project management

Project management takes time, and the amount of work involved is often under-estimated. Make sure that the figure you include is realistic, and then double it.

Bear in mind that it is not just the project manager's time, but also the time that other members of the project team will need to give. Apart from routine work, there will also be ad-hoc demands. These may include visits from or reports to senior management, enquiries from internal auditors and others not directly involved, but who will want some input to the project or need to understand what is being done. There may also be colleagues from other organisations who are thinking of going down a similar route and who will want references or to see what you are doing.

It all takes time and needs to be costed into the project.

Users

Users will have a substantial workload of one sort or another in relation to the project. Apart from their own training, they will need to give time to assessing whether needs are being met, finding information, cleaning or validating data. These costs are rarely properly counted, let alone planned for, yet they may be quite substantial, as they may involve recruiting temporary staff to free the necessary resources.

Disruption

Implementing new systems are always disruptive. The extent will depend on the project, and needs to be assessed on a case-by-case basis. We have already considered many of the costs of that disruption, for example the time spent on validating the new system, and will consider others such as the cost of staff time for training.

There are others not directly related to staff time which include:

- lost production;
- opportunity costs – what else might have been done to give benefits to the organisation;
- missed sales;
- late billing and its impact on cashflow.

This is by no means a definitive list, and you need to look at the impact of staff unavailability and general inconvenience and decide what benefits have been lost or not realised, and show them as costs to the project. They are likely to be more difficult to identify than the costs that are directly incurred, but they should be included because they may well be material.

Temporary staff

If your organisation has got the basics right, as already suggested, then your staff should be fully occupied with their everyday work. So for them to be involved in implementing the new systems, there will be a need for staff to fill in to cover the time used. All but the smallest new systems need temporary staff to continue to operate the old systems, whilst the permanent staff work on implementing the new. As the live date approaches, most of the regular staff will be working almost full-time on the new system.

The sort of work that existing staff will need to do on the new system includes:

- agreeing details of how the new system is to be implemented;
- redefining code structures;
- redefining and rewriting operating procedures, quality manuals, etc;

- sourcing new information;
- assisting with data transfer;
- data cleaning before or after transfer;
- validation of data transfer;
- system testing;
- user testing;
- acceptance testing.

Such costs should be allowed for in planning the project and should not be under-estimated. The work described above is very labour-intensive and therefore time-consuming.

TRAINING COSTS

Training is a major cost and again the full costs are rarely built in to project budgets. Usually only the formal elements are included and the more time-consuming familiarisation and top-up training is forgotten.

Initial user training

Courses

All staff who will be working with the system need training in a formal way. This may take the form of one-to-one coaching, or it may be in a classroom setting. When considering the cost of training, remember that the cost of the tutor's time is only a small part. If you have ten people on a course, then their costs will almost certainly outweigh the cost of the teacher; their work has to be covered.

Even if classroom courses are used, there will need to be follow-up which will probably need to be personal, as each person learns at a different rate and will have different needs and difficulties. Again the time of both tutor and pupil need to be costed.

As a minimum, you probably ought to allow one day of personal coaching per person for every day of formal tuition. This may not always involve external teachers – it may be mutual coaching from your own staff. But it still has to be costed.

Familiarisation

On top of that a new user will need time to familiarise themselves with the system at their own pace and in their own way. Again this time is rarely costed, or if it is, it is grossly under-estimated. Again it is

107

probably wise to plan for at least a day, probably three, for each day of formal courses.

Even then a new user will not be fully proficient and there should be an allowance during the first few weeks of live operation for overtime or support. Proficiency comes with use, and it cannot be fully achieved before using the system on 'real' work. Again there are costs that should be built into the plan and the project assessment.

System manager

There may be two 'system' managers to consider. With most systems there should be a super-user, a system administrator who takes responsibility for the system from the user's point of view. Such a person will act as the user's initial point of contact if there are problems or changes needed, and will ensure that proper controls are operated to ensure data integrity and the like. They will become the 'expert' on the business aspects of the system and its use.

The system administrator will work with the technical system manager (often the IT manager or one of her staff) to agree changes and to resolve problems in a way that makes sense for the business needs. The system administrator therefore acts as a filter to ensure that only appropriate issues are passed through for in-house technical support, and then only once rather than each user doing so themselves.

The technical system manager will then resolve problems in-house or liaise with the supplier's technical support team, again ensuring that the problems are filtered before being passed on to the supplier.

Both these managers need training in more detail than the main body of users. Usually the technical manager will need all the training that the system administrator needs, plus extra to cover the technical issues. Where the dividing line falls will depend on the individuals – in some cases they may well take the same training.

The training needs for these two roles needs to be built into the cost, and as with all the other training, there will be a need for additional coaching and time for familiarisation. Although the system administrator and the technical manager should to a large extent be able to provide cover for each other, it is unwise to rely on single individuals. So allowance in the costs should be made for training additional staff to provide cover for these two critical roles.

Support

Any staff, technicians or users who will be supporting the system managers will also need specialist training on the internal operation and application of the new systems. These people will often be the first port of call for help, and therefore need to be well-versed in the details of the new systems. They should be available from the early stages of the implementation so that they can grow their expertise as the system develops.

ON-GOING COSTS

Training

Training does not stop once the system goes live. There is a continuing need for training and this should be budgeted into the lifetime costs of project.

New starters

It is too often forgotten that new staff will need training, and unfortunately they are often left to pick up the job as they go. This is neither fair on the individual nor cost-effective for the organisation. So training costs should be built in for new starters and like the initial training should allow for:

- formal teaching either on-site, at the system supplier or a third-party training centre;
- coaching both as part of the formal training and as on-the-job training;
- familiarisation – the new starter has more to learn as they need to learn the organisation's approaches as well as the system. Their system familiarisation may therefore take longer;
- time out for existing staff to support and coach the new starter.

Continuous staff development

Even existing staff will need training during the life of the project. It may take the form of remedial training for staff who have developed poor habits, are not making full use of the system or are simply ready to develop new skills and make more advanced use of the system's capabilities.

As with all training, there will be formal training, coaching and familiarisation time, along with support time from colleagues. The costs should be built into the plan.

System updates

During the life of the system there will be changes. Some will be to accommodate new legislation, but many will be to add new functions or to use more capabilities of the system. All but the most trivial changes will need some training of all staff associated with the system with the usual impact on costs and for the same reasons.

All this training has a cost, and it should be built into the budgets, and used to assess the viability of the new system. It should not be thought that these costs can be reduced by cutting down on the amount of training – the costs will in practice be greater, but will be less obvious as they will be lost in reduced staff and organisational performance.

Downtime

It is quite possible that there will be costs associated with downtime during the life of the project. This should be possible to minimise by careful selection, implementation, testing and by making changes to the system outside normal working hours. However it is an imperfect world, and particularly during the early live operation of new systems, there may be difficulties.

This raises two cost issues. What is the cost of not having the system available, and should some contingency be built into the costings to take account of that?

Also, there should be a plan for how the organisation will continue to operate in the event of significant downtime once the system is live. This may be a combination of a disaster recovery plan for coping with a major problem such as a fire, coupled with a plan to revert to manual systems should the system be unavailable for whatever reason.

There should be an allowance in the on-going costs for testing both the disaster recovery and the manual fallback systems. It is time-consuming but cheaper to find out that the recovery procedures do not work at a quiet and scheduled time rather than when really needed. Finally, remember there will be a need for staff training (and to recognise associated costs) in these procedures and systems – new starters in particular will not be familiar with the old manual systems.

CASE STUDY

Ambulance services

Most ambulance services in the UK now have computerised control rooms for their emergency service. These include despatch and signalling systems so that they know what resources are available and where. Many use satellite vehicle tracking systems and computerised maps, so that they can see the location and status of their emergency vehicles at all times.

But they can all revert to the paper-based system that they used before the sophisticated technology. The forms and procedures sit in the desk of every controller, so they are instantly available.

They test their fallback capability from time to time to make sure everyone is familiar with it, and that they can switch straight across without compromising the essential 999 service.

Air traffic control also have the same ability. They may not be able to handle quite the density of traffic on the manual systems that they can with their computers. They can however keep aeroplanes flying and do so safely.

Maintenance

Maintenance of technology, for instance hardware and software, is usually properly built into the cost estimate. However the in-house costs of maintenance are rarely (in my experience, never) accounted for, yet they are likely to be greater than the third-party costs.

Every upgrade to the system will involve in-house costs. These include:

- staff time to test the system – both technicians and users;
- staff to implement the new version;
- cost of advising users of the changes and their implications;
- changes to documentation.

Apart from the costs of new versions, there is also expenditure associated with resolving problems, minor changes to the set-up of the system, adding and deleting users, housekeeping associated with the systems and the data. No system that is genuinely being useful is ever static for long. Individually, these elements may be small, but those odd hours or half-days add up to a significant sum over the lifetime of the system. They should be costed in and allowed for in the cost-benefit assessment.

111

Further development

As already said, no useful system ever remains the same for long, and nor do the requirements of users of such systems. We are increasingly having to respond to a fast-changing business environment. We expect our people to adapt, and they expect their supporting systems to follow suit.

Hence there are likely to be substantial revisions to a system over its lifetime. Some may be achieved by modifying the set-up, others by enabling so far unused capabilities of the system and others will require significant development work. In practice, such changes should be costed as an information management exercise in their own right, but allowance should be made when planning the original system for these costs. They are, after all, part of the lifetime cost and should be built into the viability assessment.

Consumables and other charges

Again, allowance is made in most project budgets for a consumables element that should consider:

- Stationery – especially pre-printed forms and cheques. Also bear in mind that the costs of running printers are not insignificant. They can vary from around one pence per page for a normal black and white page printed on a laser printer to over £1 for a colour transparency using some printers.
- Disks are not normally a major item unless there is a lot of data distribution. This can become an issue if you are distributing large graphics files on high capacity disk cartridges or tapes.
- Line charges can mount up even on a normal telephone line and should be accounted for. If high performance lines are used, then they should be costed in both the one-off costs and the on-going costs. Also bear in mind that if there are any problems with the set-up of data communications, it is possible to incur initially high costs, for example, when ISDN adapters do not release the line when there is no traffic. These problems can usually be resolved, but allowance may need to be made for high costs in the first few weeks.

These costs are unlikely to make or break a project, but they should be budgeted for, and as with all good management, there should be someone who has clear responsibility for managing that budget. If allowed to fall in general overheads they will not be managed and will therefore be higher than necessary. All expenditure should be managed properly.

Upgrades

Plans need to be made and costed for the growth of the system over its life. It is likely to have to accommodate more data and more users over time. It may be that the initial system will cope, but in many cases it will not. In which case any equipment and software may have to be upgraded to a larger, faster version to retain satisfactory performance. A realistic estimate of such growth and the cost of meeting it should be included, bearing in mind that all the costs of disruption and training will have to built in.

Bear in mind that if a system will support growing needs over a period, then it might be argued that the initial specification was excessive and therefore more expensive than it need have been. The cost of starting with an oversize system has to be weighed against the cost of upgrade during its life.

Ideally, as with all cost and benefits that are to be incurred over time, the figures need to be adjusted to a common base, with clearly stated and justified assumptions. The most common approaches are *discounted cash flow* and *net present value* which are outlined later in the chapter (see page 118).

CONTINGENCY

Remember Robert Burns' poem – plans often go astray. So a wise project team will make an allowance for unforeseen problems. And almost any solution to a problem has a cost implication. Because the problems cannot be anticipated – otherwise they would be built into the plans – some contingency reserve has to be made.

The size of any contingency fund has to take account of the nature of the project risk. A straightforward traditional accounting system implementation is less risky than a project using leading-edge technology, and the contingency should reflect that. Assess the risk and determine how much *realistically* needs to be set aside for covering the potential problems, then build it into the costs before determining the viability of the project.

Note it should be done that way round – the contingency should not be adjusted to make the cost-benefit analysis work in favour of going ahead. Unfortunately, most projects work on the basis of: how much contingency can we get away with? It is imperative that none of the contingency funds should be used without senior management approval. Such approval should require a justification that shows that the extra investment will allow the achievement of the original objectives, and that no expenditure beyond that in the contingency fund will be required. The investment already sunk into a project is not a justification for further expenditure; only the cost-benefit analysis can be. It may be better to write-off the original expenditure, to learn from it and do it again, but differently. All too often cost-benefit analysis is done in a way not to *test* whether a project should go ahead but to *show* that it should. Make sure your investment appraisal properly tests the viability of your project.

With all the realistic costs included, over-optimistic benefits avoided, a proper assessment of the risk made and a sound investment appraisal showing a worthwhile return on investment, such problems should be avoided.

BENEFITS

Having frightened you with the scope of the real costs, the time has come to address the benefits. Hopefully the message will be positive, but it is all too easy to over-estimate the value of the benefits. All too often information-related projects do not reduce costs as far as expected. Indeed for organisations at Level 2 or beyond, the opportunities for reducing costs within their existing organisation are minimal at best.

Therefore wider benefits need to be found. It is difficult because many are apparently intangible: improved customer service, faster turn-around, better quality products, etc. We need to find ways of balancing such benefits against the costs, and of monitoring them, so that we can recognise whether we have achieved them or not.

This means that any benefits are likely to be much more difficult to quantify. Even more difficult is weighing one benefit against another, as they may be different in nature and contribute to different strategic objectives. We need to find methods for making some sort of objective relative assessments between different benefits. Later in this chapter, we will consider some techniques for identifying the benefits gap of different options. One option that should always be considered is that of doing nothing – this gives a baseline for assessing all other options.

Cost reduction

Do not overestimate the cost reductions that will be achieved. Bear in mind that many organisations already have administrative systems that will have eliminated obvious overheads, although they may have acquired new burdens.

Even if there are cost reductions, they may well not be cash-releasing as the savings are so fragmented throughout the organisation. A re-engineering exercise at a hospital supported by new approaches to information management was calculated as £40,000 less expensive in a full year. But that was not cash that was available: rather it took the pressure off a dozen different departments, and allowed them to get on with just a little bit more of their normal work. It was still valuable.

So do not expect a lump sum that can be spent on other things or used to offset the costs of the new system.

User expectation and satisfaction

With a new system properly implemented, there should be an improvement in user satisfaction. That user satisfaction should come from meeting user expectations better than the system that was replaced. It should also come from better support for users' work, which should result in improved performance through better, more informed and more timely decisions.

Again it probably will not be cash-releasing, but should enable higher performance to be achieved, and from that improved performance will come increased profits, more patients treated – or whatever the objectives are.

SMART objectives

As has already been said, the organisation should have SMART objectives which will measure its success. Some estimate has to be made of what improvements in those objectives are worth: in a commercial organisation, that can probably be stated in terms of improved profits (or reduced losses). Such monetary value is easy to assess against the costs. In not-for-profit organisations, the improvements may not be so readily expressed in financial terms – but it is possible.

Consider a hospital department. It treats a number of patients in a year at a given cost. If it can treat a few extra patients for the same cost, using new systems, the benefit is the extra money that would have been needed to treat those extra patients without the new facilities. So it can be expressed in financial terms by asking what would have been the extra cost to achieve the same improvement in performance using the old approach – in other words, what is the financial saving that can be attributed to the new system?

Differentiation and added value

A similar approach can be taken with strategic changes. The question is what financial benefit has accrued as a result of the project in hand. The benefit may be a mixture of profits from increased sales (or less reduced sales) or increased profits because the extra value to the customer allowed a greater margin than would otherwise have been possible.

Again in the not for-profit-area, consider the extra activity (as with cost reduction) that has been made possible by the extra funds that have been made available because the funding body is prepared to pay more for higher quality services.

Information products and services

Where the new systems have produced new information-based products and services, the benefits are rather more clear as they are simply the extra profit from the sales of the new products.

Reduced fire-fighting

Do not underestimate the benefits from closer control and better management. There should be a direct link to improved performance that can be costed and included in the benefits.

TESTING BENEFITS

Benefits can only properly be tested if there are SMART objectives where improvements can be seen as a result of the changes being made. The project benefits too should be expressed in the same way – SMART objectives for improvement in SMART objectives!

As phases of the project are implemented, changes of the objectives related to expected benefits should be continuously monitored. They should form part of the project management process. Both achieved and expected benefits should be reviewed formally if there is a need for extra funding for the project – the extra funding should only go ahead if the benefits justify the extra cost.

INVESTMENT APPRAISAL

A key responsibility for any manager is to ensure the most effective and efficient use is made of the organisation's resources. Finance is a key resource, and it is necessary to be able to demonstrate that good use is made of it.

As there are many imponderables about the results of information-based projects (and others), it is vital that a sensitivity analysis is performed on the costs and the benefits in the first instance, and then on the assumptions made for assessing the return on investment. Return on investment, essentially, is what benefit the organisation is going to achieve, expressed as a percentage of the costs. For example, if we put money on deposit, the return on investment is the interest rate that the bank or whatever will pay us for giving them the use of our money.

Because the benefits and costs will happen over a period of time, there is a need to make assumptions about inflation and interest rates over the life of the capital investment. As these can only be guessed, it is wise to perform a sensitivity analysis by considering ranges, and seeing what the impact of different rates will cause on the return. In many organisations, the rates to be used will be pre-defined, so that all investment decisions are made on the same basis. Where this is the case, then such rates should be used. Where they do not exist, then a decision as to what values should be used must be made at the highest level within the organisation.

Even when the rates are prescribed, sensitivity analysis should be undertaken: it will give a guide to the viability of a project as actual rates become known.

The simplest appraisal methods total the value of the benefits over the life of the project and its operation, and express them as the percentage of the costs incurred over the same period. This however does not take account of the varying value of money over time and generally is not used for major investment decisions. Instead techniques that convert all values to an equivalent current value are used.

Investment appraisal bases

The most common bases for investment are based on similar thinking – they are just expressed in different ways. The main appraisal methods are:

- discounted cash flow;
- net present value;
- internal rate of return.

Discounted cash flow

Discounted cash flow takes account of the fact that cash received in the future is of less value than cash held now. And the longer it is before such cash is received, the lower its value.

Future costs and benefits are estimated as far as value and timing are concerned. Discounting is then used to bring them to their equivalent value at a common point in time. It is similar to compound interest, but reversed. It must take account of both the possibility of inflation and any uncertainty.

Net present value

This method takes this approach and brings future monies back to today's values. There is a simple formula to be applied to each period's benefits and costs: in other words, benefits in one period less costs in same period. The formula is:

Present value = Future net benefit / $(1 + \text{interest rate})^n$

where *n* is the number of periods at which the benefit will be achieved.

This will need to be applied to the benefits and costs for each period (normally years, but may be smaller intervals at periods of high inflation). Initial investment is applied in period zero. The costs and benefits are then totalled to give a net present value for benefits and costs.

These present values could then be expressed as a return on investment and compared against targets imposed by the organisation for capital and other expenditure. They should also be used to compare different options (one of which may be to do nothing and simply invest the money at a target interest rate) to find the one that gives the best return.

Internal rate of return

This approach works on the basis of determining the rate at which the investment earns a return. This is achieved when the net present value is zero. The approach is calculated by trial and error by trying various rates and calculating net present values.

There are many tools available to facilitate the calculation of discounted cash flows, net present values, etc. These vary from tables and specialist finance calculators to software that runs on personal computers. Indeed most of the leading spreadsheets have functions to assist with these calculations.

The details of these calculations are covered in more detail in *Finance for the Non-Financial Manager* (see *Further reading* later in this chapter) and in many other books on finance and business mathematics. All managers should familiarise themselves with these matters.

ANALYSIS OF QUESTIONNAIRE 5

1 No. These days it is very rare for significant savings to be achieved directly by implementing new information systems. In my 20-year experience, one of the main faults is over-estimation of the cost savings. This, coupled with a separate under-estimation of the real costs for most projects, makes their financial justification tenuous, unproved at best.

2 Yes. Ask the question, 'How much would it cost to achieve the same performance (however expressed) using the existing organisational set-up?'

3 No. You must understand **all** the costs associated with the new system both one-off and on-going for its lifetime. You can bring the savings that will be achieved by removing existing systems into the benefits side of the equation. But the true costs need to be understood so that they can be managed during the full lifetime of the new systems.

4 No. Initial training is only the starting point. There will be a need for top-up training to give users new, more advanced, capabilities and to familiarise them with new versions of the software or processes. There will also be the need for training of new-starters, promoted or transferred staff and for remedial training.

5 No. Remember there are many costs which will fall on other groups outside the project team. The disruption caused by existing staff

giving time to the project will have a cost. There will also be opportunity costs caused by the new information systems – including lost sales or slower cash flow.

1 Re-assess the costs and the anticipated benefits for existing information projects.

2 Determine target return on investment or internal rate of return required in the light of the project risk and the economic environment.

3 Conduct an investment appraisal for the existing information developments.

4 Take management decisions to continue or kill projects on the basis of what the return on investment that will achieve. Use the money saved on more effective strategic options – assessed in the same way.

FURTHER READING

John Harrison, *Finance for the Non-Financial Manager*, Thorsons/Harper-Collins, 1989

All managers need an understanding of finance. This book is a useful background designed for the non-finance specialist. It is pitched at a suitable level on all aspects of finance. It adopts a practical approach with many worked examples. It avoids jargon and it would be a useful addition to any non-finance manager's bookshelf.

It covers all the capital appraisal methods outlined above with clear examples. It should enable any manager to undertake this work on his or her own project with minimal input from finance specialists. Specialist advice will be needed only to set out the rates to be applied and the target rate of return that the organisation requires to achieve.

SUMMARY

The main concern is to ensure that all costs have been properly considered and that the benefits are realistic and also costed. That way a proper investment appraisal can be carried out. Investment appraisals are rarely carried out effectively for information-related projects. Many would claim that they are, but I have seen few really thorough business cases. Most are designed to allow the project to go ahead – not to make an assessment about whether it should.

The full costs need to be considered. Most of the costs that do not fall on the project budget are not considered in any meaningful way. They have to be picked up by the affected department, whether they have budgeted for them or not. This means many one-off costs are paid for out of revenue income.

The full costs must be taken into account and include:

- *Initial one-off costs:* these are usually reasonably well-defined, but it is not unusual for unforeseen or even unrelated capital items to be sneaked in under the banner of the project.
- *Implementation costs* are where many of the real costs are ignored. Some that affect the project team, and their departments, are included, but the budget for cost of disruption to other departments is rarely adequate.
- *Training* also tends to be skimped, both in practice and in the planning of the budget. It will be a significant cost, but the cost of not doing it is greater and more insidious. On-going and top-up training are rarely budgeted for, but allowed to fall on other parts of the organisation.
- *On-going costs* are often largely left to take care of themselves. They simply come out of next year's budgets. Some consideration will be given to them during the assessment of the options, but they are never monitored specifically after the system has gone into live use.
- *If full lifetime costs* were considered, most organisations would be more circumspect about how they invest in information management. It would probably make senior management look more closely at how it is being used, and the benefits would probably be greater as a result of a more corporate and thorough view of the needs and opportunities.
- *Benefits rarely measured* may be costed in a spurious way, but they are not tested as a matter of course during and after the development project. They need to be made more measurable and used as critical performance measures for the project.

As costs are usually under-estimated, most projects overrun their budgets. However careful the original business case, the extra monies are made available with little re-examination of the return that will be achieved on that additional investment. The sunk costs are the justification, but they should not be, as it may well be a case of throwing good money after bad. I have seen projects swallow £500,000 and deliver nothing. Yet the management team would not cut their losses, because they would lose face – 'It might come right' – or even better, they cannot afford to waste half a million pounds. So they take the cost up to a million pounds with no discernible benefit, and then an external audit makes them scrap it. The senior management team lose their jobs, and the organisation has wasted a million pounds. It is an all too common result unfortunately.

But using standard appraisal techniques that would be used for almost any other major expenditure, it can be avoided. But it does require monitoring before, during and after the project is complete.

WRITING THE SPECIFICATION

At the end of the day, a specification is a working document and need not be a literary masterpiece.

INTRODUCTION

Many managers are not happy about writing formal documents. Most are even more uncomfortable at the prospect of writing what they see as a complex technical document such as an information systems specification. There is no real need to fear writing such documents, if you adopt a structured approach to its contents.

I appreciate that, as an author, I am perhaps more comfortable with the craft of writing than most people. However writing any fact-based document, whether a book or a specification for an information system, is a craft that can be quite easily learned to the level required. Most people are comfortable talking face to face with a friend or colleague: write in much the same way as you talk and you will be very close to what is required.

The problem is getting started, but the approach suggested here should get over that resistance, because you will do it step by step, adding more detail on to what starts as a simple framework. As you go, you will add more elements to the framework, and detail to other parts. Eventually, you will have all the elements detailed, and you can then just polish it, or even better, get a colleague to review it and to suggest any clarification that might be needed.

At the end of the day, a specification is a working document and need not be a literary masterpiece. If the meaning is clear and unambiguous to its intended readership, then it is good enough. That is its overriding purpose; anything else is mere gloss.

The objectives of this chapter are to help readers to:

1   appreciate what a specification has to achieve;

2   structure their thoughts and requirements;

3   determine the contents of the specification for an information system;

4   understand the language that should be used;

5   become more comfortable with the craft of writing.

QUESTIONNAIRE 6

Writing the specification

1. Specifications need to say exactly how new systems should work.
   a Yes?
   b No?

2 Do information system specifications need to be written in technical language?
   a Yes
   b No

3 Specifications should include:
   a Essential requirements?
   b Desirable requirements?
   c Potentially useful facilities?
   d All of the above?
   e None of the above?

4 Any competent manager should be able to write an information systems specification.
   a Yes?
   b No?

LANGUAGE AND STYLE

Structure

With writing, as with many aspects of analysis and planning suggested in this book, we start at a high level and work down into more and more detail. It does not matter whether it is a one-page paper for a client or a complete book – I find this approach works for any scale of work. I know many other people who work this way, and I know a few who do not. It is those in the latter group, with rare exceptions, who tend to find writing more difficult.

By building a structure in this way, I find I can race through the sections which I understand well without having to worry about the gaps I am leaving. I can then research the missing bits and fill them in as I become comfortable with what I need to include. Eventually, I have all the holes filled, and I can then read through the whole thing to make sure that it flows properly, nothing is missing or out of order and that the language is reasonably polished. With word processing, it is easy to move complete sections around if they are in the wrong place.

Plain and simple

This approach requires you to write in your natural style. If you are writing different sections at different times and are not using your natural style then there will be no consistency of style between sections. As a result it will not read easily when you have finished and will require more polishing to ensure that the meaning is clear. It takes a very skilled writer to write something in a manner that is not their own and make it consistent.

KISS

Keep It Simple and Straightforward. This should be the watchword for any writing. There is a tendency to write differently from the way one speaks, but there is no need. All that is needed is a little tightening of the structure, and grammar, which will come more easily with the written word than with speech.

Many people become pompous when they write. It is equivalent to adopting a 'posh' voice on the telephone – it sounds contrived and artificial and becomes the butt of humour. Keep the words and phrases simple. For example, try to use simple words, such as 'better' rather than 'improved' or 'enhanced', except when you need another word to avoid too much repetition.

Remember George Orwell's advice in *Politics and the English Language* (1946).

(i)   Never use a metaphor, simile, or other figure of speech which you are used to seeing in print.

(ii)   Never use a long word when a short one will do.

(iii) If it is possible to cut a word out, always cut it out.

(iv)   Never use the passive where you can use the active.

(v)   Never use a foreign phrase, a scientific word, or a jargon word if you can think of an everyday English equivalent.

(vi)   Break any of these rules sooner than say anything outright barbarous.

Yes, you should try and make your writing grammatically correct – but far more important is to get over your meaning clearly and unambiguously. You are not trying to write a literary masterpiece. You are trying to make your needs clear – clarity of meaning is the one absolute requirement in writing a specification. So remember KISS and it is easy!

CONTENT

What is required

Measurable

Decide at an early stage how you are going to measure the success of the solution. What are the critical success factors for this project? Each project will be different, but they will all need to achieve a return on costs based on some measure of the benefits. Therefore in the specification there will need to be some quantified measure of the benefits.

> *. . . clarity of meaning is the one absolute requirement in writing a specification.*

Most suppliers will be reluctant to commit to measures outside their control. So if achievement of the planned benefits is dependent on users meeting their targets, then it is unreasonable to expect a supplier to take on that part of the risk. So you will need to find intermediate measures of benefit which are under the supplier's control.

These may include:

● Timings of response on computer- and other equipment-based elements with an agreed load – be clear about how many people will be using the computer at the same time and what they will be doing on it.

- Throughput or capacity.
- Quality of data, less than 1 per cent duplicates on a supplied or cleaned database or returns from a mailing list, for example.
- System availability during working hours.
- Response time to fault call, or more importantly, time-to-fix which is the time from the initial call reporting a problem to its successful full resolution. There may be considerable differences – I have seen response times of two hours routinely lead to end-of-next-day fix times because the person initially responding did not carry the necessary spares. Be aware also that such times are usually quoted in terms of working hours – usually 9am to 5pm, whatever your normal hours! Eight hours' response frequently means 'next day'.
- Some measure of usability scoring, probably in terms of improvement over the system being replaced. The conditions for this would take some negotiating with the supplier, but it should be possible. Usability saving would probably require that the users evaluating the system should have been given the recommended training by the supplier. It could use some of the techniques discussed elsewhere in the book. Many reviews in magazines now quote a usability score for comparison purposes, so there is some precedent.
- There will be other measures that should be considered, but bear in mind that these should be under the supplier's control. They might include response times, elapsed time for certain operations or clerical processing, sizing of computer systems, quality measures such a number of duplicates or missing information records. Each project will have different criteria.

Unambiguous

The requirements stated in the specification should be as clear and unambiguous as the writer can make them. Whilst I encourage the specification writer to be as precise as possible as to what is required, there is also an onus on those responding to the specification to understand it. That means they cannot hide behind any ambiguity of the writer's, in their response to the specification, they should state the assumptions they have made where it is incomplete or ambiguous. Indeed, I would recommend that a statement is included in the specification or other tender documents putting the onus on the bidder to resolve any omissions or clarify meaning where necessary.

Essential

The specification should focus on the essential requirements. It should not be peppered with those requirements that 'would be nice' or 'hoped for'. If it is not necessary, then it should not be in the specification.

This will make the specification easier to write. It will ensure that the specification team and the users have focused their thinking. It will also make the specification easier to evaluate as there will be fewer elements to score. In any case, the evaluation will give much greater weight to the essential than to the merely 'nice to have' which will have little or no impact on the final result. That is as it should be – our whole thrust should be to eliminate the non-essential in all aspects of the business. The choice should be made on the basis of what is essential – if the lesser elements come into play, then either the evaluation criteria are faulty, the solutions are equally satisfactory, or we have lost sight of what we are trying to achieve for the business.

Desirable

If after reading the previous section, you really *must* include those 'nice to have' elements, then can I suggest that you put them in a separate section or even better an appendix? Then they can be used to fine-tune the selection once you have done an initial evaluation and eliminated the clearly unsuitable proposals.

The specification should focus on the essential requirements.

Personally, I would not waste my time. If they are not essential, then they should have no bearing on the suitability of the solution. They will simply be an extra cost – in training, implementation, time or other resources. They are a distraction now and in the future.

It would be nice if . . .

Do not include under any circumstances. If it is merely nice to have, then it is redundant. Forget it. No excuses, no justification, no arguments – cut it out, and fast! It is a complete waste of time thinking about it.

Business-related: the 'what?' and 'how?'

Express the requirements in terms of what you are trying to achieve for the business, and focus on what the project must achieve. Leave how it is to be achieved to the proposer – they should know their systems, and probably the related technology better than you. Leave them room to innovate on your behalf and encourage them to do so.

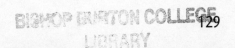

You can encourage suppliers to innovate, especially in a technical sense, by focusing on what the business and the users need from their solution. You will need to test their proposed solutions with key users as part of the evaluation process. The suitability of the suggested approaches will be a measure of how well the potential supplier has understood your business needs.

If you have followed this book through so far, you will have sought and found creative ways of redesigning your business processes and you will be looking for suppliers who can match your creativity with imaginative, and practical, solutions of their own.

Technology issues

If there is a technological element or link with the proposed information management system, then this section will be essential to ensure that any new elements are compatible with what is already in use.

If there is a technology strategy in place or the new systems need to fit with what is already in place, then there will be a need to make this clear. This may restrict suppliers in what they can offer or whether they wish to bid at all. Do not let suppliers browbeat you into accepting solutions that do not fit with your technical strategy. If you are using mainstream technology, then there should be no need to compromise your stated strategy.

If you have an IT department, then this section will probably best be written or approved by the IT manager. If you do not, then make this section simply a statement of what is currently in use. Put in a requirement that the proposed solution should make use of what is already there, and that any additions are also fully compatible with existing systems. Make it clear that the onus is on the supplier to install the new solution, without disturbing the operation of current systems and to demonstrate that they have done so.

How it is to be achieved

As a management team, you should have been creative in developing new processes for which the new systems need to provide support. Be clear about what those systems need to achieve to allow the new processes to achieve their objectives. But do not be too prescriptive.

You should have chosen suppliers with a proven track record as well as creative and practical approaches to your sort of requirement. Leave them to use their expertise on your behalf and to innovate around your needs. It may be that they will find even better ways of doing things than you could have imagined. In any case, you will not accept a solution that is worse than the one you would have designed.

The specification should therefore concentrate on *what* is to be achieved, and allow the bidders to concentrate on *how* it is achieved. Then when the supplier has been selected, you will work together to meld the two sets of ideas into an even better whole.

ANALYSIS OF QUESTIONNAIRE 6

1 **No.** Surprisingly perhaps, one should not try to write a definitive specification. There are several reasons. First, it is not practically possible to do so, as any implementation will have to compromise to a greater or lesser extent – needs will change to some extent in the time from writing to live operation. But no one group has a monopoly on wisdom or expertise, and it makes good business sense to use the expertise of the people providing the new system. Therefore, they should be encouraged to take the specification and the business objectives and use their skills to produce an even better solution. But the business objectives should be well defined and measurable.

2 **No.** The specification is for a *business* system and should be written in business language with which the manager and supplier are comfortable. Make the success factors by which the work is assessed business-oriented, then the technical issues can largely take care of themselves (but take advice from competent specialist advisers, independent of the suppliers, if necessary). Then monitor those objectives and ensure that they are achieved.

3 **Essential requirements.** The system should be designed to meet the essential and not be cluttered with essentially peripheral elements that will always reduce the performance for the main functions. One of the biggest reasons for the failure of information systems projects is that the requirements and user expectations are allowed to grow during the procurement and implementation (see Edward Yourdon *Byte*, September 1996).

4 **Yes.** If it is written in business language and in the manager's natural style, then it is possible. Avoid the temptation to adopt a 'technical' or 'management guru' language or style.

ACTION PLAN

The aim is to get your ideas and requirements on paper.

1 So start writing the specification right at the beginning of the project as the basic strategy starts to become clear.

2 Build a high-level framework and add to it as your research and ideas develop.

3 Change the structure as necessary (the detailed structure of this book is not the same as in my original proposal nine months ago although its purpose is the same).

4 Flesh out the sections that you can, raise questions for further investigation in those areas that are unresolved.

5 Keep at it and it will all come together.

6 Do not expect to start at the beginning and write all the way through to the end. You will always find parts that you do not properly understand – do not let them get in the way of writing up the rest. The more you get on paper the less daunting it will look!

7 Above all use your own natural language and if necessary get colleagues to proof read it. Ask for constructive criticism and do not feel threatened by such advice. By the time this book is published it will have been read and amended by several people other than myself. It all goes to make it a better and clearer result.

FURTHER READING

Barbara Minto, *The Pyramid Principle, Logic in Writing and Thinking*, FT/Pitman, 1987

This book is an excellent introduction to the craft of researching and writing structured documents. Barbara Minto adopts a similar top-down approach to that which I recommend. She explains why it is appropriate for communication and how it works as a tool for clarifying thoughts and ideas.

If you find writing complex papers difficult or simply wish to be better at communicating your ideas then read this book. It may not turn you into an award winning author but it will make your writing easier and more effective.

SUMMARY

Writing a basic specification is not difficult, and any experienced manager ought to be able to learn the skills needed. The language should be that of business, not technical jargon. Indeed the specification does not require much technical content at all.

Specifications should be written by breaking down the requirements from the top. It is only necessary to include the essential, as the decision is to be taken on how well the proposed solution meets those essential requirements. Desirable and possibly useful requirements will only confuse the issue. Stick to the point.

The requirements should include measurable success factors that can be used to evaluate the project after the work is completed.

CHAPTER

7

BUYING
SOLUTIONS

*. . . the aim must be to
purchase a solution to a
business need, rather than
simply to buy a product.*

INTRODUCTION

As discussed with regard to writing a specification, the aim must be to purchase a solution to a business need, rather than simply to buy a product. An appropriately organised specification is part of the answer, and a suitable approach to procurement will help ensure that you meet your needs.

This chapter explains how to buy information systems without having to be a technical wizard. Some knowledge is obviously useful but as long as the specification and subsequent contract are sufficiently clear, then a satisfactory system should be forthcoming.

The objectives of this chapter are to:

1 illustrate a general-purpose procurement approach;

2 show how a non-specialist can get a satisfactory technical solution;

3 provide an auditable and demonstrably fair tendering process.

QUESTIONNAIRE 7

Meeting business needs

1 Do you have documented standing financial instructions or procedures for tendering or procurement?
a Yes
b No

2 Can the files from previous projects be used as a starting point?
a Yes
b No

3 Do those files contain a review with findings and recommendations of how to improve things in future projects?
a No
b Yes

4 Have you started looking at possible suppliers and their solutions for your next project?
a Yes
b No

5 Documentation should be:
a Complete?
b Neatly typed?
c Formal?

6 The process should be flexible and accommodating
a Yes?
b No?

7 Selection criteria should be established during the evaluation of proposals
a Yes?
b No?

COMPETITIVE TENDERING

Why?

You want suppliers who can meet your requirements in a creative and effective way. And you want the best possible solution. As in sport, competition brings out the best performance – the truly creative thrive on a challenge and what better challenge than to win a major contract against your peers?

You want the supplier to respond to your needs, rather than having to fit your needs around their offering. If they are the only bidder, especially if they know it, then they will be less flexible on meeting your needs and on the price.

Documented process

The process should be properly documented. If you have quality procedures or formal procurement rules, then the documentation standards may well be defined. Even if you do not have such a framework, then you should adopt a formal documentation approach.

This will serve several purposes. It will allow review by auditors and others to ensure that the bidding was fair, and that an appropriate decision was taken. It will provide a record of what has taken place, should there be any dispute at any stage of the purchasing and implementation stages. It will also provide for review of the effectiveness of the process and a background for training and future purchasing. All major programmes should be treated as a learning exercise; there are always be lessons to be learned and improvements to be made for subsequent projects.

TIP

Documentation starts early

Start a formal file as soon as any work starts on a project. Important thoughts and documentation will be lost if there is nowhere to keep them. The initial notes are likely to be scrappy and rough, but they are the seed for what is to come. It may well be necessary to go back to those original ideas – in a major project, it is all too easy to lose sight of what the original idea was. You need to be able to check that you have not departed from important elements of the original concept, or that the changes that you have made are appropriate and justified.

You will need the background as the project grows, so that you can explain it to the growing number of people involved in the work. Whilst it may be possible to carry it around in your head, much of it any way, this is not desirable from the organisation's point of view. The information needs to be shared (we have talked about corporate memory), so that the organisation is not hostage to one individual's continued good health and good will.

Standing financial instructions

If your organisation is large, it will almost certainly have developed formal policies for a variety of matters, including finance-related issues such as purchasing. Any procurement process should be built around those instructions, which will be checked by the auditors for compliance. They will be based on experience and be designed both to protect the organisation from bad practices and even fraud, and to provide protection to individuals by allowing them to demonstrate good practice.

They should be followed if they exist – if they do not, then they should be developed with appropriate advice from finance, auditors, internal audit and legal staff. Any good books on procurement and finance should provide suitable guidance.

Auditability

The aim with any large-scale procurement and implementation should be to make the process as open as possible, and to ensure that it can be audited to demonstrate good practice and sound corporate governance.

This will require good record-keeping and a rules framework agreed and documented before the start of the process. This will involve, amongst other things, having a clear tender process. The evaluation criteria for the proposals and presentation must also documented before the closing date for the receipt of bids. Then they should be followed unaltered, except in the most exceptional circumstances and then only if it can be demonstrated that the changes were fair to all prospective suppliers.

Public-sector procurement

Although many consider the public sector to be over-bureaucratic, it does have a sound approach to procurement, especially where it is of high value. Although there have been problems with some projects, especially with regard to IT, these have usually occurred where the rules have been relaxed or ignored.

The approaches adopted by government and similar agencies have several strengths. They require a clearly documented specification, they are usually open to all suitable bidders, the process is designed to be equitable to all bidders, and the final decision can be justified and the whole process audited. The latter is particularly important in the public sector, as employees are spending public money and have to be able to demonstrate due care in its use. They are also subject to greater supervision than most commercial companies.

That is not to say that there are not problems. It can be bureaucratic, and there may be a tendency to go for 'safe' decisions rather than better, but slightly risky solutions that may give greater benefit. However, such problems are not intrinsic to the approach, but rather a consequence of the culture of the organisation. The same problems exist in many so-called 'commercial' organisations.

There is much that the average private-sector organisation can learn from the public sector with regard to purchasing.

Broadly speaking, the approach for larger procurements is as follows.

1. **Business case**
   There is usually a requirement for a formal business case and option appraisal that considers the costs and benefits. The option proposal requires the do-nothing option to be considered as a reference for the other alternatives.

2. **Purchasing team**
   The purchasing team always requires a project sponsor who will be a member of the executive board and will act as the formal 'customer'. There will also be a project manager as well as representatives of key user groups.

3. **Specification or statement of requirements**
   There is always some form of documented operational requirements agreed at a senior level.

4. **Advertise the project**
   For all but modest purchases, there will be a need to advertise the project to comply with the EU/GATT regulations for public procurement. This will usually be in the official journal of the European Union. The advertisement may seek expressions of

interest, or it may invite prospective bidders to send for the full bid documents. Which route is chosen depends on the number of companies who would be competent to bid.

5. **Expressions of interest**

If there are many companies who could bid for the work, a full open bidding process could be expensive and time-consuming. Expensive to send out many copies of a large specification and time-consuming to give due consideration to the evaluation of dozens (or more) proposals. Instead, a brief outline of the work can be given and interested parties asked to demonstrate their competence and the availability of sufficient resources, in terms of both people and financial resources to undertake the work. Such expressions of interest should be brief – for most projects, an extended letter should be sufficient.

6. **Seek proposals**

These expressions of interest are then used as a basis to select a shortlist to be invited to submit full proposals. The procedure from here is much the same for all procurement, public or private sector, with often just an extra couple of steps for public sector purchases.

7. **Proposals**

8. **Presentations**

9. **Negotiation**

These three elements are common to all purchasing and will be covered later in more detail.

10. **Memorandum of specification**

At this point, public sector procurement diverges slightly from routine private sector practice. By this stage, the final shortlist of possible suppliers has been reduced to those few (typically less than four) who can fulfil the requirements equally well. Rather than select on subjective judgement, a formal memorandum of specification is agreed with each supplier. This sets out what it is to be delivered, when and how. It will form the basis of the final contract.

11. **Invitation to tender**

The final shortlisted suppliers are then asked to tender against the agreed memorandum of specification. At this stage, the only determinant is the financial terms, so the lowest bid wins. Previous stages have been concerned with the functional competence of the proposals. Those surviving to this stage have equally competent solutions, so there is no need to consider any other aspect but the costs.

12. **Award contract**

As with any procurement process, the contract has to be formally awarded with all the appropriate legal aspects covered.

Number of bidders

Preparing proposals is an expensive process, as is evaluating and documenting them. So I would recommend that a minimum number of bidders should be invited to submit proposals. You should invite submissions only from suppliers who genuinely have a chance of winning the contract. Otherwise you are wasting their time and your own.

If that means there are only two realistic candidates, then so be it. Even if standing financial instructions say that there should be three, in some cases it may be that only two proposals should be sought. However, it may be necessary to get high-level clearance to do so, and in any case a proper justification for the limited number of bidders should be documented. This will then allow auditors and others to ensure that corporate governance has not been compromised.

For most projects, five bidders should be more than enough. It is difficult to do justice to more, and it should not be difficult to get the shortlist down to that level. If there are many more or there is a need for open bidding, then an initial stage should be undertaken. Expressions of interest or a small proposal against an outline specification should be sought. The aim of such an exercise should be simply to qualify the potential bidders in terms of financial and other resources, expertise, experience, availability of a suitable product or service and understanding of the key requirements. From the evaluation of such submissions, it should be possible to produce a shortlist of suitable bidders to receive and bid against the full documentation

TIP Expressions of interest

Ask for limited and highly specific information that can be readily tested against predefined evaluation criteria. For all but the largest projects, it should be possible to ask for the response to be kept down to a two- or three-page letter, perhaps with supporting brochures and other material.

Be strict about your evaluation. If you have asked for information and it is not there; score the supplier down. If their response is longer than requested, or not in the format required, then again score them down – or if the number of respondents is large, ignore them completely. They have failed the first test in meeting your needs!

PROCESS

The purchasing exercise should be treated as a project in its own right and planned and managed accordingly. It may be a sub-project of a larger project to include needs assessment, specification, procurement and implementation, but it should be planned in detail within an appropriate framework.

As with all projects, there should be a steering group with responsibility for delivering the work within agreed terms.

Terms of reference

A steering group or project team, like all committees, should have formal, written terms of reference agreed at the highest level possible within the organisation. As a general rule, committees should have a finite life with a clear task to perform. Standing committees all too easily become talking shops that achieve little in the way of results.

> *The purchasing exercise should be treated as a project in its own right, and planned and managed accordingly.*

The terms of reference should set out what the steering group is to achieve and by when it is to have completed its work. This should include the final review of its work, which should be agreed and signed off by the same management body that originally set up the group. Delegated authority should be explicitly set out in the group's remit.

Personnel

The people forming the committee may well be the same team as for the earlier stages in the overall programme from strategic planning to specification. They will have the advantage of having a detailed knowledge of what is required and why; but there is also a risk that they have become too close to the challenges and will not be as dispassionate as they will need to be.

Most important is that there should be a high-level manager with sufficient authority to make all decisions albeit requiring ratification by the board or some other top management group. One of the strengths of many public sector procurements is that the framework insists on having a top manager to act as the overall 'Customer'.

The team should be as small as possible, whilst having representatives with the key skills required. These skills would include project management, procurement, technical IT skills if relevant and of course, user experience and knowledge. Bear in mind that it should be possible to bring in other people on a temporary basis when other skills are required.

Timetable and diaries

One of the first tasks must be to decide the key dates and get them into everyone's diaries. The key dates include:

- initial meeting to allocate tasks and to agree programme;
- progress meeting dates if the process is going to be lengthy;
- meeting date to agree list of invited bidders;
- date of meeting to agree Invitation to Tender documents;
- agreed date for sending out Invitation to Tender;
- bidders workshop date (if necessary);
- closing date for return of proposals;
- date of evaluation meeting;
- presentation date for shortlisted bidders;
- presentation evaluation meeting;
- date for re-evaluation of cost and benefits based on preferred solution;
- date of board meeting (or of another appropriate body) for ratification of final decision;
- date to award contract;
- final meeting to review procurement against original objectives.

Internal communications

The procurement team should meet at key points to agree the approach for the next stages. If any member of the group has any contact with bidders, formal or informal, they should share their notes of the discussions with the rest of the group. There should be a single centrally held file for the project where brochures, correspondence, notes of discussions, etc., can be kept together. This will simplify the review process and any subsequent audit that may be undertaken.

The exception might be with regard to personal assessment of the bidders or their approach. This should be saved and incorporated into the formal evaluation of the bids. Each member of the procurement team should form their own opinion of the possible suppliers for the initial evaluation stage. Only after that, should a joint view of the bids be formed.

Rules

All members of the group should understand their role, and particularly the rules about discussion with bidders. It is particularly important that all bidders are given the same opportunity and that all are treated alike.

It may be that whilst the suppliers are preparing their proposals, all enquiries and contact should be through a single member of the project team. This will make it easier to ensure that a consistent approach is taken with each bidder.

In any case the team should decide what information can be shared and what should be kept confidential. For example, it is usual to keep the names of bidders confidential. However, it would be reasonable to give suppliers a feel for the number being asked to bid, or the number who have been shortlisted. In the latter case, particularly if there is only a single supplier being asked to make a presentation or take part in more detailed discussions, it may be better to state that there are 'no more than three on the shortlist' than to admit to one and weaken your negotiating position.

There will be other issues on which you will have to take a view as to whether the information should be shared. Whatever you decide, make sure it is understood by all members of the team and that it is carried through fairly.

Finally, whatever your standing instructions say, no member of the project team should accept gifts or hospitality from the bidders. Perhaps the only exceptions are the normal courtesies of coffee and a light lunch if the team is spending the day on the suppliers' premises for demonstrations, etc. Whilst this is especially important during the procurement, it should be made clear what is acceptable or not at any time.

Documentation

These last two points lead on to the subject of necessary documentation. We have already stressed the need to be able to audit the procurement process properly and to demonstrate proper corporate governance. Good documentation is essential for that, but at the same time there is a danger of slipping into bureaucracy for its own sake.

The main requirement in my view is to make and file contemporaneous notes of all important discussions whether internal or with possible and selected suppliers. However they do not need to be perfect prose or to be typed – as long as the meaning is clear, readable handwritten notes should be sufficient.

As has already been said, a file should be started and maintained from the start of the process. But the aim should be to keep it brief and to the point, without missing important notes of discussions. Good notes are vital to effective negotiation, as you can then 'call in' off-the-cuff verbal promises made by salesmen and other representatives of suppliers.

Keeping notes

I use a bound notebook rather than loose pages for all my project notes. I start a notebook right at the beginning of the project, even before analysing the needs, and use it throughout the life of the project. This has the main advantage that notes do not go astray and I have a full chronological record of discussions, thoughts, meetings, etc.

It is invaluable in meetings and especially negotiations to be able to go back to the notes of a meeting several weeks earlier and correct someone's recollection. Good notes are a powerful negotiating tool.

In that context, record all telephone conversations with suppliers and especially any verbal promises as you talk. It does not matter if they are scribbled. If the initial scribbled notes are not clear, and they contain promises or other important ideas, then make a tidy note as soon as the call is complete while the memory is fresh. I have been able to get suppliers to fulfil verbal promises, through having good notes of conversations.

At the end of the project that personal notebook should go into the main project file as it may be required for audit. If things have gone badly wrong, it may be needed to support litigation! It should not get that far if you are conscientious in your procedures.

Selection criteria

It is important to have the basis on which selections will be made defined formally before selection starts. In this way, you can avoid or at least rebut accusations of favouritism or lack of objectivity. Auditors may wish to see how selections were made to ensure that procedures are being followed, and, especially in the public sector, that value for money is being sought and achieved.

There are three main selection steps requiring formal evaluation rules.

Criteria for selecting bidders

In many cases, there will be a large number of potential bidders for any information management project and a means has to be found to bring this down to a manageable level.

This may be by means of an initial request for expressions of interest against some form of outline specification laying down essential requirements for possible suppliers. This is particularly appropriate, indeed necessary, where there is a wish to adopt the open bidding process often required for larger projects for public sector organisations and should probably include:

- basic competence in the particular area of interest;
- industry knowledge including similar work elsewhere;
- availability of the necessary resources: finance, people and equipment, etc., to undertake the work.

Where there is no need for such open bidding or where the list of possible suppliers is fairly modest, then a less formal internal process would work. However, although it can be carried out less formally, it should still be against clearly defined criteria, so that it can be justified to senior management or auditors and explained to unsuccessful suppliers. As with all other evaluations, the criteria and other rules should be defined and documented before starting the evaluation.

Evaluation criteria for proposals

However the bidding process is handled, the evaluation of proposals should be carried out formally and fully documented. The projects under discussion in this book are likely to be significant in value and critical to the success of the organisation. It needs to be possible to demonstrate that the process has been fair and equitable to all parties, and will provide value for money for the commissioning organisation.

Evaluation of demonstration and presentations

A similar process should be adopted for any presentations or demonstrations made by the final shortlisted suppliers. The evaluation criteria can be built into the overall proposal model to give an overall assessment for the whole of the invitation to tender process.

Identifying potential suppliers

The first step has to be to identify possible suppliers. Some may be obvious as key players in their field, but there may be many other, possibly more specialised or smaller, providers. Initially, the aim should be to identify as many as possible suitable companies before reducing them to a manageable list with a very specific match to the requirements.

Of course, if the work has been openly advertised in appropriate journals and expressions of interest sought, then this stage can be ignored as the initial 'long list' will be self-selecting.

Contacts and referrals

Most managers will have a wide circle of contacts, both within their own organisation and with suppliers, competitors, customers and professional advisers. All of these may be able to suggest possible sources of the necessary expertise, and perhaps more importantly, those to avoid.

A judgement has to be made about the quality of any advice from such sources but then, as a means of identifying names for further investigation, it can be highly effective. Referrals and recommendations from trusted colleagues should be regarded particularly favourably, if they are suitable.

Directories

The information technology industry and associated organisations are well served by directories. There are also directories aimed at particular industries which will include specialist suppliers to that industry – again, these may well include providers of information management expertise.

Trade and professional associations

Apart from the information-related associations, there are also your own trade bodies who may be able to provide lists of suitable suppliers with expertise in your industry. They should be consulted – if you are a member, it is in your interest to get maximum benefit from your subscription!

Advertisements

Many suppliers will advertise in the specialised information and information technology magazines, as well as in the trade press aimed at your own industry. Whilst it will give you little real information about the supplier, it does provide a basis for inclusion on the initial list.

Magazine reviews

Magazine reviews are useful as a basic starting point, but treat them with care. If they are reviews of technology, they tend to be written by enthusiasts. They are also written by journalists who will not have the same business needs as yourself or your organisation. You need to be able to read between the lines – what is important to the writer may be irrelevant to you.

For example, I recently read reviews of software for producing presentations. From my experience, most people use it to produce overhead projector transparencies. Far fewer use it to deliver presentations directly from the computer. The reviews gave much higher scores to those with the fancier fades and merges between slides than to others which were easier to use to produce quality printed slides. Yet the latter feature is more relevant to the average user who cannot make use of the clever slide transition effects. The reviewers were enthusiasts for computer technology, and one suspects would always choose a computer solution, even if paper were more appropriate!

So be warned: most magazine writers on computer matters are in love with the technology. And remember love is blind!

Yellow Pages

Like most of the foregoing sources, the *Yellow Pages* are merely a starting point. Further investigation will be needed.

Bidders' shortlist

Once an initial list of bidders is available, then contact needs to be made with them. And that is when formal evaluation starts. How responsive are they? If the contact is by telephone, were they polite and, more importantly, interested? If the first person could not answer your questions, did they pass you on to someone who could or did they try and waffle their way through? Do they return calls?

Be formal from initial contact

Be as formal as possible from the initial contact. Score the responses as you make contact and use those results to evaluate the potential suppliers.

Decide what will be important to you and your project before making contact. You might want to include, especially using the telephone:

- politeness;
- ability to speak to the right people;
- knowledge;
- initial suitability of their offering;
- attitude – friendly, helpful, even fun!

Having decided on your key factors, score them on a simple 0 to 10 range. Zero would be complete indifference or acknowledged unsuitability of their products.

I would recommend that initially you ask for a brief set of information, company size, suitable products or services, etc. You will need to give an outline of your requirements – volunteer the same information to all suppliers, and seek the same. You will quickly get a feel for those who are capable, as they will quickly get to your key issues without jumping to conclusions. In fact the questions they ask are likely to be more revealing than their answers to yours.

Keep notes of your discussions for future evaluation. In fact I score their attitude during those discussions and record them on my brief, handwritten notes which then go in the project file.

From my experience, a significant number of possible providers will rule themselves out on that first contact. Some will do so by acknowledging that they are not suitable, but many more will do so simply by their attitude and indifference to your enquiry! It always amazes me how difficult it is to buy from some people, even when new business is scarce – you do not need to deal with such people. I would go so far as to say that you should not do so, because their indifference is likely to be reflected in all aspects of their work.

Avoid salesmen and demonstrations

You should avoid salespeople; at least until the bid invitations have gone out. You may be prepared to meet them to resolve any queries they may have about what is required (more about that later), so that they can make as accurate a proposal as possible – that is after all in your interest.

Similar advice applies to attending demonstrations or going out to 'find out what is available'. This is the wrong approach. You will end up designing your problem (albeit subconsciously) to meet the

solutions that took your fancy. Find out what you *need,* and then
make sure what you purchase satisfies that need. If you are innovating
and moving on to higher levels of information management, it is
probable that what you need will not be available 'off the shelf'.

Inviting proposals

There is no magic in buying information services: it is much the same as
buying any expensive products or services. It requires a blend of business
understanding, technical knowledge and good purchasing practice.

All the selected suppliers should be treated equally, and the first steps
are not to involve any of them in the specification process and to
ensure that all are sent the invitation to tender documents at the same
time. The one exception is if a suitable supplier comes to the project
team's notice at a late stage.

Such a situation should only arise in exceptional circumstances if the
initial bidder selection process is undertaken carefully. However, if a
late entrant is included, they may receive the bid documents late, but
they will still be required to meet the closing date for receipt of
proposals. Any flexibility with the closing date to accommodate a
particular supplier will be seen by the others and by outsiders as undue
favouritism – it will undo all the good work in ensuring high standards
of corporate governance in procurement.

The information required to support the specification is straightforward.

Summary

There should be a brief, one- or two-page, summary of the
specification and the requirements. This will allow suppliers to decide
quickly whether they really want to bid for the work. You do not
want suppliers to waste their time producing unsuitable proposals,
and you are even less likely to want to spend time evaluating
proposals with no chance.

Background

There will be the need to give suppliers a feel for the organisation, its
strategy, its competence in relevant areas and its culture. These will all
have a bearing (or should) on how the bidder approaches the work.

The proposals should reflect those issues, and at evaluation you should consider carefully how well the suppliers have understood not just the technical issues, but also the cultural and other 'soft' issues that are, in my view, more important to the success of any information management project.

The documents should also give some background to the project, its overall objectives and why it is being undertaken.

There may also be some technical background to put the whole thing in perspective. This should include some of the history of the existing systems and the longer-term technological strategy.

Specification

This is described in detail elsewhere, and it should be complete and with clear performance requirements. There should be no doubt as to how success for the project will be measured.

It should also not be so specific in its requirements that it favours a particular solution. It should give room for suppliers to innovate in the way they provide the solution within a required performance framework.

It should *not* be a copy of someone else's. All organisations are different and what is right for one may not be for even an ostensibly similar organisation. Unfortunately, many organisations do copy the specification and then wonder why their staff do not 'own' the solution and why they do not achieve the benefits they expected. They will not gain competitive advantage by copying their rivals or similar organisations serving different customers.

Proposed project timetable

This should set your view of the timetable for implementing the information systems defined in the specification. It cannot be firm as it will be very dependent on the selected solution, but it gives the supplier an idea of how you see the scope of the project.

However, if some of the benefits are dependent on achieving particular elements of the project by a particular time, then this should be made very clear. If these cannot be achieved, then the cost and benefits appraisal may have to be re-examined to ensure that the project is still viable.

Tender rules

You will need to be explicit about any rules that you wish to make for the tender process. This will include how queries will be resolved, rules about gifts or other incentives, collusion between suppliers or between supplier and staff in your organisation.

You may wish to make it clear that any agreements between bidders with regard to prices or even as to who should bid should not be permitted. Discovery of any collusion between bidders would exclude such bidders immediately. Bear in mind that cartels are forbidden under European Union regulations in any case.

It may also be a requirement that bids are presented and made in a particular way, for instance, all bids must be sealed.

Sealed bids

Your standing financial instructions may call for bids to be submitted in sealed envelopes with no external marking to identify the bidder. There may also be a requirement that bids will all be opened at a formal meeting. Such an approach is sometimes required by public and voluntary sector procurement rules to help ensure and to demonstrate fair play.

If either or both are applicable, then the rules should be clearly stated in the bid documentation. For example, it may be a requirement that packages must be submitted for tender with no additional marks that may identify the sender.

Any breach of such rules should exclude the proposal from consideration.

Format of proposal

I would recommend that you set out a required structure for the proposal that matches the structure of your evaluation model (see Appendix E). This will make it easier to compare proposals and to formally evaluate them.

I would also recommend that you insist on a one- or two-page summary to cover the key issues. This will again make it simpler to compare and evaluate proposals.

Information required

There will be key information that you require from all bidders. Typically this should include, amongst other more specific needs:

● financial performance of the bidder;
● organisational and management structure;

- experience with similar projects;
- help desks, support, and problem escalation and resolution procedures;
- references.

Selection process

This should describe the selection process as it is relevant to the bidders. As already mentioned, there will be more involved for the organisation inviting the tender.

Timetable

The procurement timetable should be clearly stated, especially the key dates that the bidders need to have in their diaries:

- date of any bidder's workshop to explain the project and answer questions in an open forum – only if felt appropriate;
- closing date and time for receipt of proposals – essential;
- date of presentations for shortlisted suppliers – essential if they will be required.

As much notice as possible needs to be given to potential suppliers, because you want them to be able to field the team that they will be using on your work.

What you see is what you get (WYSIWYG)

WYSIWIG is often used by the computer industry when talking about the way data is presented – it is the same on-screen as it will be when it is printed. Well, the same applies to presentations.

You should insist that the team making the presentation should be the team who will be undertaking your project. You will have to work closely with them for some time, and need to be comfortable that you will be able to work with the supplier's team. You need to be able to work with them on both the technical and a personal level.

So all the key personnel that the supplier intends to use should take an active part in the presentation. The team should not be padded with senior people who will not be seen again to give spurious credibility – if they are there, they should have a genuine role in the implementation stage.

So ensure that you give them as much notice of key dates as possible – that way they have fewer excuses for not fielding your team rather than the sales team.

Equal opportunities

There is a requirement on employers to demonstrate that they have non-discriminatory employment practice. You may wish as part of that policy to require suppliers to demonstrate or certify that they do not discriminate on the basis of ethnic origin, religion, disability or even age and in other ways.

Collusion and gifts

Many organisations have strict rules about staff accepting gifts from suppliers to reduce the opportunities for undue influence. Similarly, there should also be a requirement for bidders to bid independently without forming cartels – which is against the law – or otherwise co-operating. This latter may take the form of agreement not to bid against each other and therefore reduce competition. If such practices are discovered, then both suppliers should be excluded from all current and future work. You may also wish to advise the appropriate authorities and to re-examine any bids for other work that they have won.

Workplace rules

If you have workplace rules about alcohol or smoking or indeed any other matter, they should be made clear to the prospective supplier. It may have an impact on the staff they choose to do the work and the approach they adopt. That will then have an impact on the proposal.

Intellectual property

If there is a design and development element to the services to be provided, there may be an issue of who owns the rights. It will particularly relate to copyright of software developed especially for you, the client.

Suppliers' standard contracts will usually seek to retain copyright on all their work, and in any case it will remain with them, unless expressly transferred in writing. If the development is merely modifications to an existing piece of software (especially if it is standard packaged software), then it is probably reasonable for the supplier to retain the rights as it would be practically impossible to separate the different elements.

However if the software is being written specially against your specification, then the issue is less clearcut. If the new software is innovative and the design is largely the client's, then the client should probably seek to have the copyright transferred. This is especially important if the new system is such that it will give your organisation a competitive advantage over your competitors – you do not want them to be able to go and buy the same solution 'off the shelf'.

This will mean of course that you will have to bear the full costs of the development as the supplier will not be able to spread them over anticipated future sales. Many software packages are based on work done especially for one customer and then developed further to make it more generally applicable. Often the first customer will get their development at a reduced cost as they are underwriting the provider's product development. That is fine if you are comfortable with essentially the same system being made available to all your competitors.

In any case, most writers of software will use standard software components that they have developed in the past and over which they will wish to keep control – they are commercially valuable to them. In which case the developer should be prepared to license the client to use the components for internal use within the organisation, but not for commercial exploitation, without some separate agreement with regard to rights and royalties.

Whatever applies, the issue of copyright, and patents if applicable, should be addressed at an early stage, as it could have a significant impact on the cost and approach adopted by suppliers. Do not automatically assume that you have to have rights transferred – you can agree to license just the relevant parts of it for a given time. You could have the rights to the software in your industry for five years if that gave sufficient protection, and it should be much cheaper than outright transfer! Think it through and make it clear what you actually need.

Confidentiality

This should be a two-way process. As customer, you require your supplier to respect your obligations under the Data Protection Act. With an information-based service, you may also require their solution to comply with the requirements of the Act and any other policies of the organisation. If that is the case, the policies should be made available as part of the invitation-to-bid documentation.

In some instances, suppliers and their staff will have to have suitable clearance under the Official Secrets Act. If they are not already cleared, they will have to be willing to undergo formal vetting procedures. The supplier may need to seek the agreement of appropriate staff before bidding. In any case if clearance is required, thought will need to be given as to when that process will be started, as it may take some time and have an impact on the project start date.

Insurance

Any supplier should have third-party cover for the normal third-party risk to their staff and clients through the normal course of their work. If there is a particular risk or requirement that needs to be covered, then this should always be made clear and a requirement made for appropriate certificates to be shown at a suitable stage. Make the cover required appropriate to the risk – the risk of expensive personal injury or other third-party damage claims are greater when using a building contractor than, say, a management consultant.

It may be that the supplier will have to take out additional cover for your project and clearly will not do so until the contract has been awarded. Make it a condition of the contract that the certificate must be produced with one month of the contract award, or – if the supplier fails to do so – you will take out the cover and take the premium and other costs from the payments due to the supplier.

Professional indemnity

Again, most major suppliers will have professional indemnity for the normal scale of their operations. You may wish to see that cover exists much in the same way as for third-party insurance, and again if the project is larger than usual or more risky, then the supplier may need to take out additional cover.

If it is important, treat much as discussed in the previous section on *Insurance*. Bear in mind that if problems get to the stage where claims on professional indemnity insurance are made, then there have been substantial failures on both sides. It is as much the client's responsibility as the supplier's to ensure that the solutions adopted are correct for the organisation. Using a third party does not absolve management from responsibility. They should exercise due diligence in their own role as managers of the organisation.

Initial contact

Remember that assessment of potential suppliers starts with the initial contact. Make a note of how easy it is to get the information you require. Was the telephone answered quickly, and was the telephonist friendly and helpful?

Were you put through to the right person first time, or were you sent all around the telephone network? Did the person to whom you spoke understand what you were trying to get over, but without jumping to conclusions? Did they send information as promised, and was it sent promptly? Did they follow up a few days later to make sure it was what was required and to answer any questions that may have arisen?

Make a note of your reaction to them during this initial contact and all the pre-bid interaction. Make sure other members of the team who may be speaking to potential suppliers also keep notes on their experiences. You will ultimately need to feed them into the selection of the initial shortlist and later into the final evaluation of the favoured supplier.

As pointed out previously, keep notes of all such conversations, especially where they make promises or offers that they may later 'forget'. It is very impressive in a negotiation when you can say that on a previous date, possibly a year before, and at a specific time a particular individual said, 'We do not charge for. . .' It takes the legs from under the other's negotiating position!

Handling queries

Whilst bids are being prepared, potential suppliers will need to resolve queries. They should need to ask for clarification about aspects of the proposal. It is practically impossible to make a specification so clear and tight that no questions will arise. In fact as we have already suggested, it is probably undesirable, as we want to use the suppliers' expertise to produce an innovative solution – they cannot do that with a tight contract.

It is imperative that all bidders are treated equally. As already proposed it might be preferable that a single person handles all queries about the bid. That way a consistent approach is easier to achieve. They should work within clear groundrules about what information may be given.

Equality of treatment does not necessarily mean that all bidders have to be given the same information. All the unrequested information should be identical, as should the answers to the same question from different suppliers. But, if a prospective supplier does not ask, the information does not have to be offered.

However, there will be cases where bidders will raise fundamental questions which, if misunderstood, will alter the whole nature of the solutions that will be proposed. There will also be instances where the specification turns out to be incomplete for some reason – perhaps there is a set of questions that keep being asked or a change in circumstances. In that case, additional documentation may need to be prepared and sent to all prospective bidders.

For large procurements, it is not uncommon to organise a bidders' workshop to which all potential suppliers are invited. This follows the issue of the specification and is an opportunity to clarify issues in public. This ensures all bidders receive the same information. It usually takes the form of a short presentation on the business requirements, and then an open question and answer session on the documentation and implied issues. Such a workshop may be an effective use of your team's time if the requirements are complex or the number of bidders is large.

When answering questions, keep a note of what answers you give. It will make it easier if someone else asks the same question, and it will protect you if you are challenged for not being even-handed. It is no accident that police officers' notebooks are numbered, with date of issue recorded, and have to be returned without missing pages. It (almost completely) prevents additional information being added to notes retrospectively and thereby improves their standing as evidence.

Sending out invitations to tender

As a general rule all Invitations to Tender should be sent out at the same time. This is to give equal opportunity to all parties. You may wish to send them by some form of delivery that requires a signature to confirm receipt. Again this will ensure that any disputes about unequal treatment can be resolved.

There is one exception where it may be necessary to send out an invitation pack separately. That is when potential bidders make themselves known after the first packs have been sent. In that case, they should be sent a pack, but they should still be required to submit their proposal by the same deadline as the other bidders. This should not occur because someone has been added to the bidding shortlist by the client – that would be a failure of your process for selecting the shortlist and could raise serious questions about the probity of it. If it is felt necessary, then the procurement process ought to be abandoned and resumed after the preparation of a new shortlist of bidders to be invited.

Aborted procurements do happen for all sorts of reasons, and I have seen them from both sides. It is never a happy experience for anyone. It wastes a lot of valuable time all round. Procurements should go strictly by the book.

Demonstrations and presentations

Treat presentations and demonstrations in exactly the same way as you do the main procurement. You will need to predefine your evaluation criteria and be clear about what you want out of the meeting.

You should be in control, so take control from the start. Under no circumstance, let the supplier browbeat you into doing it their way. It is your project, your procurement and it will be your solution, so make sure you work to your agenda, not that of the suppliers. Even if they are totally ethical or even altruistic, their agenda is not the same as yours.

Framework for bidders

Make it clear what the programme will be, even if you are visiting their premises for a demonstration. Send them a copy in good time along with a list of questions that need answering and points that you wish to cover in the presentation and especially in demonstrations.

In a demonstration you may wish them to take you through business processes as close as possible to those the systems will be supporting in your organisation. If you do, make it clear, and give them a copy of the procedures – or an outline of it, if it is still under development.

For presentations, set out how long the meeting will be and how much time they have to make a presentation. After that, you will have a question and answer session up to the scheduled finish time. An hour and a half is usually long enough, and you can then have a break between each presentation, and still have four in one day. That should be plenty – most should have been ruled out at proposal stage. You should invite only the presentations that you believe can deliver what you require. As with the proposals, you should not waste time with suppliers who have no chance – they will not thank you for wasting their time either. If there is only one, then so be it – but you do not have to tell them!

Let the presenting suppliers know the framework in good time.

Preparation

Apart from preparing lists of questions to be given written answers at or in time for the presentation, you should also prepare the questions that you wish to raise face to face. These should focus on the issues in the proposal with which you are uncomfortable. Answers to the big questions should be given in written form before the presentation.

The same chairman and support team should be appointed for all the presentations. A decision also should be taken about who will ask which questions and of whom, as far as is possible.

Bear in mind that you do not need to ask the same questions of each supplier. Rather you should use it as an opportunity to probe the weaknesses that you suspect from their proposal (or that arise in the presentation).

You may wish to run a rehearsal. At the very least, you should have a briefing session the day before, just to make sure everyone is clear about responsibilities and objectives.

Make sure you have room, and that the presentation facilities such as overhead projectors, screens, etc., that you have promised will be available. Order tea or coffee, as suppliers will often have travelled considerable distances, and lunch, if necessary.

Evaluation

You will have identified your evaluation criteria in advance and probably incorporated it into your overall assessment model. You should arrange to do the assessment as soon as possible after the last presentation or demonstration. Make sure you include compliance with your proposal framework as part of that evaluation.

Some points to bear in mind with regard to evaluating presentations are questions like:

- Were they on time?
- Did the presentation simply repeat what was in the proposals?
- Did the presentation add to the proposal?
- Had they complied with the requirement that only relevant people should be used?
- Did all the supplier team contribute effectively? Or was it a one-person show?
- Were their responses to questions to the point and satisfactory?
- Did the written answers they provided fully address the questions?

On the day

The team should get together before the meeting and ensure that they are comfortable with their role and that all the facilities are as they should be. Make sure you have spare flip-chart pens, etc. – they always run out at the most awkward time (when I am presenting, I always have spares in my case).

Make sure that receptionists know what the timings are and how the teams are to be delivered to the presentation room. Also make clear to support staff what information they can give to the visitors – probably not the names or numbers of other presentations. Warn them to be careful about leaving details on their notepad – all good consultants and salesmen are adept at reading upside-down!

When asking questions, do not always ask them through their team leader. Ask them directly of other members of the team, and sometimes ask them questions outside their speciality. Are they a team, or are they there as makeweights to back up the leader? When asked a question outside their field, a competent member of the team should be able to make some relevant comments, and then pass it on to someone who can answer it more fully. Be firm: do not let the team leader jump in to take questions directed elsewhere. Also watch other members of the team when they are not answering questions their body language can tell you a lot. When salespeople make promises that technicians will have difficulty keeping, there will be inadvertent winces from the technical people on the team!

As an aside, you may be wondering, why the secrecy about who is bidding or presenting? If the shortlist is known, bidders can modify their approach to compete with rivals, at the expense of meeting your needs. This can go further, and if bidders know that the others are all high-cost players, then there is scope to set their bid price relatively high. Of course if you were to inadvertently let slip that there was a low-cost supplier amongst the bidders . . .

What you see is what you get

For the presentation, insist that only the people who will have significant involvement with your project are to be involved. Also make sure the key people are there – if the date of the presentations or demonstration have been announced in the bid invitation documents, there is little excuse for them to not be present. Do not let them field the sales team, and then use different people to deliver the system.

Negotiation and contracts

'Keep detailed records of meetings and all other contact with possible suppliers from the start', is my principal advice as far as negotiating is concerned. For contracts, I would suggest that you focus on what you want to achieve for your business and express it in measurable terms that you and your colleagues understand. Just as you have done so far.

Concentrate on the critical success factors. There will be key measures that sum up the success or otherwise of the project. They have to be ones within the supplier's control and not be dependent on the performance of the organisation. What are the supplier's Vital Signs from your organisation's point of view? Identify what you would use to manage their performance on this work if they were an in-house department.

I will not attempt to teach a manager, who is senior enough to have the responsibility for such a project, how to negotiate the details. He or she should already have experience of negotiating contracts of lesser value. In any case, it is beyond the scope of this book and there are many other good courses and books on the subject.

Nor will I write the contracts. That too is a big specialist field. Use a solicitor who has experience of the information field and is especially familiar with the licensing practices and the intellectual property issues surrounding software, training courses and the like. Leave the legal side to the specialists: if you are part of a large organisation, there should be standard purchasing contracts and, anyway, you should have support on the legal front. But examine it in detail at an early stage, ideally with the proposal. Do not leave it to the end – you will need time to negotiate the terms.

Trust

Bear in mind that the contract will only come back into consideration if mutual trust breaks down. As we explore later, managing the relationship between customer and supplier is all-important to the success of an information management, indeed any, project. The secret is to work with suppliers who you feel you can trust, and then work hard at building and maintaining such a relationship.

The secret, as we will see later, is good communication.

Open-ended

Avoid open-ended contracts. Make sure that there will be no doubt that the work has been completed to a satisfactory standard. To do that you need to build in deliverables that are measurable or concrete. If the contract is open-ended, you will get hit for additional costs due to variations or add-ons. As we will see later, keep focused on the objectives and do not add things because it 'would be nice' – the cost of such additions is out of all proportion to their value.

Anyone who has building work done, an extension perhaps, knows that the profit for the builder is not in the initially contracted work. It is in all the bits and pieces that were missed or changed during their work. The same is true for most projects – in fact, we are seeing it on a large scale with some of the facilities management contracts or 'outsourced' functions that have been so popular. Many are costing a lot more because of what was missed from the contract, or, more usually, because of changes outside the contract.

ANALYSIS OF QUESTIONNAIRE 7

1   **Yes.** There should be clear rules relating to financial matters for any organisation. These should be appropriate, formally documented and above all, used. They ensure proper controls, and protect individuals by making clear the limits to their responsibility and authority. If they do not exist create them, at the very least for your projects.

2. **Yes.** This is a good idea, because we are talking about information management and learning from what has gone before. If procedures have been adopted in the past, then new work can build on what has gone before and avoid some of the mistakes made by predecessors. But do not simply copy what they did. Use it as a starting point and improve it – no process will have been 100 per cent perfect.

3. **Yes.** Even better is to have a formal assessment of previous projects. Much can be learned from the problems and mistakes that were made. Only by sharing knowledge about previous mistakes, can we avoid repeating them. Remember:
    'Experience is the name every one gives to their mistakes.'
    Oscar Wilde, *Lady Windermere's Fan, Act III*

4. **No.** Start with a clear mind focused on the business objectives. For that you do not need to know what is on offer. Let suppliers show you how they meet your needs. By looking at solutions prior to the bidding stage, there is a likelihood that you will prejudge the result or bias the requirements towards a particular solution. It may be subconscious, but it will happen.

5. **Complete.** The internal notes of meetings, telephone conversations, etc. need not be typed as long as they are legible. They should be created at the time of the events they record and filed in the project file. All members of the project team should adopt the same standards.

6. **No.** Once it has been started, the procurement process should be rigidly formal. Flexibility leads to the possibility of bias, opens the

opportunity for collusion and a loss of auditability. It becomes difficult to prove that decisions were taken in good faith and equal treatment given to all interested parties.

7. **No.** As with the overall process, the selection criteria should be defined and documented before the proposals are received (better still at specification stage) and should not be revised once proposals are received. They *must* be finalised before the closing date or the receipt of any proposals, whichever is the earlier. That is why good practice can be clearly demonstrated.

1. Review standing financial instructions and any other procurement-related procedures. Bring them up to date.

2. Set out the additional rules that apply to the projects in hand.

3. Start a project file and pull all documents, notes, etc. together.

4. Define the process to be used for the current project.

5. Define the pre-qualifying and proposal evaluation criteria. Formally document them and build the evaluation model using your preferred spreadsheet (see Appendix E).

6. Start the procurement process. Identify possible bidders.

FURTHER READING

Martin Wilson, *Getting the Most from Consultants*, Pitman, 1996
A shameless plug for my own book! With many information management exercises, there will be a desire to use consultants. This book is aimed at enabling the reader to make the selection and use of consultants as effective as possible. It seeks to ensure that as much expertise is retained within the organisation as possible, and that the organisation and its people learn from the experience.

It also shows that successful consultancy needs good clients. It shows how you can be a good client and not waste money on using consultants for work that could be done in-house: use consultants for their expertise, not as another pair of hands.

It also stresses the different roles of managers, consultants and contract or freelance staff. Essentially, consultants advise and manage themselves, managers manage the business, and contract staff are managed by those managers as an alternative to permanent staff.

SUMMARY

The procurement process should be formally structured with clear rules and documentation. If there are existing rules such as standing financial instructions, these should be used. The aim is to produce a process that is auditable without being bureaucratic.

The number of bidders should be kept to a manageable number of no more than six or so. If there are many potential suppliers or a need for an open bidding process as there is with public-sector procurement, then it may be necessary to use a preparatory stage by asking for expressions of interest to prequalify the bidding shortlist. Similar rules should be adopted for the expression of interest as for the final tendering process.

It is important that there are clear rules as to what information may be provided to bidders, and it may therefore be appropriate to use a single person to co-ordinate communications with bidders. All discussions with bidders should be documented, as they may make promises or provide information that will be useful in later negotiation or selection. Whilst records need to be kept, contemporaneous handwritten notes will suffice – there is no need to waste time and resources having everything typed. Just make sure it is readable.

Evaluation criteria for all stages should be predefined before the stage starts. Ideally, all criteria should be established at the specification stage and before any suppliers are considered. However that is probably not realistic beyond the expression of interest or initial bid stages. Presentations and demonstrations should have their assessment framework decided before the first of such meetings and then be used for all of them.

It is recommended that no demonstrations or presentations are attended until after the full proposals have been evaluated. This will prevent inadvertent bias being applied to the specification, evaluation criteria or assessment. It is the organisation's business needs that determine what is required *not* what is on offer.

Use the suppliers' expertise to refine the solution without redefining the business objectives.

Make sure the contract is tight with clearly defined and measurable performance criteria. The success factors, as far as possible, should be such that the supplier can manage their achievement and not be dependent on the client's performance. If the supplier will not accept such measures, then question whether you should use them.

CHAPTER

8

MANAGING THE
IMPLEMENTATION

*This chapter aims to provide
a framework for the
management of any project.*

INTRODUCTION

Although the failure of technology is often cited as the cause of unsuccessful information systems projects, it is rarely, I would venture to say never, the primary cause. I have been brought in many times to act as a trouble-shooter on projects that have got into difficulties. Sometimes the difficulties have been due to inappropriate technological choices, but those choices have usually been made in a vain attempt to overcome management or other people problems. By far the majority of my trouble-shooting has been to sort out difficulties due to poor user involvement or, in most cases, simply due to ineffective management of the project.

My experience is that the most obvious symptom of a project in, or heading for, difficulties is the absence of real communication. There is perhaps a lot of shouting, but no real interchange of views or plans to resolve the problem. Customers stop talking to suppliers, users are not talking to the project manager or technicians. And managers trying to dictate results in the face of overwhelming evidence that they cannot be achieved and nobody is listening in any case! Everybody is blaming everybody else for the failures. If there must be blame, then it should fall on all involved in the project. Failure by an individual needs to be allowed to go unaddressed by other members of the team for it to cause a serious problem for the project, hence it is a collective failure. Laying blame is a counter-productive process.

The aim should be to design the management process to spot potential problems at the earliest possible stage and to take corrective action. A positive approach to difficulties will ensure that the project is implemented effectively, and will in many cases throw up new ideas and opportunities.

This chapter aims to provide a framework for the management of any project. There is no fundamental differences between the project management of a major civil engineering work such as a dam, and a small project to reorganise an office layout. An information management implementation is similar to them. The only difference is the scale of the resources and time involved, and the nature of the technology. But the technology does not affect the project management; it only affects the technical processes of the project. Whether a task has been completed to specification may be a technical judgement. The answer as far as the project plan is concerned is simply yes or no – has the objective been achieved?

All managers are expected to manage projects from time to time, so project management should be a core skill. This book cannot cover all that is involved in project management, but it seeks to guide the manager through the basics and into good practice. Further reading is suggested to extend the reader's understanding of general project management and associated issues. Managers should ensure that they have a good grounding in project management techniques, because their roles are increasingly becoming project-based.

The objectives for this chapter are to:

1 demonstrate that project management should be within the competence of any good manager;

2 show that managing an information systems project is no different in principle from any other project;

3 allow managers to organise the project team;

4 provide some techniques and advice on project planning;

5 suggest approaches for identifying and coping with risk;

6 guide the manager through the challenges of managing a project.

QUESTIONNAIRE 8

The challenges of managing

1 Project management is a black art that needs specialists.
   a Yes?
   b No?

2 Once established is the plan fixed?
   a Yes
   b No

3 If the supplier offers to manage the project, do we need a project manager?
   a Yes
   b No

4 Can we add in some of the 'nice to have' things that the supplier is offering during the implementation?
   a Yes
   b No

5 We have spent a lot of time and money on a project. It is still not complete, and it does not look like achieving all the benefits we anticipated. What do we do?
   a Kill it
   b Review it
   c Reassess the investment decision
   d Carry on as best we can

PROJECT STRUCTURE

High-level commitment

No project should go ahead without high-level commitment to its objectives and the provision of the necessary resources. All but the smallest information management projects should be actively supported and directed at the highest level within the organisation. Remember we have recognised that such projects should be designed to support corporate business objectives, and that senior managers are the final arbiters of the corporate strategy.

The senior management team are therefore the eventual 'customers' of any information management exercise. Only they can really judge the long-term relevance of such work to their longer-term plans and whether the benefits justify the costs.

> *No project should go ahead without high-level commitment to its objectives and the provision of the necessary resources.*

The high-level commitment has to be more than superficial and has to demonstrate genuine interest in the effective implementation of the proposed plans. They have therefore to understand why the work is desirable, and what it will achieve in a business sense. If they do not understand that, then senior management is failing in its principal duty to show due diligence in the management of the organisation's resources.

Senior management also has a responsibility to show leadership. That has to be active and to be substantially by example. If they are not interested in the changes happening within the organisation, why should anybody? If senior management knows and cares what is being done, and demonstrates that in a genuine way, then those most closely affected will be more prepared to drive the changes through.

Steering group

All but the smallest information management programmes should have a steering group to direct the work on a day-to-day basis. The role of the steering group is to provide high-level oversight of the project to ensure that the work is headed for the right target. It also has a strategic role with regard to interpretation of the specification, the underlying requirements and any changes that arise. It has the final responsibility on such matters and should have delegated authority through the senior management representative to take decisions within the project's terms of reference.

The detailed management of the work should be the responsibility of the project manager (and his team leaders on larger projects) with support from the supplier's project or account manager and her team.

The committee should be as small as possible, whilst having representatives of the key groups. A team of around five or six is usually enough to cover the key areas effectively; more and it starts to become unwieldy and a talking shop, fewer and there may be insufficient expertise or authority. The members are likely to include:

Senior management

The steering group needs a senior management representative for a variety of reasons. The senior manager will act as project sponsor and represent issues relating to the project to the board or executive management team of the organisation.

As a member of such a group, they will also have delegated authority to make day-to-day project decisions on behalf of the senior management team and without reference to it, within agreed terms of reference. Appropriate authority is essential to the smooth running of any programme of work. Without it, delays are inevitable as the steering group will have to keep coming back to the board for approval or clarification of its actions.

There are other benefits of having high-level representation on the steering group as they will be able to keep the group apprised of strategic and other relevant developments. Similarly, the senior manager will be able to inform the board's thinking from his or her experience, as information management projects will often be of strategic importance.

Finally, having a senior manager take an active role in projects that cause changes will send a message to affected staff that the organisation places considerable importance on the success of the work. Too often, the senior management team shows only cursory interest in information systems projects. This is demotivating for the project team and it tells other staff that this is another technically based initiative from the computer department of no business relevance. Is it then not surprising they are half-hearted and do not work to make a success of the new systems?

Users

Users need to be properly represented, but that does not mean that a member from every team affected should be included on the steering group. That would often make the group too large. The users' delegate(s) should have a good overall picture of the requirements and should be trusted by all user groups to represent their interests fairly on a day-to-day basis. In any case, all affected users should be closely involved in the programme of work and their views taken through other forums. From time to time they may be asked to attend steering group meetings relevant to their particular interests.

Technical specialists

As with users, there should be a representative with broad knowledge and understanding of all the technical issues around the work. They may need access to colleagues, or consultants, with a more detailed understanding of particular technical matters. Such experts can and should be used as part of the wider implementation team and where necessary be involved in the work of the steering group where their expertise is required.

Project manager

Clearly the client-side project manager is a key member of the steering group. The skills and role of project managers is explored in more detail shortly.

Supplier

There are arguments for and against making the suppliers part of the steering group. I tend to suggest not making them part of the steering group but including them in the smaller project management group.

Others

It may be necessary from time to time to co-opt other skills on to the committee to cover particular issues. Rather than make them full-time members, they should be members only during the relevant phases of work. However their involvement should be planned, as it will be necessary to keep them informed about the project and the underlying thinking. This will allow them to make their contribution appropriate and to the point without a lot of additional briefing.

Project managers

Supplier

Very often the selected suppliers will include project management costs in their bid, and it is tempting to leave them to run the project. Indeed suppliers will often encourage customers to think in that way. It is in their interest as they can manage the project to give their needs priority over those of the client. And what happens if there is a problem – whose interest will the suppliers' project manager champion?

So it is essential that there is a knowledgeable project manager who can protect the interests of the client. Many suppliers will welcome having a principal contact who is on the spot, and can ensure that the client meets their obligations so that the project runs to plan.

Client

The project manager is the key appointment if the implementation is to be effective. A good project manager is invaluable and should be guarded jealously by the organisation. The skills needed by the client's project manager include:

- diplomacy;
- business sense across all disciplines;
- approachability;
- ability to understand the technical issues;
- organisational skills;
- negotiating skills;
- strong-mindedness or resoluteness;
- open-mindedness;
- flexibility;
- toughness;
- sensitivity;
- independence;
- good inter-personal skills.

Yes, many seem to be in conflict, but that is the nature of project management and a good project manager has to be an all-rounder. The project manager has to be able to switch from one to another as the needs demand, and this may be by the minute.

TIP

Internal project managers

It is very tempting to second the project manager from within one of the user departments because 'they know the job'. However it is usually a mistake.

Someone from the user departments may well have knowledge of the requirement, but they will have to go back to that department after the project. That means it will be unfair to expect them to be even-handed during the project. Many people in that position will, albeit unconsciously, avoid upsetting their colleagues and tend to make decisions that favour their own department. Others will bend over backwards to be fair, and go too far, so that their own department does not get proper treatment.

As an alternative, it may well be tempting to use someone from the computer department, but that raises the concern that the project will then be seen as a technical exercise rather than a business-oriented project. The project *must* retain a business focus, however technical the issues concerned.

Ideally, then, the project manager should be external to the departments concerned and not be seen as a technician. The ideal candidate would be someone of sufficient authority who can be seconded full-time for the duration of the project. They should have no responsibilities in their base department, otherwise the project will be neglected when problems arise 'back home'. Otherwise it may be necessary to bring someone in from outside with suitable skills on a short-term contract.

High-level reporting

If there is effective delegated authority, then formal reporting to the board can and should be kept to a minimum.

The high-level reporting can then be largely informal, through the board member on the steering group. The formal reporting should focus on the key aspects that will concern the board. These will include expected completion date, costs and expected benefits compared to the plan. These should be supported by a brief commentary of what is being done to correct any problems and the expected result of those changes. This approach is explained in more detail in Chapter 2, Vital Signs Monitoring.

If there are substantial increases in the planned costs, or likely to be reduced benefits, then this should be a subject of a separate brief paper, detailing what it means to the planned cost-benefits and recommending a course of action. This should be treated as the investment appraisal for the original project – does it meet the organisation's expectations for authorising capital expenditure? If it does, then well and good, but if it does not, then a decision may have to be taken to abort the project. That contingency should be considered in the risk assessment, and outline plans made in case it is necessary.

At key milestones, the project plan should include just such decisions. There should be a formal high-level decision to go or not go at these points. Too many projects develop a life of their own, and the overspend is compounded because no-one is strong enough to cut the losses – so good money is thrown after bad.

PROJECT PLANNING

There should be no mystique associated with project planning and management. It is something we do all the time from childhood. Everybody has planned a holiday or a picnic – they are simple examples of project planning! The list of clothes to take and jobs to do before leaving is no less than a project plan. The plans used for larger projects are not really very different, although they may be wrapped round with technology, bureaucracy and the inevitable jargon.

There are a lot more tasks which have to be monitored and more complexity in the relationships between tasks. However, there are tools and techniques for helping with that and in any case as the project gets larger and more complex, then large sections of it should be delegated. The project manager can then manage the big picture at a high level, whilst team leaders manage the detail. If this sounds familiar, it is the same approach outlined as Vital Signs Monitoring in Chapter 2. The basics of management are much the same whatever the task – project planning and management is management!

There should be no mystique associated with project planning and management.

Formal project plan

An approach to project planning that works for me and many people I know is to start with the big picture and to break it first into large sub-projects and then to break those into smaller elements. That top-down disassembly continues until the whole project is reduced to manageable tasks.

So the overall project may be to implement a complete new computer-based sales system. I would start by breaking it down into, say, hardware, software, business processes, etc. Then I would break software down into product lines, customers, sales staff, etc. The breakdown can be fairly arbitrary to start with, as it should result in much the same tasks whatever route is taken. Tasks will have a dependence on each other – the software cannot be loaded, until the hardware has been installed as a high-level example. The new dependencies will then give the plan a new structure that is different from the starting point, but which will be more valuable for the management of the work.

By breaking it down into small, manageable elements, it is then possible to estimate the resources and elapsed time required to complete each individual task. These can then be aggregated to get an estimate of the total resources required to deliver the project. However, simply totalling elapsed times will not give a good approximation to the total elapsed time for the work, unless it is a one-person project. This is because many tasks can take place at the same time. So a different approach is used.

Understanding how each task depends on others leads to techniques based around Critical Path Analysis (CPA) and Program Evaluation and Review Technique (PERT). The two approaches at a basic level at least are very similar. They rely on recognising task dependencies, so that they can be modelled and the best possible elapsed time identified. These days they are usually modelled using a computer and project planning software which allows the critical path to be determined. It can be done manually, but it is tedious and does not lend itself to revision as the project unwinds and actual data becomes known. Also this planning software will usually take account of resource availability in its calculation of the critical path.

The critical path comprises those tasks which cannot be delayed at all without delaying the whole project. In a complex project, most tasks have some float in their starting or completion time which does not affect the overall schedule. Items on the critical path do not have that flexibility.

However I do not intend to go into detail about CPA and PERT, as I do not have the space. I would recommend that inexperienced project managers read the book by Philip Baguley, *Managing Successful Projects*, listed in the *Further reading* section.

Deliverables

All tasks should have clear deliverables. This should not be a problem, as we have detailed them in our work preparing the specification. A deliverable is anything that can be seen to have been produced without any doubt. For example an agreed, and signed off, list of codes or a demonstrably working link between computers in remote offices. They are deliverables – a meeting is never deliverable, but the decision resulting from it might be. Minutes of meetings, similarly, are not deliverables as they do not take, of themselves, the project forward.

SMART objectives

The project as a whole should have clearly stated SMART objectives and the achievement of these objectives should be monitored at appropriate points during the work. Some will be similar to deliverables, but the majority should reflect business benefits to ensure that we are not only doing things right, but doing the right things.

Many information management projects will be a phased series of mini-projects, and the results of each phase should be tested against the relevant objectives. Problems are easier to correct at this stage than if they are left until subsequent phases are completed – the corrections may have a ripple effect through the later work and need corrections made in the later phases.

Ideally, objectives should be tested before implementation by using walk-through with users and other relevant groups to ensure that the proposed detailed approach will meet their needs. These are a step-by-step examination of the proposed solution, the environment in which it is to be applied and with the people who will have to use the system. In that way, many problems or potential operational difficulties will be spotted by the end-user who will have to work with the systems on a day-to-day basis. It is an approach I use more and more and at earlier and earlier stages with clients – it is the best way of avoiding unworkable solutions I know as it involves the user in the design in the most meaningful way possible.

Schedule or timetable

Although the tasks are the result of breaking the main project down into sub-projects and then tasks, that is not the way to apportion time, or resources. Having identified the tasks, then each should be assessed on the basis of who will do it and how much time, realistically, it will take. This is then aggregated, using project management software in most cases, to determine the minimum possible elapsed time for the whole project.

It is very tempting at this stage to play around with the individual tasks to shorten the elapsed time to meet the original 'guesstimate' for the completion date. Do not do it! Almost invariably the first task-based estimate for project completion will still be too early in any case and will not be achieved. Trying to fine-tune individual tasks to get the plan to say what you and the board hoped will be a mistake. Face the difficulty upfront, once, because it will only get worse as the project keeps slipping and you keep having to ask for extensions.

If the realistic deadline is a real problem, then the scope or scale of the project may have to be revised. It may be necessary to work back from the deadline and decide what can genuinely be achieved in the time available. This will require all parties to reconsider what is really essential and what is 'merely' desirable. Many projects fail because expectations are too high, and in fact unachievable. It is all too easy for 'needs' to be added, merely because they are possible, not because they are really needed. These should be eliminated during the specification phase or during negotiation with the supplier. This project planning step is the last sensible opportunity to eliminate excessive requirements. Dropping elements during the project looks like failure, and it is. It sends the wrong message to management and users and will not do your career much good!

Resources

Much the same goes for resources as for time. Identify who and what will be required and their availability. Most project management software will then smooth the workload across the available resources, and coupled with the time estimates, produce a date for earliest possible completion.

Again, it may be tempting to try and fine-tune the availability of resources to improve the timetable. But even the first estimate is likely to be over-optimistic about what can be achieved; expecting more will make the plan extremely sensitive to the slightest snag.

It must be remembered that almost any planning will be inaccurate to some extent, so trying to get unrealistic precision is a waste of effort. Accept that management is a crude art and needs to be applied in big lumps, if it is to be effective. Project management is akin to steering a large ship, it needs substantial inputs and the effect is not obvious for some time – it is certainly not like a racing car where small, delicate inputs are required and felt immediately.

Err on the slightly pessimistic side and you will be less disappointed. You might even bring the project home ahead of schedule; you will not if you pare time and resources to a minimum. As a project manager, you are there to manage the risk and that may mean you have to make your colleagues, and your boss, aware of the real position, rather than pandering to what they imagine is the situation.

Supplier and client roles

With the best will in the world, the supplier and client will have different objectives and the roles need to be kept separate. The supplier will probably have many concurrent projects, whilst the customer is only concerned about one of them – theirs.

The suppliers' project manager will wish to keep the suppliers' cost down and ultimately to protect the suppliers' interests. Suppliers want their project managers to use their resources in a way that suits the supplier.

On the other hand, the customer wants those resources made available when they need them even if it conflicts with the suppliers' commitments on other projects.

The roles are separate, although there is much common ground. However, the different objectives are justification enough to require separate project managers. They should and usually do work closely together with considerable co-operation, But when the going gets tough, they will fight for their own interests, and usually find an acceptable compromise.

Agreement

There must be agreement on the objectives, deliverables, resources and time from all the key interest groups involved in the project. Without such agreement, there will be endless squabbling about the availability of people and other resources. In particular, the concerned groups should include:

- Users – both managers and the individuals involved in all relevant aspects of the plan.
- Technical staff – their agreement is needed in particular for compliance with the technical strategy and the resource implications. This applies not only to the computer department,

but also to all other departments, who may have a specialised input such as: estates, finance or human resources.

- **Board or executive management team** – their agreement is needed especially for the expenditure, benefits and the delegated responsibility and authority. They need also to be committed to make any decisions referred to them in a clear and timely way.
- **Suppliers** – these have to agree to meet all the agreed aspects of the specification as well as to agree to make sufficient resources available to meet their part of the plan and to facilitate others in meeting theirs. This agreement will be largely explicit during the negotiations of the contract and the project plan.

This agreement should be formal and the project should ideally be signed off by all parties to its implementation. Similarly, any significant changes made later should also be in writing and formally agreed. That way there is less room for argument – unfortunately, however hard one tries, some room will always be found.

Vital Signs Monitoring

If you have detected hints that suggest the Vital Signs Monitoring approach is appropriate to project management, then you would be correct. It is a highly appropriate tool as we have a plan with clear measurable objectives and other measures to guide us along the way. These can be readily monitored and they will quickly highlight problems.

The two main measures that will be used for routine project management are completion dates for tasks and budget or resource input measures, for example, time or material costs. Once a reasonable-sized project is running, completion dates should be coming up almost daily; if they are not, then it is possible the tasks have not been broken down to a sufficiently detailed level. With key indicators needing to be checked every day, there will be early warning of any problems.

As part of the weekly project meeting, then an assessment should be made as to whether the completion dates for longer tasks are still achievable. If they are not, then decisions need to be taken as to whether additional resources (such as overtime) would bring it back to plan, or whether the slippage will have to be accepted and accommodated. This brings us back to the Cycle of Control we discussed early in Chapter 2 (see page 33). We will need to replan on the basis of the new data we have and assess what effect it will have on the final outcomes. Will the project be late, or over budget (the two tend to go hand in hand)? Is it still worthwhile? What does it do to the expected benefits?

The same Vital Signs-based approach should be applied to monitoring the performance against the agreed deliverable elements. Are they achieving the expected performance? And will this provide the benefits that were envisaged in the original investment appraisal? These can be monitored as elements of the project are completed, but they will be on a longer cycle than the project management details.

However as the assessment of performance and benefits are made, then the project investment appraisal should be reconsidered to check that the work is still economically viable. If it is not, then a proposal should be put to senior management that the project be revised or killed. Such considerations should be made at the earliest opportunity before further investment is made and probably wasted. Too many projects continue after it becomes clear that the expected benefits are unlikely to be achieved – usually because no-one is prepared to admit that a mistake was made. So the mistake is compounded by wasting further time and money.

Sunk costs are not a reason to continue!

Expenditure already made on a project (sunk costs) is never sufficient justification for further investment. The decision as to whether further spending is appropriate should be on the basis of a complete reassessment of the investment decision. Simply, do the likely benefits justify the new increased total cost?

Research shows that sunk costs play a major part in most decisions relating to continued investment. All too often, no-one is prepared to say that an earlier decision was flawed or that circumstances have changed. The decision becomes too institutionalised, political or emotional for anyone to argue against continuation.

Do not fall into the trap. If you and your team cannot stand back and be objective about a project's future, then find someone who can.

This then might be a good time to review Chapter 2 and make sure you are comfortable with the Vital Signs Monitoring approach. It will be invaluable in your day-to-day project management, and the rest of your management responsibilities.

Informal aspects

Usually the supplier and customer teams will develop close working relationships and these should be encouraged. It effectively means a single team. Especially on long projects, some social contact is useful to help encourage that team spirit and mutual trust and respect.

Often the suppliers' staff will be living away which can get lonely. From time to time on a long project there is no harm in organising some social activity where it does not compromise the relationship. Apart from having meals with customers, I have often worked on projects where, as the suppliers, we have been treated almost as one of the customers' staff and been invited to social activities. At other times we have organised ten-pin bowling or golf matches between supplier and client.

It is all about communications and will contribute to the success of the project.

Flexibility

All projects need to change to some extent during their implementation. So flexibility of approach is important, but not at the expense of allowing the scope of the project to creep or to lose sight of the real objectives. Sometimes genuine opportunities for new ways of doing things that will benefit the original aims will be found – test them against the objectives and investment appraisal and if they are beneficial go for them.

However do not let the attitude develop of 'if we just do this we can. . .' This is a prime reason, in my view, why projects are late and over budget. We did not let the 'it would be nice' elements into the specification: do not let them creep back in during the implementation – they will be even more expensive at that stage.

RISK MANAGEMENT

Unless it is trivial, the project will not go to plan. However well the project is planned and managed, there will need to be changes and management action taken to achieve the best result. This can still result in the project coming in on time and to budget. To do so will have required a good understanding of the risks and careful planning to avoid or mitigate possible problems. This can best be achieved by identifying difficulties that can be foreseen to a greater or lesser extent.

Project management is as much about managing the risk as it is simply about bringing the projects to time and budget. There will be times on complex projects where trying to meet time and budget constraints will severely compromise the success of the project. I have seen many projects brought in on time and cost, but which were complete failures. They were a technical implementation only because they had not taken the people along with them. And a technical implementation is no use to anyone. Information systems are of value only if they are used effectively by people in pursuit of business objectives.

If meeting the deadline means leaving the eventual users behind, then be late if the other risks are acceptable.

Potential problems

With any non-trivial project there will always be challenges, but these can be mitigated by effective risk analysis and good preparation. Difficulties only become a problem if there is no plan for dealing with them. Most potential difficulties can be foreseen or at least imagined – in which case plans can be laid for meeting them.

Triage

One of the key problems is unrealistic expectations, especially by future users of the system. These have to be managed to avoid disappointment and demotivation. As has already been mentioned in identifying needs and preparing the specification, some form of triage analysis of needs should be made – this should be on-going during the life of the implementation and indeed during live operation (see Chapter 6 page 127). Business needs change almost on a daily basis and therefore which of the three triage categories an identified requirement falls into will change as the business environment and the organisation changes.

As a reminder, the three triage categories are:

- **Essential:** without meeting this requirement, the new systems will not meet the needs of the business and achieve most of the expected benefits.
- **Important:** these requirements will make the system more useful or more pleasant to use, but it would work satisfactorily without meeting them, in other words they are not essential.

- **Nice-to-have:** all those other requirements that would be useful occasionally, make things prettier or would be nice to have, but without which the system would be fully functional and still work well.

With requirements identified in these three categories, the project team are in a position to make contingency plans which allow them to drop any elements from the 'nice-to-have' category (which survived specification and project planning) when things get tough. If the situation gets desperate, then the 'important' elements can be dropped without risk to the basic success of the project. And that is the main point – managing the risk to the project and the organisation by knowing what is essential and what is merely gloss.

Risk areas

We have already agreed, I hope, that project management is about managing risk. To do so, requires the principal risk factors to be identified and some assessment made of the nature of their possible impact on the plan and achievement of expected benefits.

Some of the possible risks might include:

- acceptance by users of the need for the work;
- the willingness and capability of users to take their part in the plan's execution;
- business issues such as a market changes, changing regulatory or political environments;
- the sophistication of the technology and everyone's understanding of it and the ability to achieve the anticipated results;
- availability of the expected resources;
- the role of key people both internally and at the chosen supplier – consider the impact if they became unavailable for some reason (illness, resignation or other demands).

'What-if' exercises

You will need to test your estimate of where risks might originate and the scale of their possible impact against the plan. The effect of these risk factors on the plan, the costs and hoped-for benefits need to be assessed.

Do not just consider each potential problem in isolation, as many will have knock-on effects that will create additional difficulties. Consider problems in combination so that their interactions are understood.

Indeed in the worst cases it may be that the project will not be viable, so it will be necessary to repeat the cost-benefit analysis for some of the worst-case scenarios.

Contingency plan

Once you have understood the possible impact of risks on the plan, it will be possible and desirable to create contingency plans to respond to problems. Being prepared will help you mitigate the effects of problems. It will also prevent you taking decisions that leave you vulnerable to risks.

For example, a pension trust company was in the process of implementing a new pension administration system to replace the bureau service provided by a third party. It had to give at least three months' notice to the provider of the service. Three months before the planned switch over, there seemed to be no reason not to give that notice. However, we declined to do so because the slightest hiccup could have left the trust without any administrative capability. It was considered better to leave the decision to give notice until the new system was actually operational. It meant that additional costs were incurred, but it removed a major risk. In practice, it turned out to be a wise move as there was a minor problem and the new system was two months late. Actually, that was not bad on a completely new, specially written system working to an incredibly tight timetable of eight months.

MANAGING THE PROJECT

Communication

Communication is the key to success. Do not hold back on problems, but share them with all interested parties. That way there are more heads working on the problems and expectations are realistic.

Users

Keep users informed of the progress of the project, and involve them as much as possible in the decision-making and evaluation of the developing solution. As elements are completed, test user satisfaction both subjectively and objectively to ensure that you are on line to achieve the expected benefits.

Listen to users' concerns and ideas. Understand them and use them constructively. Do not let the project's scope creep. Manage user expectations and fulfil them as far as possible without extending the scope of the work. The secret is to explain: explain everything.

Suppliers

Work together closely, share your concerns and listen to theirs. If you can mitigate their problems, then do so and they will respond in kind. If there are problems, be honest about them, do not let them grow out of proportion. The sooner a problem is exposed, the sooner it is resolved and with less effort than if it is ignored.

Keep talking even if things get difficult. There is almost always an answer if both parties want to find it.

Management

Keep other managers informed about progress of the project and solicit ideas. Senior management particularly should be kept fully informed, even if it is informally. They will worry about what is happening if they do not hear anything and assume the worst.

Make the whole process a two-way communication, and most problems will resolve themselves naturally.

Milestones or management decision points

At key stages of the implementation, there should be a formal decision taken to continue or abandon the project. These key stages will usually fall where there is a major tranche of the investment to be made. The business strategy, project and its objectives should be reviewed: are they still valid and in line? If they are and the benefits justify the costs, then a decision by senior management should be made to continue the project. Without such a positive reaffirmation of the organisation's commitment, then the project should not continue. No project should continue by default.

If there is further investment to be made, whether originally approved or because of changed needs or costs, then a management decision is needed. The decision should not be made by the project group, but by senior management. It should be made on the same basis as any other investment decision – are the returns justified by the costs?

Few information-related projects are sufficiently strict about proper cost-benefit justification.

ANALYSIS OF QUESTIONNAIRE 8

1. **No.** Project management is essentially basic good management practice – which is largely common sense. There are tricks and tools, but it should be possible for any experienced and competent manager to learn those skills quickly. Managers' roles are increasingly becoming project-based, as more and more of their work is about enabling change. Their work consists essentially of an on-going series of projects, rather than day-to-day management of a relatively static process or organisation structure.

2. **No.** Project management is about managing risk. The objectives should remain largely unaltered, but there will be a need to revise the plan to work around difficulties of one sort or another. Indeed, the plan should be constructed in such a way that it includes contingency plans for foreseen possible problems. But there will also be unforeseen problems, and the planned response will have to be accommodated in a revised plan. But the business objectives should stay the same – otherwise it is not the same project!

3. **Yes.** Supplier and client wish to see a successful completion of the project, but they do so for different reasons. They will also have different difficulties and conflicts. Clients must ensure that their needs are fully considered if the going gets difficult, and so each requires their own spokesperson with an intimate knowledge of the project. In other words, their own project managers with appropriate authority to speak and act in the clients' best interests.

4. **No.** This is one of the biggest causes of cost and time overruns on information systems projects. And it causes reduced performance on the main requirements. Stick to what was planned and leave 'improvements' to a separate, properly planned exercise that goes through all the viability checks that were used on the original work. Users' expectations have to be managed, otherwise there will be a lot of effort expended on 'gloss' that adds nothing to the original objectives.

5. **All but the last (carry on as best we can).** If an information management project is not delivering the benefits, or is costing more than planned, then it may no longer be viable. In any case the project should stop until it has been reviewed to determine what it will really cost, and what benefits it will achieve. Those costs and benefits should then be weighed in exactly the same way as the original investment appraisal (but using the latest rates and targets). If it does not achieve

the required return on investment, then the project should be killed. The costs already incurred will have to be put down to experience. Obviously other strategic options may need to be considered, such as reverting to the previous system or leaving the new system as it is and making do with that – they should be considered as part of the investment and option appraisal.

ACTION PLAN

1. Appoint, with appropriate terms of reference:
   a the steering group
   b the project manager.

2. Using top-down approach identify the tasks, their inter-dependency and the resource requirements.

3. Consider the risk areas, assess the possible nature and scale of their impact and undertake a sensitivity, a 'what-if?', analysis of the plan.

4. Prepare contingency plans for working around the possible difficulties, and identify how you will pick up the problem at an early stage should it arise.

FURTHER READING

P. Baguley, *Managing Successful Projects*, Pitman, 1995
An invaluable introduction to project management. It takes the reader through the background of project management and then leads them through the issues and techniques of successful project management.

It is non-specific, so the advice is applicable to most projects. The whole thrust of the book is practical and aimed at the manager who needs to adopt a project management approach for perhaps the first time. But it will be equally useful to the manager who wishes to brush up their project management skills.

J.R. Turner et al (ed) *Project Manager as Change Agent*, McGraw-Hill, 1996
Project management is about much more than the technical skills required to bring in a project to time and budget. It requires the manager to be highly adaptable. This book will show why and help the reader to understand the wider challenges of project management.

A project manager has to understand change, the impact on the organisation and most importantly on people. If a project manager, indeed any manager, fails to win support of the rest of the staff then the result is likely to be less than effective.

This is a comprehensive review that bears study but it is not the lightest of reads. But it should be accessible to all those who have what it takes to be effective project managers.

E. Obeng, *The Project Leader's Secret Handbook/All Change*, FT/Pitman Publishing, 1994

This is somewhat unusual as it is two books bound back to back. *All Change* is described as a novel and a step-by-step guide. *The Project Leader's Secret Handbook* is more conventional except that it addresses change management form the individual's point of view rather than that of the organisational needs.

They are readable books and if you like to explore unusual approaches then these titles will give you a different slant. It will not be to everyone's taste but there is some good advice in them for anyone who is prepared to overlook the unusual presentation. Once into *The Project Leader's Secret Handbook* then it will seem more conventional than first impressions suggest.

SUMMARY

All but the most minor projects should have demonstrable, high-level commitment, otherwise resources will not be available when needed and other staff may not give their part in it due priority.

Projects should have a steering group with clear terms of reference established for the duration of the project only. Their role is not so much to manage the project on a day-to-day basis, but to provide a forum to resolve conflicts and to decide issues relating to the project strategy – it should therefore be representative of the eventual system's user group. The steering group will have the delegated authority to take all reasonable decisions relating to the project without reference to a higher body.

The client should have their own project manager to protect their interests, and to ensure that the client delivers its promises to the suppliers. The project manager will be part of the steering group and report progress and other issues to it. However, the project manager will have the day-to-day management responsibility and authority for the project. It is not wise to rely on the suppliers' project manager, as such a person's loyalty has properly to be to their employer. There will be situations where client and customer priorities will be in conflict, and these will have to be resolved by mutual agreement by the two project managers.

There should be a formal project plan which should be monitored using the Vital Signs Monitoring approach detailed in Chapter 2.

At key points, there should be a formal review as to whether benefits are being achieved and costs are on budget or better. Finally, from that a formal minuted decision should be taken as to whether the project should continue. If a project is not achieving its objectives, it should be reassessed for viability and if it is no longer viable, it should be killed. Previous expenditure is not a reason for keeping an uneconomic project alive in the hope that it might be all right in the end.

Project plans should have contingency plans in place. Project management is as much about managing risk as budget or timetable. Therefore, a detailed assessment of possible risks should be made and their impact on the project considered. If the effect is significant, then measures should be devised to highlight the problem at an early stage and plans should be made for coping with difficulties should they arise.

Communication with everyone, suppliers, users, management and others is the key to success. Make sure everybody understands the importance of the work, their role in it and how it is progressing. And do not be averse to asking for, or accepting advice and support from others. Manage the risk.

WHEN THINGS GET TRICKY

Many projects run into some problems, and the test of a real project manager is how he or she copes with that challenge.

INTRODUCTION

Many projects run into some problems, and the test of a real project manager is how he or she copes with that challenge. As already pointed out in the previous chapter, project control is as much about managing risk as achieving deadlines come what may. It is when problems arise, and they will, that making decisions to minimise the consequences becomes particularly important.

If there has been good communication, then there should be goodwill all round and the desire by all parties to find a workable solution. It is through the difficult time that effective communication becomes even more important.

The objectives of this chapter are to help the reader understand:

1 how to identify possible difficulties as they arise;

2 what to do to mitigate such problems;

3 how to handle complaints from the supplier;

4 appropriate ways of making complaints to the supplier;

5 the importance of keeping good communication, even when all parties are under pressure.

QUESTIONNAIRE 9

Handling difficulties

1 Should the first question, if there are problems be: 'Who is at fault?'
   a Yes
   b No

2 What is the biggest single cause of difficulties?
   a Communication
   b Technical issues
   c Suppliers
   d Users
   e The IT department
   f The project manager
   g Senior management

3 Is the customer always right?
   a Yes
   b No

4 When a complaint needs to be made it should be made:
   a Firmly but quietly?
   b Publicly and angrily?

CATCHING PROBLEMS EARLY

The key to successful project management, indeed any management, is to catch deviations from plan at the earliest opportunity. This requires a proactive approach to management. A manager should not rely on what has happened, but watch what is happening and what is likely to happen in the near or longer-term future.

Remember the Cycle of Control from Chapter 2? We have a project plan with meaningful achievement measures. The aim is to perform the plan as well as possible, and at the same time monitor what is being achieved against the planned performance measures. Note this is continuous during performance of the plan, it is not retrospective in a weekly or monthly project review. This means corrective action can be taken immediately a deviation from plan becomes manifest. Too often the problem will be left until the progress meeting, and only be seen and acted upon after it has grown for a week or more.

In Chapter 2 we set out the Vital Signs Monitoring approach and reiterated its use for project management. Properly used it will reduce the likelihood of delayed response to problems.

> *The key to successful project management . . . is to catch deviations from plan at the earliest opportunity.*

Early response means that corrective active can be smaller and more effective – it does not need so much backtracking to restore the situation.

Once control has been taken, then the results of the action need to be fed back into the plan to identify any knock-on effects of the problem on the overall plan. This may change some of the achievement measures and therefore the monitoring of subsequent performance. Hence the closed loop of the control cycle.

BLAME

The aim is to keep the project moving forward as efficiently and effectively as possible. Trying to lay the blame will not do that – it is a totally counter-productive exercise. More important is to understand the problem and its consequences and then to decide, as a team, on a course of action to resolve it.

So any investigation should focus on:

- How did the problem arise?
- What is the nature of the problem?
- What are its implications for the rest of the project?
- What action can be taken to correct or mitigate the problem?
- What are the consequences of those actions?
- Can the project continue? Is it still viable; in other words, will it still deliver benefits that are justified by the cost?

The last point is important: too many information management projects exceed budget and do not achieve the expected benefits. In many cases, if the final result was known, the project would never have been started. During many such projects, the members of a project team know that the benefits will not justify the costs, but let their heart overrule their head and let the project continue. Every time additional expenditure is considered, the whole economic justification of the project should be reviewed. If it no longer makes sense, then the project should be aborted and the financial losses minimised. Unfortunately it rarely happens early enough, if at all.

COMMUNICATION

I have had to sort many troubled projects, and in pretty well all cases, communication had broken down. Not just between customer and supplier, but even between members of the project team. Everybody had got to the stage where they did not want to talk about it, and they did not want to face up to the implications and their role in the problem. This kind of situation tends to be exacerbated by a 'blame' culture in many organisations; who can we make scapegoat, even though it was a team responsibility?

HANDLING COMPLAINTS

Often suppliers get unhappy with their customers not delivering their part of the bargain. This is the principal cause of complaints from suppliers. In any information system implementation, there will be elements that only the client organisation can deliver. This may be anything from creating space for the equipment to providing details of code structures or datasamples or even live data. If the customer is late, that wastes time and resources for suppliers. Suppliers do not want

197

projects to overrun, because they will want to be using the same staff on a project for someone else. Your delay is going to cause difficulties for another customer.

So if the supplier project manager raises such issues, do not take offence. Simply sort it out – get the project moving and juggle resources if necessary, so that it does not happen again. Make sure that there is a clear action plan with dates and who is responsible, so that there are no excuses for not knowing what is required and when. These should have been in the plan or the results of meetings between the supplier project manager, client project manager and any affected staff.

It is up to the project team and the senior manager representative to make it clear to all staff that the project is a priority and that agreed targets should be met. Too often the lack of such clear leadership means that users put the project tasks to the bottom of their in-tray. This is especially likely if they feel peripheral to a project seen as belonging to another group.

If there are complaints from suppliers or from elsewhere within the organisation, then they should be addressed quickly and effectively without recrimination or seeking to lay blame. That achieves nothing, the problem will still be there and getting worse, and you will have generated resentment which will reduce future co-operation. The quicker and more fully it is resolved, the less it will cost in the long run.

Too often we try to get away with as little as possible when resolving complaints and then have to come back and do more, often several times. A complaint must be resolved immediately and completely first time.

MAKING COMPLAINTS

In any substantial project, there will be the need to raise issues with the supplier and some may be formal complaints. However a formal complaint is often a sign of a failure of communication. Such problems are usually allowed to happen by inaction by both parties – communication is a two-way process.

A complaint must be resolved immediately and completely first time.

Most difficulties when they reach the stage of a formal complaint have been well-known for some time. They should therefore have been raised informally or at least through different channels much earlier. A formal complaint should not hit a supplier out of the blue – it should have been discussed before. A complaint therefore should become formal only if the supplier has not taken action agreed at the earlier stage. The customer has to be absolutely honest about their role and be sure that they are not even part of the problem.

A formal complaint should be in writing and should set out the facts, the action agreed, the action taken and the results. It should not threaten or use emotive language, but should simply be a statement of the problem possibly with a recommended course of action. It must not get personal. Most suppliers will respond positively to such an approach and address the problem. Then get on with other aspects of the project whilst they sort it out. Do not start recriminations or bad-mouthing the suppliers, as you still have to work together on the rest of the project. The success of the project should still be your over-riding concern.

If the supplier does not sort out the problem, then one has to wonder whether the procurement was undertaken properly, or whether you as the customer are, in part at least, responsible for the problem. If references were taken up, you would know how well the suppliers' previous projects had been managed and how problems had been resolved. If they had worked well then, but are not now – what is different? Possibly the staff the supplier is using – but the main difference is the customer!

Complaints on either side are usually caused by lack of clarity as to what is required and expected on both sides. It is a failure of specification, project planning and communication.

So, communication is the key to avoiding complaints. It is also the key to resolving difficulties – when a problem arises, all the team should be talking more, not less. This requires an open and trusting environment which happens only if there is a commitment to achieving success rather than avoiding failure and blame.

ANALYSIS OF QUESTIONNAIRE 9

1 No. The aim should be to find out what the difficulty is and to find out how it might be resolved. Placing blame will not contribute to solving the problems which must be the over-riding priority. If you have a blame-laying culture, people waste a lot of time covering their backs, rather than admitting the problem and seeking to sort it out. This means that the problem will be more serious when it is discovered, and energy will be wasted on non-productive activities such as individuals proving they were not at fault.

2. **Communication.** Or rather more correctly, lack of effective communication. Problems rarely appear out of the blue, and if there is effective communication, people will spot them earlier and be better placed to resolve them. Most problems can be avoided if people air their potential difficulties and seek a mutually acceptable solution.

3. **No.** Many difficulties are caused by customers who fail to live up to their commitment to the project's implementation. Most of the problems below cost suppliers time and money – if they happen more than very occasionally, suppliers would have good justification for charging for the lost time. Customers' failings can take many forms, but some of the most common are:

   a. Not undertaking their part of work to agreed timetable or quality
   b. Being unprepared for meetings
   c. Cancelling meetings at short notice
   d. Claiming more competence than is justified
   e. Moving the goalposts during the implementation.

4. **Firmly but quietly.** A firm but cool response is far more effective than one made in the heat of anger. You can negotiate far more effectively if you are cool and in control of your emotions. And a complaint is a negotiation which needs communication channels to remain open. The priority must always be to find a satisfactory solution to the problem, and thereby keep the project on course.

SUMMARY

The aim must always be to catch problems early. That is why we have spent so much time on using the Vital Signs Monitoring approach and identifying possible problems and how they can be detected.

Seeking to find out who or what to blame is counter-productive. Laying blame makes people less inclined to co-operate with identifying the scope and nature of the problem. They are too busy protecting their position.

By all interested parties keeping in close touch throughout the project, many problems will be picked up early. Sharing knowledge and keeping users, suppliers, customers and others well-informed means that each can spot issues that may cause them problems. By discussing those issues with the other parties, a satisfactory solution can usually be found.

Occasionally, problems will get to the stage where a formal complaint is required. It is at this point that properly documented projects score, as they have an audit trail so that the problem can be properly understood. Any formal complaint should be supported by a written statement of the problem and a request for appropriate action. Again the emphasis should be seeking to find a solution. Complaints may need to be made firmly, even forcefully, but it should be in a cool and considered way with no anger (as far as possible).

If complaints are made against you and your team, then the response should be positive and cool. The aim is always to find the common ground and from there build a solution to the problem that led to the complaint. Quick and complete action is much better (and considerably cheaper in the long run) than a series of half-hearted responses.

REVIEWING THE IMPLEMENTATION

Systems should . . . be reviewed at regular intervals during live operation to ensure that they are still meeting needs.

INTRODUCTION

Before the project is signed off and final payments made to suppliers, it must be evaluated against the original objectives. It is at this stage that the stress on measurable success factors becomes clear. Without them, how can we determine that we have achieved what we set out to do?

There are a variety of techniques which can be used, some of which will mirror those used during the investigation and specification stages. The results will contribute to the planning of the next phase of the information management strategy and provide a guide for those undertaking subsequent projects.

But it is not just on completion of the implementation that the systems should be reviewed. They should be reviewed three to six months after going live to identify adjustments that are required. All systems will have snags that can only be identified by using systems for real. It should be planned to resolve these snags as soon as possible – they should not be fundamental changes.

Systems should then be reviewed at regular intervals during live operation to ensure that they are still meeting needs. The requirement will also have to be re-examined to ensure that they are still valid and that the system is responding to those developing requirements. Over time, a system will degrade as the needs that it was intended to meet change. Even with modification, this will happen, until at some time a fundamental respecification and implementation of new systems will be needed. The whole planning and selection process will then need to start over again.

The objectives of this chapter are to:

1. stress the need to measure the success of the work against its original objectives;

2. enable subsequent project teams to learn from the successes and failures of previous projects;

3. suggest techniques for reviewing a system against its objectives.

QUESTIONNAIRE 10

Techniques for evaluation

1 When should information systems be reviewed?
   a On completion
   b After a few months' live operation
   c At regular intervals, say annually
   d Never

2 What should be reviewed?
   a Functionality
   b Suitability for current needs
   c Business benefits
   d Procurement processes

3 Is it possible to evaluate improvement in performance of an information system against measurable measures?
   a Yes
   b No

4 Who should undertake the reviews?
   a The original project team, because of their detailed knowledge
   b The team about to start on a new project
   c An independent team

WHEN TO REVIEW

Reviews should take place regularly but there are some key points at which a system appraisal should be required.

Post-implementation audit

The most important time to undertake a system review is shortly after the information management system has gone into live operational use, but before the final payments are made to suppliers. The completion of a review, and any remedial work should have been built into the specification and contract as part of the final acceptance testing.

It may be that it should be carried out in two stages. First, an initial, mainly functional, review for acceptance immediately after it is live. This should then be followed, a few months later, by a user evaluation against broader headings to gauge how successfully the projected benefits have been achieved. This should also throw up opportunities for further refinement in the light of operation experience. This will then provide a starting point for the on-going development process that all systems require.

Planning cycles

All organisations have some form of regular planning cycles. These will have both a strategic and an operational element. Information management strategy and operational needs should form an integral part of such plans. We have already explored how inseparable information management is from other aspects of business operations – it is a key part of any manager's function.

There will therefore be a need to conduct information-related reviews as part of the planning process. Probably the key planning time is the annual business planning exercise. It is my view that this is in fact an on-going process throughout the year (see the Cycle of Control in Chapter 2, pages 33–35). All that should be required at the year end is a snapshot of current thinking for the formal annual document which is usually called the 'business plan'. However I do accept that the preparation of such a document is also an opportunity to take stock in a more considered way, and to ensure that the vision for the coming year is revitalised.

As part of this business planning round, all the information management support should be reviewed as to its suitability for the new vision. This should be supported by a detailed review of older systems (say, more than three years old) and of the implications of any substantial changes to the organisation's strategy or business processes.

When there are major upheavals in the way the organisation operates, then a fuller review of information management needs in all related areas should be made. These may be the result of merger, major repositioning of the business, new products or services, new organisational structure or business process re-engineering or other cultural changes. Such profound business changes will require development of the business process which will impact on the information support required. In any case, new plans will require a proper appraisal of the costs and benefits which should not ignore matters such as information systems support, training and other functions. The full impact should be considered.

On-going review

Even without such changes, all information systems should be formally reviewed on a regular basis. There will be a steady divergence of the business requirements and the capability of existing systems to meet those needs. This will happen even with proper maintenance and development of the systems.

This decay will take place at different rates for different functions. Finance systems may be fairly stable, at least as far as the main accounting function is concerned, but information-dependent services to customers may change rapidly as the pace of change in the market continues to accelerate.

Full user-satisfaction testing should be carried out for each major system at least every two years. Annually would often be preferable. This testing should consider how well the system is meeting users' current needs and should also seek to establish how well it will meet needs over the next review period. Users will have some feel for the impending changes in the way they operate and what support they will need. They can allow the information manager to establish whether a full reappraisal and a possible replacement of the system are likely to be required or whether the system can continue to be developed to meet changing needs.

Managers should be encouraged to undertake such reviews themselves – the whole purpose of this book is to help equip managers to deal with their own information management needs. Indeed they should be encouraged to work with colleagues in other areas when doing so. That way there will be a more corporate view of information management requirements. It should not be left to IT managers to initiate this – it is a business management requirement that is being reviewed, not a technical issue.

IT managers should however take responsibility for reviewing the technological support for information management with user managers. They should not lead the users' satisfaction reviews with their technical agenda.

Some user-evaluation techniques have already been considered and further ideas are suggested in subsequent sections.

Note that so far we have only suggested assessing the users' view of the suitability of the existing systems, not the detailed requirements. There should be an on-going process of reviewing needs, improving processes and practices and questioning the need for information. This will highlight changing needs, and these should be incorporated as part of an on-going development programme. All staff, and especially managers, have a responsibility for making continuous improvement, either incrementally or through more fundamental changes of working practice. These changes should be reflected in the support infrastructure, including information needs.

Problems

Day-to-day problems and complaints should also be used in a positive way. They should be logged and analysed, as they will highlight several important issues:

- Training needs: are people having problems because they do not understand what they are doing?
- Have there been changes in working practice that mean the system no longer fits properly?
- Has the system never worked properly?
- Is there inadequate development effort to keep the system suitable for changing needs?
- Is replacement simply overdue?

If the problem is that the system is failing to meet the business needs, then a more detailed investigation of requirements is required. In the first instance, there should be an evaluation of users' satisfaction as a benchmark for the replacement or redeveloped system. Then it will be necessary to make a broad-brush assessment of the needs, and then to

> **Day-to-day problems and complaints should . . . be used in a positive way.**

consider alternative strategies from doing nothing, through more development of existing systems to complete replacement. These should consider the costs and benefits.

That initial study will determine the possible ways forward, and you can then start again at Chapter 3.

WHAT SHOULD BE REVIEWED?

Processes

After each project, it will be necessary to examine what lessons can be learnt for future work. Some are essentially one-off exercises that should be undertaken when the system has settled down into live operation.

Planning and needs definition

First, one should consider whether the initial planning and identification of the needs were effective. The main questions that need to be answered are:

- Were there many changes to the requirements after specification and during implementation?
- Were the changes due to oversight or real changes to users' needs? Had the underlying business requirements changed?
- Were the changes during implementation due to limitations in the chosen solution? Could these have been avoided? How important were these changes?
- Was there an improvement in the users' satisfaction with their support systems? Re-evaluate their satisfaction as for the baseline and compare results.

Procurement

Again, there are some key questions about the procurement process:

- Were the proposals received relevant to the specification and other documents? If not, then perhaps more work is required on choosing the shortlist of invited bidders in future.
- Were there are a lot of queries during the bidding stage? Again, it may be that the specification was incomplete or unsuitable bidders had been chosen.

- Is there a good record of why the selection decisions were made and are they clearly justified? Would you be happy for them to be audited? If not, then evaluation and record keeping will need to be improved.
- Was there full compliance with existing procurement rules, the tender rules and other rules defined by the project team? Do the failures compromise auditability and good corporate governance? If the answer is 'yes', then there needs to be a general tightening up of both attitudes and enforcement. This should be applied from the top of the organisation.
- Did the rules work? If not, and they did not cause auditability problems, are changes needed to streamline or simplify the rules?

Implementation

A similar exercise needs to be carried out for the implementation phase. Some of the questions that need to be asked include:

- Was the project delivered to time and budget? Why not and how could it have been improved?
- Did the project achieve the planned measurable benefits. If not, why not? And what could have been done to ensure that it did? Were the planned benefits unrealistic or irrelevant, and how could that have been avoided?
- Does the implemented solution meet user expectations? Were their expectations realistic, and could they have been better managed?
- Have the costs achieved the return that was planned for them? If the costs have increased from plan, have the achieved benefits, and therefore the actual return, increased in proportion?
- Do the benefits achieved justify the costs on the basis used to give the work the go-ahead? If not, why was the underperformance not identified earlier? Should the project have been abandoned to mitigate the costs?

Note that all the questions are about finding out what was achieved and what problems were encountered, then why these things, good and bad, happened, and how that understanding can be used to improve future projects. There is no searching after who did it – we should not be seeking to apportion blame, but to find ways of doing things better in future. It is a learning exercise.

Business process

There should be an on-going review of business processes. They should be challenged frequently and fundamentally. It is only through such

questioning that working practices, product and service quality or
corporate and individual performance can be improved.

Information systems

Both shortly after implementation and from time to time in the
future, it is necessary to review the information systems. This will be
much as for needs assessment in earlier chapters. But some of the
questions that need to be asked include:

Performance

- Does it work as fast or as accurately as required? This may change
  with time. What seems fast initially may seem slow with growing
  experience and expectations.
- Is it available when needed?
- Can you use it from wherever you need to?

User satisfaction

- Is it convenient to use?
- Are users happy with it?
- Is user satisfaction growing or declining?
- Do users actually use it?
- Are they happy with the form of presentation of the information?

Requirements

- Does it meet users' requirements?
- Does it support your routine work effectively and as completely as
  possible?
- What else is needed?
- What is no longer used or required?
- Who else could use the same information or even the same system?
- Could the information be used to add value to our products or
  services? Would it be useful to customers and appropriate to let
  them have it?
- What do users do with the system and what do they do outside it?
  Should the latter be incorporated?
- How do users use the information? To whom do they pass it?
- Have the requirements moved on?

TECHNIQUES FOR REVIEWING INFORMATION SYSTEMS

Introduction

This section can only give an overview of some of the techniques that can be used to evaluate information systems. Further reading is suggested to allow interested managers to extend their knowledge further. Many of the techniques may be familiar from other purposes. All should aim to eliminate 'fuzzy' results, and as far as possible measure what is happening.

Questionnaires

Popular though questionnaires are, they are of very limited value. If you wish to prove a judgement already made, they are ideal: it is possible to design the questions to lead to almost any result!

Questionnaires seem to be falling out of favour for the reasons as described. More direct approaches are made to the people whose view is being sought.

Focus groups

Focus groups are just such an approach, and within limitations, are useful for getting at some of the less obvious issues that would never be picked up from more structured interviews or questionnaires.

A focus group consists of a small group of people with similar interests facilitated by an independent chairman. The aim is to understand the underlying issues of a particular area of interest. The chairman's role is not to take part in the discussion, but to ask open questions to keep the discussion moving forward. Once the discussion is under way, it will usually feed upon itself so that the matters that are of concern to the participants will be exposed. These are their primary concerns, rather than responses to the project teams perception of those concerns. They may be very different.

Performance measures

I have a friend, an engineer and a senior manager, who argues that you can find measures for any role or function within an organisation. I have never been able to floor him! For any job or function we have discussed, he has been able to come up with useful ways of getting quantitative results that are relevant. Sometimes it requires lateral thinking, but there always seem to be sensible answers.

Analysis and evaluation

I suggest a similar approach to analysis and evaluation of user satisfaction as that adopted in Appendix E for the evaluation of proposals. Break down the broad areas of interest, usability, flexibility, suitability, etc. into more detailed questions. These could be given weights as in the evaluation model but it may be more appropriate to treat them as having equal weights (still adding up to 1 or 100 per cent within a heading) as the main concern is to detect changes in perception rather than absolute values.

If you decide to use weights then they must be agreed by all parties otherwise it will be believed that you are using the weights to support your own objectives.

Then use standard survey techniques although I would be very careful of questionnaires unless they are validated by the use of focus groups or other interactive methods. Questionnaires tend to give the results they were designed to give – so they are very useful for proving some predefined view! There is much to be said for using disinterested parties to conduct the survey as users are likely to be more open with people that have no axe to grind.

Use the same evaluation model (as far as possible) for each re-evaluation of the same systems then the results will be directly comparable. By comparing the results from two analyses separated in time it will be possible to identify changing perceptions and developing difficulties. These will highlight the issues that need to be addressed. As described in Chapter 2, Vital Signs Monitoring, it will be necessary to look behind the bare figures and understand what is really driving the changes. It may be that the business processes have changed and the systems are no longer as suitable as they once were. It may be that users are becoming more sophisticated and their expectations have risen, or it may be that users have got into bad habits, or new staff have started and there is a need for some re-training.

Bear in mind that the analysis will be of systems, user sections, IT and other support departments and even individuals and so should be treated in the same sensitive way that personal appraisals are handled. It may be desirable sometimes for external help to be used to give comfort that only aggregate results are being passed back and that individuals who may be the source of critical comment are not identified.

Using the findings

The findings should be formally documented, so that they can be used for personal development of all staff involved in this work. Indeed, there is an interesting information and knowledge management exercise that should be done. It would need to suggest ways that project review findings can be captured, stored and used effectively by as many people as possible – in some organisations that do such reviews, the findings once considered by the team (and sometimes senior management) just get filed, never to see the light of day again.

> *The findings should be formally documented, so that they can be used for personal development of all staff involved in this work.*

Instead, all new project teams should be required to examine documentation for the last few projects, especially the final review findings, and develop new policies and approaches based on that experience. They should also review all the documentation for the systems that they may be replacing – from initial study through to post-implementation findings, any subsequent modification specifications and on-going system reviews. That will give them a feel for why the system is as it is, and they can then concentrate on deciding what will be required to meet future needs.

WHO SHOULD UNDERTAKE REVIEWS?

Ideally, it should not be the implementation project team that undertakes the post-implementation review, as they will have been too close to it, for too long. They have expended too much emotional energy on the project and it would be unreasonable to expect them to be objective. From my experience, they will be tired in any case and just want to see the back of it.

I would suggest using the team who are about to start on the specification, procurement and implementation of the next new project. They will then be able to apply any lessons that they learn on their new project. This will increase the value of the review process and ensure that knowledge is disseminated as widely and quickly as possible. Many of the techniques they use in the review they will also need to apply in determining the needs and potential benefits from their new system. Again a valuable practice.

For on-going reviews, a group should be created from outside the user team for the systems to be reviewed. This will give an objective view, but of course the review team should be supported by users and by any specialist support needed from the IT or other departments. It should be reviewed in the light of the overall strategic vision for the organisation.

ANALYSIS OF QUESTIONNAIRE 10

1. **All of them except 'Never'.** Information projects should be reviewed at all points: after implementation before making final payments to the supplier to ensure that they have met their performance measures; after a period of live operation, when it has settled down to test whether the expected benefits have been achieved. On-going reviews are needed to identify development needs and suitability for changing business requirements.

2. **All of them.** Everything should be open to review. Each project has valuable experience which should be used to support the planning and execution of subsequent projects (not just information systems).

3. **Yes.** There are techniques for evaluating soft issues such as user satisfaction in a reasonable objective way. And as discussed elsewhere, there are ways of measuring benefits in a way that can be tested.

4. **The team about to start on a new project and/or an independent team.** After a considerable period of time and a lot of personal involvement, it would be difficult for the implementation team to undertake a truly objective review of their project. Their thinking would inevitably be coloured by how difficult aspects of the project had been. Using a team independent of the original project is ideal and it presents a useful opportunity as a learning exercise for teams about to start a similar project.

The main tasks that should be undertaken after reading this chapter include:

1. **Undertaking a post-implementation review for the most recent information-based project.**

2. **Reviewing existing systems from the point of view of:**
   - **user-satisfaction (as a bare minimum)**
   - **real information needs**
   - **business process and their consequent information requirements.**

3. **Examining the procurement process for the last project.**

SUMMARY

Reviews of all systems are needed at regular intervals during their lives. A key point is after the new information system goes into live operation. This is a full functional review of the system against the project objectives, costs and success measures set out at the start.

After a few months of live operation, the project should be assessed for the benefits it has achieved. These should be compared with the anticipated benefits used in the initial investment appraisal. At this point, a re-evaluation of the investment decision would be wise, to see how well the actual results compare with the forecast. The information gained from such an exercise will enable better investment decisions in the future.

These should be repeated from time to time during the life of the system. At the same time, the then current needs should be compared to the system. Eventually it will become clear that the system no longer meets needs and that replacement is due.

Reviews of systems should be undertaken by a group other than that responsible for its implementation. This will give greater objectivity, as the project team will have invested considerable emotional energy in the implementation. Such reviews are a useful learning exercise for the team that are about to start the next project.

SUMMARY

Information enables better decisions to be made and makes opportunities possible.

We have explored information and its management in the broad context of general management. The aim has been to encourage the general manager to appreciate that they both need to use and manage information but that they do not have to be frightened of it.

All through this book it has been stressed that information and its close relations, data and knowledge, are not technological or even technical issues. They are the very basis of good management and decision-making. Information enables better decisions to be made and makes opportunities possible.

We argued that few organisations have moved far in their use of information in the 30 years or so that they have been using computers. The problem has been that managers have not treated data as the valuable (and expensive) resource and raw material that it is. We set out Seven Levels of Information Management (see pages 16–22).

1 Compliance
2 Operational management support
3 Added customer value
4 Competitive advantage
5 Strategic insight
6 Transformation
7 The Knowledge Net

Most organisations are still only thinking in terms of Levels 1 and 2 with some attempting Levels 3 and 4. Few have gone beyond that. So there is still a huge opportunity for anybody who has the imagination and will to grasp it.

Vital Signs Monitoring was detailed as a means of eliminating the bureaucracy around Level 2, and by doing so, moving the business towards Levels 3 and 4 by giving managers more time to look for new ways of improving their service, whilst at the same time improving current performance.

By understanding the nature of competitive strategy and their own business, it is hoped that managers will begin to see that information and the consequent understanding does provide opportunities. Furthermore, information in itself has potential as a product, if it is treated appropriately. An increasing share of commerce is in intangible products and related services – most are information-based or rely on information and related technology.

When planning information systems, investment appraisal is rarely carried out effectively. The full costs are rarely considered and the benefits are overstated and usually unmeasurable – 'better', 'faster' or 'improved' – they are rarely stated in terms of increased activity, profit or other measures. We detailed the wide range of costs that will be incurred and showed how even not-for-profit organisations can produce financial measures that are appropriate to their purpose.

. . . information in itself has potential as a product, if it is treated appropriately.

Specifications need to be kept simple and focused on the essential business needs. They should be written in plain language and the requirement should be expressed in business terms, concentrating on *what* has to be achieved. They should not be technical documents. We largely leave the *how* to the supplier, whether internal or external.

We set out a step-by-step process for purchasing solutions that meet the business's needs. The whole process is auditable, and ensures proper corporate governance. To keep control the purchaser needs to buy a solution, not be sold a system. That means: buying starts with knowing what is wanted, untainted by what is on offer.

Similarly, managing the implementation of an information management project should not be beyond the scope of any competent general manager. Indeed, the Vitals Signs Monitoring approach discussed earlier comes back into play here as the key project management tool. When things get tricky, then communication needs to be stepped up to find a mutually acceptable solution. But by using the suggested management approach that highlights problems at an early stage, the effect of problems will be mitigated. If the project manager has followed the advice, then he or she will have plans to cope with most eventualities, and more importantly will be able to avoid disasters.

As this book is about information management, then much stress is placed on extracting the information contained in the experiences of the project. Review techniques are suggested that will allow the next project team to learn and avoid the mistakes (inevitable) made by their predecessors. So the organisation will get onto a virtuous circle by using information. It will be building up organisational memory, so that there needs to be less trail-blazing in the future. Just think where we would be if the early explorers had not made maps and kept journals!

Finally, we consider generic opportunities for making the most of information now and in the future. A comprehensive model of how the development of leading edge information systems could be developed in a manageable and affordable way is embodied in a Corporate Information System. This can be started today to deliver benefits almost immediately – yet it will expand as the capability of the organisation develops. It will give anyone who follows it through a head start on most rivals.

Forecasting will always be wrong, but we can be fairly sure that the world will get smaller through communications. And our access to knowledge and information will grow enormously. The challenge for you is to make the most of it and where appropriate lead it. Go for it!

CORPORATE INFORMATION SYSTEMS (CIS)

How can one meet the new information needs, and at the same time protect the majority of users of the systems from major change?

INTRODUCTION

Most established organisations who have had computer systems for many years have what are described as 'legacy systems'. These are usually old systems that have been meeting the operational needs of the organisation for a long time. They have probably not been upgraded for many years beyond the minimum needed to keep them operational. They are often basically sound, if hardly state of the art. In many cases, they are written in obsolete programming languages by people who have long since left the organisation, and are frequently poorly documented – this makes any change an adventure into the unknown!

The problem is that replacing them is a major task likely to affect everyone in the organisation. Yet their time is running out as the organisation goes through fundamental change in its processes to meet rapidly changing customer and market expectations. The systems' inability to meet the new needs may be demonstrated by a proliferation of small local systems probably developed on personal computers by individuals for their own or departmental use.

How can one meet the new information needs, and at the same time protect the majority of users of the systems from major change? How can one ensure that everyone is working from the same information? The Corporate Information System (CIS) model proposed in the next few pages is one possible framework. It is an approach that can be implemented in many different ways to meet the specific needs of most organisations. Importantly, it is an approach that is technically neutral – it does not assume or require a particular technological approach.

THE CHALLENGE

It has been said that there are no problems, just challenges. Coping with legacy systems and inadequate information is just such a challenge. It need not be a problem as there are obvious solutions – they may be expensive, disruptive and unwelcome, but they are solutions and many organisations have bitten on that bullet. The following ideas are hopefully more manageable and therefore more welcome.

The nature of the challenge is two-fold with related consequences (see Figure 12.1).

Users want and need information from across all functions of the organisation to support their planning and decision-making. Unfortunately, as far as most of the systems operated by the organisation are concerned, they have little or no direct access. This makes them reliant on others who are busy with their own problems. In theory, users may have access to the necessary systems but due to lack of expertise, they remain unused.

For the most part, staff can only be casual users of most of the systems: 'computer literate' as far as their own systems are concerned, but 'casual users' of the other facilities because they only have need of occasional use of them. As casual users, they do not have the familiarity that is needed to exploit fully the capabilities of those other systems, all of which will almost certainly be different in the way they operate and how information is extracted.

Even if such users were to be trained in all those functional systems, they would not be able to make effective use of them, simply because they do not use them often enough for the training to stick. It is unreasonable to expect a non-specialist user, however well-trained, to do so.

Furthermore, the data in these operational systems are structured to meet the purposes of functional departments rather than general analytical and management requirements. For the general user, the data may be incomplete or in an inappropriate form; for example, without key data items to provide linkage to data in other systems. Difficulties such as these will also inhibit the general user from trying to use the systems to support their own planning and decision-making.

Training is expensive and as already implied, it is only effective if it is supported by regular exploitation of the skills it creates. Organisations

223

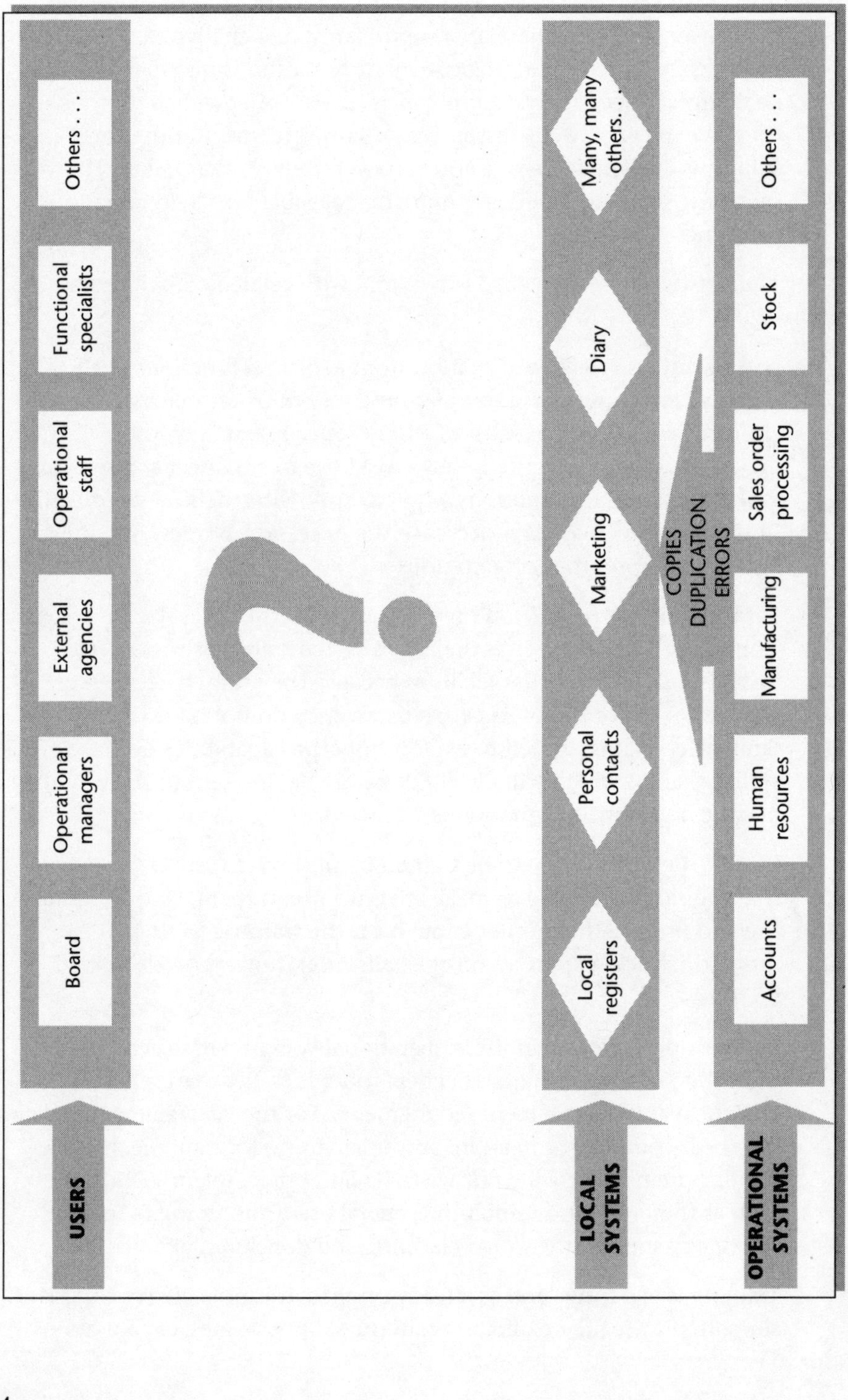

Fig 12.1 THE CHALLENGE

USERS

Board | Operational managers | External agencies | Operational staff | Functional specialists | Others . . .

LOCAL SYSTEMS

Local registers | Personal contacts | Marketing | Diary | Many, many others . . .

COPIES
DUPLICATION
ERRORS

OPERATIONAL SYSTEMS

Accounts | Human resources | Manufacturing | Sales order processing | Stock | Others . . .

need to maximise the return on their training investment, which therefore needs to be put to the widest possible use. Training someone to use systems that they see, at best, for only a few hours each month is pretty much a complete waste of money. However if that training can be exploited more widely and more often over a longer term, then the benefits will far outweigh the cost. We will return to this a little later.

It must be remembered that there are also potential and actual users of information locked in the operational systems. Such users may be 'customers' of an internal department which has to prepare returns (often manually) to outside bodies, such as corporate headquarters, government, regulatory bodies and the like. These outside bodies, too, have a need for accurate and timely data. Often the direct benefits to the supplying organisation is limited at best, but the cost of not providing the required information to suitable quality can be enormous. For example NHS Trusts, as part of their contracts with purchasers, are required to give detailed activity data to support the purchasing body's planning of future health service needs. In the last few years, purchasers have been building in a 'fine' for inaccurate or late information as they consider, rightly, that the return is part of the contract. Typically, the cost to a Trust of not meeting that requirement is around two per cent of contract value – a not insignificant sum on a contract often worth more than £1 million per year. So the needs of external users should not be overlooked.

The second main strand to the challenge are the systems already in use and which have usually been achieved over many years. Traditionally, they were implemented to meet the needs of each function with little consideration of the requirements of other departments. This separation has led to a raft of difficulties that only now are we attempting to address. Indeed it is a similar driver to that leading the move towards business process re-engineering and its successors. It is all part of a growing interest in adopting a more holistic approach to management and organisational development.

The traditional separation of functions has often led to a series of problems:

- Inconsistent and duplicated data. Because each system is separate, there are copies of some of the same data in more than one system which is often transferred manually with inevitable errors. This leads inevitably to inconsistency as each system maintains its data to different rules and from different sources. Rarely is the data reconciled between systems. All this leads to a considerable amount of duplicated effort in that data maintenance and in explaining difference in reports from each system. Often this has to be done every month.

- Incompatible systems. This prevents users learning a common means of accessing the data or for the systems to share or exchange data to avoid the problem of duplicated and inconsistent data.
- Separate development means that the systems diverge over time as different requirements are pursued. After a few years, any possibility of linking or merging systems has been lost as a result of the different agendas that have been followed. Again this compounds the earlier problems and makes them more deeply entrenched.
- No cross-functional analysis is possible, except by heavy manual processing or by creating new systems to make use of data extracted from other systems. Often that data is entered into the new systems manually from paper-based reports, leading to further problems of inaccuracy, data inconsistency and duplicated (or worse) work.

Many, probably most, organisations have implemented office automation at some level, usually including all or some of:

- word-processing;
- spreadsheets;
- data management tools;
- personal organisers;
- mail;
- graphics;
- and other facilities.

Most of these functions are purchased from a single supplier, and in any case they usually run on a desktop computer under some graphical user interface such as *Windows* or the Macintosh operating system. As a result, all the applications work in broadly the same way. This consistency of approach means that much of the training is applicable to all the software in use and any new facilities that are added. The cost of the training is therefore spread across many purposes, and the benefits are increased as a result.

However putting this increased power in the hands of users can exacerbate some of the problems already discussed. With these new facilities, users can generate their own small systems to fill the gaps left by the operational systems. Hence more problems associated with local systems such as their lack of security, data quality and integrity, duplication of effort and of course data inconsistency. Yet of course these systems represent the real needs of the user groups who create them.

Therefore, there is a need to get to grips with the management information problem. The old approach of trying to integrate the operational systems has had very limited success. Such success as there has been has tended to be at the expense of the operational function of the systems. There simply have to be too many compromises and the scale of the resulting all-encompassing 'solutions' has been too large. It was not uncommon, is still not uncommon, for organisations adopting this approach to buy all their major systems from a single supplier to try and avoid incompatibility issues – it is often less than successful. But it does mean that decisions about relative priorities have to be made across the whole organisation, rather than producing solutions that are optimal for each function. This happens not just at system selection but all through the system life cycle including implementation, maintenance and support. A huge amount of management and other time is wasted resolving conflicting requirements and yet the result satisfies nobody!

Many integration projects have been started, but few have ever been fully completed. Because of the interdependency of the various functions there are too many parties to any a decision which slows the whole process. Compound this with the common requirement of needing to implement these systems in large chunks, and the planning and implementation timescale are so long that, even if they are implemented, the organisation has moved on. The result is that the 'solution' is implemented too late and does not meet the organisation's new needs.

Furthermore, in recent years many organisations have been making rapid and fundamental changes to the way they work, so that information management projects do not have the luxury of two- and three-year (or longer) planning and implementation cycles. They need to be designed and implemented quickly – often in six months or less.

As a further consequence of these organisational changes, many of the traditional systems that have served the business well for many years also need to be replaced. If casual users are dependent on these systems to any extent, then their replacement is going to lead to major disruption throughout the organisation. They will need an input into the redesigned functional systems, re-training to make use of them and a period of adjustment whilst they learn to use the new facilities. That is all over and above the needs of the staff who will operate the system on a routine basis. The casual user will face that disruption as each legacy system is replaced. Once all the systems are updated, then the cycle will probably need to start again to meet yet newer needs!

Therefore there is a need to isolate general users from changes to operational systems outside their area of responsibility, but yet allow them access to the knowledge contained within them. At the same time, we want to be able to give functional departments the best tools for their work without compromising it by trying to meet the needs of the occasional user. So we need to add a layer to the model we proposed in Figure 12.1.

CORPORATE INFORMATION SYSTEM

That layer is the Corporate Information System (CIS) – see Figure 12.2. It is the whole organisation's window into its corporate data resource. The aim is that it should eventually provide a much more consistent way of accessing all corporate knowledge. But it does not rely on low-level integration of major data processing systems.

The integration takes places as it is needed at an appropriate level. Many of the recent management approaches such as business process re-engineering stress the need to keep the key processes lean and unencumbered by not trying to handle the exceptional conditions. And the supporting systems should be the same – optimise and automate as much of the routine parts of the process as possible to allow people, with appropriate systems support, concentrate on applying their knowledge and experience to the exceptions in a completely separate way.

Banks have done this for their routine personal and small business lending. Most personal loans are straightforward, a few key facts and some form of credit-scoring system will work as well as an experienced bank manager. So a relatively inexperienced telesales operator can give the borrower an answer immediately over the telephone. The customer gets a speedy response, and the bank has both reduced its costs and improved the quality of its service to probably 80 per cent or more of its customers. This, in theory, allows the manager to spend more time with customers with more complex requirements which make better use of his or her time and experience.

> ... the Corporate Information System ... is the whole organisation's window into its corporate data resource.

There are a couple of dangers. One is that too much experience is shed, with the result that managers still do not have time to spend with customers. The other is that the more complex customer requirement is

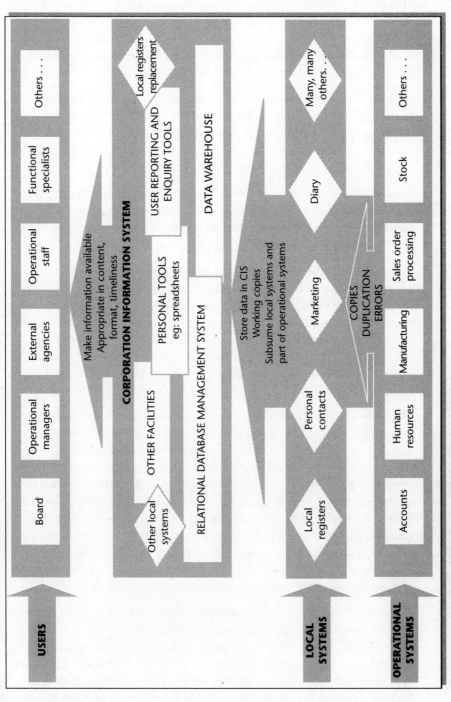

Fig 12.2 A SOLUTION: CORPORATE INFORMATION SYSTEM

not recognised and is still put through the routine processing to the annoyance and dissatisfaction of the customer. That of course is why there is the need for the processes and systems to be well-understood and properly designed in the first place. They then must be operated by staff with the training and judgement to recognise when a customer needs to be handled separately in a more suitable way.

So what is a Corporate Information System? First and foremost it is not a single solution. Different organisations will implement it in different ways for different groups within the business. Nor is it a standard set of tools, even though many systems vendors may try to sell such packages for building CIS systems.

Most importantly, it is a user-focused approach, and recognises that different users have different needs and capabilities. The system should be built to meet those highly specific needs whilst retaining an underlying general base of data, information and knowledge to support.

Corporate Information Systems are going to be complex when fully operational, but that complexity must be hidden from the end-user. Managing the intricacy will require skilled and competent information managers working with information technologists who appreciate the needs of the business, its staff, customers and suppliers. The groups responsible for the Corporate Information System between them will need to be able to talk in business terms with the board, and yet retain technical credibility with suppliers and their own technical staff.

The general manager who is going to succeed in the future will need to take on and fully understand that information management role. As this is being written, articles are appearing highlighting the development of a parallel market that is information-based and applies to all industries. Managers are going to have to cope with such changes if their career is going to continue. They will have to become information managers. It is happening now. I have been discussing this approach with clients for several years, and am currently working with a couple who are building their information management and technology strategy around a Corporate Information System approach and are actively implementing it.

The Corporate Information System will also need senior managers and directors with a vision and an understanding of how they can use information and its consequent knowledge to further the competitive advantage of the business. The board has to take that lead and ensure that those delivering the Corporate Information Systems have the skills and resources to do it properly. High-level support must be visible and real – if only lip-service is paid to this venture, then it will seriously undermine its likelihood of success. And by doing so, it will severely compromise the future of the organisation as it moves into a more competitive information-based environment in the new century. Information will be the life-blood of the 21st century organisation.

Some characteristics of a Corporate Information System

Having said that it is not a single set of tools or that it can be implemented in many different ways, we cannot be specific about what constitutes a Corporate Information System. However we can explore some of the key characteristics that any such approach should exhibit.

It becomes essential

It should rapidly become essential to the operation of the organisation, and users will come to wonder how they managed without it. Indeed the aim should be to use it as a means of presenting most, if not all, of the information that staff need to support their day-to-day function. Whilst it will not eliminate paper, it should considerably reduce the need for paper for internal purposes.

Vital Signs Monitoring will be a key role for the Corporate Information System at all levels within the organisation. It will greatly simplify the routine performance-monitoring functions of most managers by automating the work and only highlighting problem areas.

By automating much of the monitoring role of managers, it will free them to act positively to improve the performance of their part of the organisation. By allowing the monitoring to become automatic and continuous rather than, say, monthly, it will reduce the need for fire-fighting. Problems should be spotted earlier and should therefore be easier to correct. This will managers to become opportunity seekers rather than problem solvers.

Used at both strategic and operational level, it will free managers to plan for the future rather than trying to sort out last month's mistakes. All managers should then have more time to improve the organisation's performance.

Common pool of data and knowledge

Everyone will be using the same data, therefore the argument should be about interpretation or what it means. Too often without a corporate information system, managers waste a lot of time reconciling their different data and agreeing which data to use as the basis for discussion.

There will be no need for individuals to collate data for others; so much of the administrative function will be reduced or disappear. Users of data provided by others will have immediate access to the source data themselves. It will be presented in the way they need it and they will have access to the underlying detail, should they need to dig deeper.

This will mean there are no hiding places! Everyone will be able to see what everyone else is achieving. This will give truly open management and that buzzword of the 1980s 'empowerment'. Everyone will be able to monitor themselves and peer pressure and natural rivalry will drive performance improvements.

Variety of tools

Corporate Information Systems will use all the tools that are commonplace and already familiar, including: word-processing spreadsheets, query and reporting tools, and others less familiar such as data warehouse systems. They will also use new emerging technology, such as Intranets, as it becomes established and appropriate even, in time, it will probably be integrated with systems in the external organisations.

It exploits what is already in place

Perhaps the over-riding strength of a Corporate Information System is that it uses data, information and knowledge that is already available but under-utilised. Just by using what is already available, considerable benefits can be achieved. Few organisations use their existing knowledge, in all its forms, for benefits which are a fraction of what it is possible.

A corporate system uses the existing legacy systems far more effectively by providing links between them that may not be possible directly.

It isolates users from the complexity

Users should not see the underlying complexity of the technology or, as far as possible, the data complexity. The view of the data should be structured appropriately for each user group – or indeed individual. Users' routine needs for reports, enquiries or extracts should be predefined with templates in the software to provide a basis for other, more ad-hoc requirements.

It delivers user needs to their place of work

A fully implemented Corporate Information System means that users do not have to go looking for data: it is available directly to them at their desktop. Furthermore, it can be added directly into their desktop application such as a spreadsheet or a report being word-processed. Indeed that desktop could be mobile or at their home.

Information is also available when they need it; there need be no artificial reporting schedules. However for some data to be meaningful, it may be necessary to provide a copy of the live data at a known cut-off point. For instance, financial figures would be misleading if they included all the sales revenue but not all the expenses. In such cases, a copy at a known state would be more useful, but there would be an onus on the providing department to meet the timetable. For finance, for example, to ensure their data was timely, a weekly cut-off might be needed, rather than a monthly one, as is more usual at present.

It is comprehensive

A Corporate Information System should be as comprehensive as possible for all users. It should maximise the amount of data that is generally available otherwise it is prejudging and limiting the questions that a user may want to ask. If it is to be genuinely valuable and support opportunity seeking then it should not constrain users' analysis.

It is wider-ranging than existing 'packaged' solutions

The proposed approach is much more than an Executive Information System, a data warehouse or a glorified reporting tool, although it will use some or all of them and much more. It should be a fundamental part of the organisation's systems.

It will not be available as a 'packaged' solution from a single supplier. It is too specific to each organisation for that. It will need to be built for each organisation by creative and committed senior managers, information managers, IT managers and supportive users. It depends on a corporate commitment to make it work and a culture that will allow it to do so. Without that it will be an expensive white elephant.

It is flexible

Change is accelerating, and the Corporate Information System will have to be able to respond. As a consequence, users will need to be able create or amend much of their own use of the system. Hence, there will be a need for tools that allow users to write their own queries and to search the knowledge in their own ways. The questions that will be asked cannot, in the main, be predicted. Users will therefore drive the system.

This will put a premium on training, as staff will not only need competence with the Corporate Information System, but will need to be information-literate. They will need to understand the role of information, its analysis, manipulation and maintenance. Many of the semi-skilled clerical roles will vanish, – no jobs will be created, but workers will require higher levels skills. Corporate Information Systems will breed a new generation of knowledge workers who can manipulate information and create value from it: value for both their organisation and for customers.

It is home-grown

Because of the pace of change and the need for the system to adapt, it will probably have to be largely managed in-house. It will no longer be acceptable to wait weeks for outside contractors to get round to making the changes that users will demand. This system will become more critical to the organisation than any that have gone before.

It will mean that the back-up resources to manage the complexity and to take the system forward must be put in place. If they are not, the Corporate Information System will die a premature death before the full benefits are realised.

It is manageable

If it is to be maintained in-house and by users, it needs to be manageable. So tools have to be fairly straightforward in themselves, even if their inter-operation is complex. Many of the tools are already available and many readers will already be using them, knowingly or not.

One of the main beauties of a Corporate Information System is that it can be implemented incrementally by reference to the availability of capability, costs, resources and competence. It is probably desirable that it should be developed in that way, because everyone within the organisation will be breaking new ground. Everyone concerned needs to move forward together. And there will be occasions when the project will take a wrong turn, make what turns out to be an inappropriate choice, and need to backtrack and start that phase again. It will be a learning process and all learning involves making mistakes. By working incrementally, it is possible to limit the damage caused by any mistakes.

Appropriate use of technology

It is not technology-driven. Instead it needs to use well-proven tools, as there is enough complexity already in the issues around data reconciliation and user needs.

It avoids state of the art technology – instead it allows people to adapt to existing technology.

Corporate Information Systems do not and probably should not replace the key functional systems. Such systems are highly specific and effective ways of meeting major administrative and operational requirements. The Corporate Information System is more about providing access to knowledge for management decision making and planning. That is not to say that over time some of the operational systems may not be subsumed into the Corporate Information System when suitable technology and the organisation's capability come together to make it both practical and possible. But it must be for sound business reasons and not driven by technology.

A Corporate Information System as detailed here is therefore more a philosophy and strategy than a particular type of implementation. It is more about providing a consistent way of accessing data, information and knowledge resources of an organisation in a complete 'business-focused' way.

Implementation

A Corporate Information System looks complex, and in many ways it is. It will also cost a lot of money to implement fully: but then so did the current inadequate systems. But the cost and complexity of a Corporate Information System can be handled in an incremental way that proves the benefits as the system is implemented. By adopting an approach based on a series of small, even tiny, projects, everyone can learn and apply the experience to the next step. For that and other reasons, I would suggest that a 'Big Bang' approach is definitely not necessary and is, in my view, undesirable.

A Corporate Information System as detailed here is therefore more a philosophy and strategy than a particular type of implementation.

Implementation of a Corporate Information System should be at a pace that the company can afford and that allows its staff to assimilate the changes. Once all users have access to some elements of the system, then it may well be possible to accelerate the programme. By that stage, users will have grasped the concepts and be familiar with the tools being used to build the information system. The development of the system will then be more about widening the base of information to which users have access, rather than introducing new facilities.

Of course, over time, new facilities will be added, but by then, users will themselves have become more sophisticated and therefore more able to quickly learn to use new tools. From experience, once they have accepted the idea of such a system, they will quickly start demanding new capabilities. At that stage it becomes more a matter of managing their expectations, so that what is promised is practical and can be delivered!

An outline implementation programme

If much of this section looks familiar, then this book has, at least in part, succeeded. Most of these ideas have been explained and developed in earlier chapters, so that, you, the reader, can determine your own information management requirements, and work with your IT department or suppliers to implement systems to meet them.

Broadly, the steps to implement a Corporate Information System are:

1. Define business objectives.

2. Identify user needs – in outline.

3. Determine data available from current systems.

4. Reconcile existing data or identify what is needed to achieve consistent data within existing systems. This will be one of the biggest tasks, and most important as the existing systems will supply the data to be used by the Corporate Information System. It will need to be reliable when it is published more widely.

5. Identify additional data collection needs to allow linkage between different data sources. In the future, there will be a need for new data, but at this stage the emphasis should be on making the existing data work together.

6. Build an initial CIS strategy and agree objectives for initial implementation.

7. Choose basic CIS tools – make sure they are mainstream products from substantial suppliers. You will need support and long-term commitment to the chosen products by the supplier.

These will be added to over time, so only choose what is needed initially.

8. Select a user champion for the first project (Phase 1). You need a keen user who sees the benefits and will make it happen in their realm. You need early success to encourage the more reluctant users.

9. Build a project team to undertake Phase 1. Include your champion, the IT manager and a supportive member of the board.

10. Identify detailed needs for Phase 1.

11. Plan project.

12. Implement Phase 1.

13. Review Phase 1.

14. Start Phase 1 on-going development.

15. Revise CIS strategy.

16. Repeat from **8** for subsequent phases indefinitely! You will need to go back to **1** from time to time to ensure that everything fits with corporate strategy.

OTHER IDEAS AND OPPORTUNITIES

The overall purpose of this chapter is to throw in some ideas to seed the creative process.

INTRODUCTION

Most people are familiar with the needs of operational systems which are often largely Level 1 data processing systems, and do not provide much in the way of information management capabilities. These are the easiest to analyse and specify at that basic level of information management sophistication. However, as an organisation becomes more developed in its use of information management, it becomes more difficult to see or create new opportunities for improved competitive advantage. Innovation is never easy and the nearer to the leading edge one is, the more difficult it becomes – no-one else has been there before and left footprints that suggest the way forward!

The overall purpose of this chapter is to throw in some ideas to seed the creative process. Some are from experience and have been used with varying degrees of success. Many are no more than half-formed, and others may be not much more than ideal thoughts. It is not intended that you should take any of them and simply implement them on my say-so. You need to make sure that the ideas and concepts fit with your business strategy. These are merely a starting point: you have much work to do to develop them into complete workable solutions for your organisation. Many ideas will die or be killed along that road, but a few strong ones will survive and eventually flourish. Make the most of them. Good luck.

COMMUNICATIONS

Many of the fastest-changing aspects of business are associated with the hypergrowth of communications and the much vaunted Information Superhighway. This is an area with many opportunities and many pitfalls!

Expertise

Help

I use on-line access to specialist expertise to solve information technology problems for myself and for clients. I have all but eliminated the use of telephone help desks.

For example: for several pieces of software that I use; I can work at a client's during the day and keep a note of any problems I may have. As much of the software originated in the US, I can post my queries onto an on-line forum when I get back to my own office in the evening – lunchtime in the US. I could do it with a portable from the client's premises if I wished. Because of the time difference, I can often download an answer to my problem the following morning before I go out to see clients. Not only have I received advice this way, but even new copies of corrected software.

Support

Not particularly novel, but I also provide support remotely. From my office computer on my desk, I can dial in to a client's computers to investigate a problem directly on their machine. I can even watch them run through the problem and make sure that they are not making mistakes. I can fix it there and then on their machine or copy the necessary elements to mine to work on it locally. It all depends where the best tools are. I can then copy the fixed system back to the client when I have finished.

But it is starting to go much further. More and more equipment is 'smart' and uses computer technology. For example, a vending machine can diagnose that it has a problem, and dial up the support centre or advise that it needs restocking, or feed sales or usage figures to a central point for overnight analysis. We talked about timely management information – some retail point of sales systems advise headquarters what they have sold as they make the sale or at intervals during the day. This can be analysed, and the pricing at the store changed during the same day to ensure that perishable stocks are cleared or to increase margins at busy times of the day when particular goods are less price sensitive. This is already happening.

CASE STUDY

McLaren Cars

When McLaren built its $1,000,000 F1 super car, it recognised that its owners would be spread all over the world and would not be able to visit a local dealer. So it provided a capability for an owner's car to be connected by telephone to the McLaren headquarters in the UK. This allows McLaren technicians to diagnose many problems remotely, and in some cases resolve them.

Indeed, one German banker and sometime racing driver uses his McLaren F1 to commute between home and his offices – often doing 120 miles in around an hour! As there are twisty bits on his route, that of course means on the straight sections he has to do considerably more than 120 mph. After an overnight link to McLaren, the technicians suggested he had a problem with the car's on-board computer and had he noticed any problems? When the banker pressed the technicians, they said they thought there was a fault, as it was frequently recording speeds of around 200 mph or more! Most owners of such cars do not use them very often, and certainly do not regularly drive them as hard as this German owner. He, of course, had to put the McLaren people in the picture – good public relations for McLaren and the car.

Research

Much is made of the empowerment possibilities of new organisational structures and training. But little is said about the loneliness of the role of chief executives, and the many factors that limit their ability to be properly empowered.

Chief executives sit at the top of a pyramid of a people-based information process system. As information flows up, it is processed and filtered by middle managers and others, so that much of the knowledge it once contained is lost. Yet the chief executive has to take major strategic and business decisions on the basis of such flawed information.

Even worse, much of the information that the chief executive sends down to staff is filtered, softened or otherwise distorted before it reaches everybody. Even where it is received directly by staff, through the annual report or whatever, it is interpreted, explained, or added to by others in the organisation.

Now with the new communication capabilities, some information-aware chief executives (or their children!) are using the on-line world to undertake their research and to establish new contacts. It allows them to talk directly to customers, suppliers, and even staff, without someone else interpreting what is being asked or said.

Cut out the middleman

These chief executives have cut out the person in the middle. And so can the organisation. As with the Ford example (see page 93), it is possible using new information management approaches to eliminate traditionally essential middlemen. These may be internal or external.

In the Ford example, they eliminated internal functions such as Goods Inward and Purchase Ledger sections. Others have eliminated external sales agents by dealing directly using the new technology. Many have eliminated wholesalers because of the efficiency of new means of handling transactions – they can now talk directly to their customer for the benefit of both.

Remember the party game 'Chinese Whispers'? Someone whispers a message to the person next to them, and by the time it has been passed around the room, the original message is unrecognisable. Eliminating the middleman eliminates the opportunity for confusion.

Electronic mail

Many businesses have implemented electronic mail internally, and more and more are also using it for external communication. It is not a new technology, but its application is relatively recent, and it is growing rapidly. Recent industrial action in the UK postal service saw a leap in the use of E-mail. It will be interesting to see whether the Royal Mail recovers that lost business.

Substitution

E-mail is steadily replacing much of my use of traditional postal services, some of my telephone traffic and even faxes. Whilst not new, it is still not as widely used as it should be.

With the improvements that are taking place, external correspondence is becoming as fast and easy as internal communications. Why wait two days for a letter to reach a client, when an electronic mail message can be there in two minutes?

It should be understood that, unlike facsimile transmission, electronic mail allows the sending of documents or other data files whose formats can then be used by the receiver. I frequently use this method to exchange reports with colleagues.

Collaboration

So electronic mail allows collaboration in a much more immediate way than was readily possible a few years ago. And it is improving rapidly all the time.

This collaboration is not just within an organisation, or even within a country, but it can be worldwide. I have developed business ideas with people in the US that I have never met using electronic mail. This may possibly lead to new business opportunities that I would never have identified in any other way.

Internal communication

But internal communication is moving beyond electronic mail. The Internet and the World Wide Web is now moving in-house to provide similar facilities across the organisation. This is a logical extension as the World Wide Web was originally developed to allow academic and other research workers to share their papers and ideas. So using the same tools to make information available within an organisation across an Intranet and internal website is an obvious way forward.

Marketing

These new communication technologies allow direct access to the market place. First with research and access to market intelligence through on-line databases and the expertise of the participants on the Internet and more proprietary on-line services. Ask the question (in the right place), and there will always be someone who can contribute information that you would never otherwise have found. What is more, they will point you to yet more.

The technologies also give direct access to customers and potential business. They do not replace the face-to-face contact, but provide another communication route.

Most service providers do not allow or at least discourage direct mail across their services. But there are other opportunities for doing business in new ways. For example, it is now possible to distribute software (legally) and accept payment using these communication channels.

These are obvious advantages over the old technologies: there may
well be others pertinent to your business if you have the vision to see
them. *If it is already being done, you are too late to gain competitive
advantage: you need to come up with something new.*

NEW PRODUCTS AND SERVICES

Information management and the new technologies will create new
businesses opportunities. Some of these will themselves be
information-based products or services. Others will use information
and its management as added value for the customer.

Yet others will be innovative products derived from knowledge gained
by new information and understanding of that information. All will
depend on information management skills of all managers.

GLOBALISATION

Improved communications, combined with new emerging economies
around the world, are leading to a globalisation of business. And not
just for-profit business, many traditionally national or local not-for-
profit organisations are seeing the impact. American health care
providers competing for long-term care of the elderly, international
charities competing for funds and to provide services and even
religious bodies are operating across national
boundaries. All are, in some part, made possible
by new information systems.

*Information management
and the new techniques will
create new businesses
opportunities.*

The financial markets now never close. Once
governments and large enterprises had time to
consider what was happening on one stock
exchange or foreign exchange before another
opened: now they have to operate in a world where there is now
always a major market operating. It does not give them time while it is
all happening to reflect on information that has to be processed,
understood and used to take decisions. There is now much
programmed trading in shares for just such reasons – the human mind
cannot process the information quickly enough.

Similarly, business is now a 24-hour operation. Few businesses can
ignore it. And those that cannot will soon not be able to do so.

STRATEGIC ALLIANCES

With this new globalisation and rapid communication, the need for and possibility of new alliances is enhanced. And they will be transnational and across industries.

The sharing of information will be the basis for these alliances. Those organisations that will be attractive strategic partners will have good information and management systems. Information will be the currency, and as it has no exchange rate, it will be the universal currency.

DATA ANALYSIS

Much is currently being made of data warehousing and data mining. But these are not the complete solution. They will be tools to facilitate the understanding of the data available to an organisation. But they will not be the whole answer.

The answer lies with the knowledge and expertise of an organisation's people. The knowledge has to be applied to the data to create the structures for a data warehouse. To some extent, computerised data analysis techniques might assist with the interpretation of large volumes of data.

But technology will not be creative. It will show new patterns in data and from that people will make judgements on what it means. People will have to interpret and translate those patterns into business opportunities. Technology is a long way from writing your business strategy or designing the products that your customers really want.

You, a competent information manager, will be required for the foreseeable future. You may be supported by more and more technology, but it will be your knowledge, experience and creativity, and that of your colleagues and new partners, that allows your business, and therefore you, to succeed.

FURTHER READING

M J Cronin, *The Internet Strategy Handbook*, Harvard Business School Press, 1996
This is a useful insight into the possibilities of using the Internet for business purposes as it is based around case studies of organisations that have made effective use of such technology. It covers many of the issues

around using the Internet such as implementation advice and the strategic thinking behind others' developments.

The book stresses the strategic thinking that is required for successful use of the Internet. And that is vitally important with such fast-changing technology.

However, bear in mind that as this is an area which is developing very rapidly so you should not try to lift the examples straight across to your own business. Instead use them to develop your own ideas based on the state of the technology at the time you are planning your strategy. Use it as a source book rather than as a how-to guide.

D J Silk, *Harnessing Technology to Manage Your International Business*, McGraw-Hill, 1995

If your business already operates across national boundaries, or is planning to do so, then this book will provide good background reading to provide understanding of the technology-related issues in all aspects of business. It is not especially deep but will be appropriate to the general manager wanting to get a feel for the strategic challenges.

As with the previous title in a book such as this the examples will quickly date even though the underlying arguments remain sound. It is therefore imperative that it is used as groundwork for your own thinking which should be based on current state of the art and your own strategic vision.

14

INTO THE FUTURE

What will be the reality in a few years' time?

INTRODUCTION

In the 1970s, everyone in computing and business circles was talking about the 'paper-less office', and as we all know, the reality could not be further from the truth. In the 1990s, computers and photocopiers are producing more printed output than ever before. So where are we going?

As this book is being written, the hype over the so-called Information Superhighway runs on unabated. Magazines dedicated to it abound, business and computer magazines are full of it, and even the general Press has regular features about it. Families put their Christmas greetings on a Web page. What will be the reality in a few years' time?

I set out here a personal view based on 20 years' experience of computing and information technology coupled with a cynical enthusiasm for innovation and new technology. No doubt much of what I suggest in this chapter will come back to haunt me, but I can live with that. This is my exercise in crystal-ball gazing – you must make your own judgement based on your experience and expectations. You will probably be as right as anyone else!

THE NEXT FEW YEARS

The possibilities I suggest, and they are only suggestions, I believe will take place in the next ten years. I do not think that attempting to look any further forward is realistic. One only has to look at predictions for life in the 1980s made in the '60s, and they look unimaginative in parts and wildly optimistic in others. I will leave the possibility of cities in the sky or on the moon to science fiction writers and professional futurologists. Instead, I am going consider information, information technology and their impact on business and the consequent effect on working life.

Jerry Pournelle has frequently argued in *Byte* magazine that each user or task should have its own processor. I agree. He argues that there is no point in sharing processing power, as it is now so inexpensive. This suggests that the wide distribution of processing power, will continue. Indeed, it is difficult to conceive that users would give up the resource that sits on their desk or indeed their lap.

But as we have discussed throughout this book, the power of information is in sharing it and applying users' experience to turn it into a shared corporate knowledge base. This suggests centralisation, and indeed there will be a need for some degree of corporate control of what will be an important, possibly the key, resource of an organisation – its knowledge.

However this may not be in the form of traditional centralised databases, although there may be a central 'master' copy but instead knowledge pools containing routine information data requirements maintained by each workgroup or even user. Changes will be echoed over fast data links to their colleagues and the central 'master'. Using the same links they will be able to access, as required, knowledge held elsewhere within the organisation. This may not just be at the headquarters, but might be on a colleague's local machine whilst it is sitting in the boot of his car!

The information available to each user will not be confined to data held within the organisation, but may include external information providers, much as Dun and Bradstreet and others do now. Beyond that there will also be access to other people on a successor to the Internet (it may still be called 'Internet' – it has proved highly adaptable!) and the World Wide Web.

As far as the user is concerned, such data will appear as part of the larger corporate pool. They will see no difference between local, central, remote or external sources. Indeed E-mail, as we know it, will probably disappear and be replaced by a more direct inter-working (with mutual agreement) that places messages, documents, etc., directly into a correspondent's data store. We will be using a technique similar to OLE, which currently links applications on a single system, but instead linking documents, spreadsheets or records on different systems and for different users.

This will facilitate collaboration. For example: I will be able to write a chapter of a book, and a co-writer living on the other side of the world will be able read what I have written, add comments or revise it even perhaps as I write. I will not have to E-mail a copy and wait for a revised copy back. It will be much more timely.

The new technology will therefore much more readily allow knowledge-based workers to live and work wherever they like, as communications will be inexpensive and fast, so that the current limitations will disappear. However I do not believe it will replace personal contact with colleagues and customers – we need that contact to build properly trusting relationships. We will need to meet less often, and such meetings are likely to have a greater social element to enhance and strengthen those personal relationships. Routine business will use video conferencing with full motion video with much higher resolution, larger displays and better sound quality – remember we will have far more bandwidth than we do now.

I was going to suggest that we would have bandwidth to spare: but that flies in the face of centuries of development: whenever we build a new bypass or motorway, increase the power of a computer, increase storage capacity, we soon want more. Increased capacity creates the demand to use it and more! We have always been able to push technology and infrastructure beyond its limits – there is no reason to suppose that information technology will be any different.

We will be using speech or handwriting recognition, but with caveats. Increasingly, people will be comfortable with using keyboards, and it has to be realised that a competent four-finger typist can produce text as fast as most people can write legibly. So the need for handwriting recognition may not be as important as many believe, but it will develop for those applications where it would be useful – such as for portable devices.

Recognition of continuous speech is imminent, and may well make handwriting recognition largely unnecessary. However it might be a problem in an office environment with 50 people all trying to talk to their computers – it could get very noisy. And what happens when you spill a cup of coffee into your lap, and inadvertently swear – will it appear in the document? The answer might be a lip-reading computer – they already exist in prototype form!

BUSINESS

Within a decade or so, commerce based on knowledge will be bigger than that based on tangible products. As we have already explored, most industries have a growing information element – few products are sold without some information or knowledge support. Indeed the information technology industry is a classic example, but the same is true of financial services, agro-chemicals or industrial machine tools. They are having to provide information to guide the user on the safety, use and application of their products.

We will increasingly treat information as we treat any raw material. We will recognise its value, process it and sell the resulting end-product. But unlike physical products, it will be possible to sell it more than once and in different forms.

We may use the 'Information Superhighway' as a means of publishing information-based products. But we will have to solve problems about security and copyright before there will be business to be done in that way. However there will probably be a merging of television with information technology, as we have already seen with IT and telephony. They will all merge into related technology. The push from entertainment for the controls to provide protection for electronic publishing will be the main agent of change in that area.

> Within a decade or so, commerce based on knowledge will be bigger than that based on tangible products.

We will use high-speed electronic communications to work more closely with customers, suppliers, business partners and indeed remotely based staff. Indeed, it is my personal view that modern communications make national boundaries and indeed nation states redundant – but that is a topic beyond the scope of this book.

We will see an increasing use of fully automated business transactions which will probably mean a continuing and rapid decline in the number of traditional white-collar semi-skilled and even skilled jobs. The clerical function may all but disappear in medium- and large-sized organisations.

Customer-initiated transactions are increasingly common in banking with on-line banking services. These allow the customer to move money between accounts, pay suppliers, etc., without any clerical involvement by the bank. There is no reason more business should not be done in this way.

Why should a customer not use his or her own computer to access the suppliers' computer, check the stock to find out whether the item required is available, place and even pay for the order (using a credit card) without anyone at the suppliers being involved?

This could even go further. Many large suppliers have had automated warehouses for many years, so if these were linked to the sales system there would be no reason why the goods should not automatically be extracted from the warehouse, labelled and delivered to the loading bay for shipment. The only human involvement might be loading and driving the delivery vehicle.

Much manufacturing is automated, some completely so. There has been a steady growth of 'lights-out' manufacturing, where a fully automated manufacturing plant does not need lighting or heating because there are no people present. Without people, less space may be required, as the only access needed is for maintenance.

Many manufacturers also use largely automated production scheduling to decide what to make and when. These systems can determine what materials and components are required and when. It is only a small step to allow such systems to order the goods or let the supplier know what is required as in the Ford case study (see page 93).

But if we link the whole thing together, we end up with the following process.

1 A person or a production scheduling computer identifies the need for some goods from a supplier.

2 The computer or the person using a computer contacts the computer at the supplier.

3 Stock availability or manufacturing lead time can be checked.

4 An order is placed.

5 The customer's scheduling computer is updated to reflect the anticipated delivery. The manufacturing is scheduled.

6 The supplier sends the picking instructions to its automated warehouse, which sends the ordered goods to the shipper for delivery.

7 Or the suppliers send the instruction to its 'lights-out' manufacturing facility for the goods to be produced at the right time for delivery to the customer. But, of course, the scheduling computer places its orders for necessary parts and materials as in 1 for delivery at the appropriate time.

8 The goods are delivered to the customer, and payment is taken or sent from the customer's credit card or even a bank account and paid into the suppliers' account – all electronically.

The result does not need human intervention for the majority of transactions. As we have already discussed, it is already happening at lower levels with smart equipment that is self-servicing to a large extent. And it does not have to be between organisations, it could be entirely internal, so that many internal, customer-supplier type relationships will be automated.

So, in future, the emphasis for business and for those who will be employed will be much more on providing customer service, sorting out problems, new business and specialist services. The routine will continue to be increasingly automated.

From the 1960s into the 1980s, we have seen a substantial decline in the number of unskilled and semi-skilled manual jobs as automation took over. That continues to erode the need for even skilled manual workers. White-collar staff were relatively largely unaffected.

But that has changed in the last ten years. Unskilled and semi-skilled office jobs are being automated and there are signs that many traditional skilled jobs are also feeling the impact of new technology. That seems set to continue and possibly accelerate over the next few years.

But it is not all doom and gloom. New opportunities are being created and new roles developed which will tend to involve personal contact with customers or be based on exploiting information through the Virtual Value Chain.

GLOSSARY

Application software The program or collection of programs that do the work for the user, rather than for the management of the computer (utilities, operating systems, programming tools, etc). These typically include: word-processing, spreadsheets, accounts software, databases. But also included are more specialist applications for statistics, engineering, manufacturing – in fact for any profession or purpose that a user may have.

Back-up A copy of data and computer configuration, so that in the event of equipment or program failure the computer system can be recovered back to a known recent state. Most busy computers should be backed-up every night, or when major changes are to be made to data, programs or hardware.

On all but the smallest computers, back-up copies will usually be made on some form of tape for cost and capacity reasons. However, there is an increasing tendency towards the use of removable hard disks for speed and the various optical disk media such as WORM and the more recent rewriteable models.

Only on the smallest computers is it practical to make back-up copies to floppy disk. With recent advances in hard-disk capacity – disks with 1Gbyte (more than 1,000 million characters) are commonplace – it is now impractical in time and disks. The 1Gbyte example would need someone to sit and feed in more than 700 floppy disks (about 40 hours' work)!

Bundled software Software that is included with other products, usually hardware products, although sometimes software will have other software products included in the same 'bundle'. For example, many personal computers come with 'bundled' software to get the user started – often these are office automation suites that include word-processing, spreadsheets, presentation graphics and a database.

Business process engineering (BPR) A fundamental redesign of how a business works. It is not about improvement but transformation. The term was coined by Michael Hammer.

CD-ROM Compact disk – read only memory. Similar to the audio CD, but containing data that can be read but not written to or updated.

CISC Complex instruction set computer. Many computers such as the IBM PC and its derivatives have used CISC, that is, microprocessors (chips) that have powerful instructions, each of which can initiate a lot of processing. In the days when programmers worked at low level, CISC made it easier to write programs.

Componentware As software needs to increasingly work together, there is a new type of software which is not a complete application in itself, but forms part of applications. For example, word-processors originally came without spell-checkers so add-in software was written to do the job. Then they were incorporated into the word-processor where they fitted better. But then along came spreadsheets, databases, desktop publishing programs, etc. which also had spell-checkers built in. So more recently there has been a move back to using separate, more capable, components which are used by several applications.

But the thinking goes further so that now a word-processing program, a complete application in itself, becomes a component of an accounting application for producing standard letters.

So componentware is software designed to work as part of another application.

CompuServe A provider of on-line services, perhaps the longest established of the major players.

DAT Digital audio tape. A small, high-capacity tape that stores its data digitally (i.e, as discrete values) rather than as a continually varying analogue signal.

It is commonly used as a high-capacity storage medium for backup purposes.

Data warehouse Is where a copy (usually) of the (essentially numeric) corporate data is held in a specialised database to allow complex analysis and cross-tabulation of data to support planning and monitoring.

Decision support systems Early attempts at providing information to support the decision-making process.

EIS or executive information system A development of the earlier **decision support systems** but particularly aimed at high-level strategic planning. Now most EIS products at least pay lip-service to **OLAP** and data warehousing.

Ethernet A standard for network infrastructure that can be run across most cabling standards including optical fibre, twisted pair, co-axial cable and thin coaxial (Cheapernet). These transfer data at speeds between 10 and 100Mbps (Megabits per second and 1000 Mbps ones are appearing).

ETLA Enhanced three-letter acronym – see **TLA**. The IT industry has been so fond of TLAs that it is running out of letter combinations, and so is having to upgrade to four letters.

Facilities Management Where an external body manages a facility, say a computer centre, on behalf of a organisation. The idea is that the third-party is a specialist and has economies of scale not available to the client, hence will be more cost-effective. Experience is mixed at best.

Field upgradeable 'Field upgradeable' simply means that an engineer can come on-site and upgrade the machine to a higher specification, without it having to be replaced or taken back to the workshop.

FUD Fear, uncertainty and doubt. Something salesmen and suppliers the world over have sought to instil in potential customers' minds about the choice they have just made or the product or supplier they are proposing to use. A negative approach to sales, but so rife in the IT industry it acquired its own acronym!

GUI Graphic user interface. These include *Windows* on personal computers or *X/Windows* or *Motif* on Unix-based computers.

IM or information management This is explained more fully in Chapter 1. It is the use and management of the information and knowledge resource of an organisation.

Information Superhighway The links between organisations that provide information services, individuals and business and other organisations. It is worldwide and provides access to more knowledge and information than most can handle.

Often it is still more of a country lane than a motorway, let alone a superhighway. At best it is a congested trunk road.

It is much hyped: as an idea has much to commend it, but like many roads it is attracting traffic faster than capacity can be built. As a result, there is growing disillusionment amongst early adopters.

Internet The basis of the Information Superhighway. It is not owned by any organisation, rather it is a huge number of inter-connected computers. It is essentially egalitarian, and as a result somewhat anarchic, but it has seen phenomenal growth in the last few years.

Internet provider Organisations that are set up to provide access to the Internet and form part of that network of separately operated computers.

Intranet An Internet-like network for use internally within an organisation normally supporting Web pages.

IS or information systems The hardware, software and manual processing used to convert data into information.

IT or information technology The technology used to support **IS, IM** and communications. It is part computing, part telephony and part almost anything else from a pencil and paper upwards.

Legacy systems Existing application programs that have been in use for a long time. Many organisations that have been computerised for many years continue to run very old programs. These often do not use the latest technology, but because of the wealth of experience and expertise built into the systems, they are difficult and expensive to replace. Eventually the time comes when they have to be.

Middleware Much the same as componentware but usually providing a link to specialist facilities such as hardware or database management for writers of applications. It saves them considerable development time.

MIS or management information system Much the same as executive information or decision support systems but tend to be associated with legacy systems.

Modem Used to convert digital data that a computer can convert into a form that can be sent across a telephone line and back again. One is used at each end of a computer-to-computer link across the telephone network. Used to access the Internet and other remote computers.

Multimedia Software that uses sound, video, text, graphics and so on in combination to provide new ways of presenting information and interacting with it.

Netbrowser A software program that allows a user to access the Internet and particularly the World Wide Web.

Netware Novell's network operating system. One of the leading systems for networking personal computers.

Network computer The Network Computer (NC) is being promoted by some as the successor to the personal computer. It is based on the premise that most personal computers are linked to networks or central computers and therefore do not need their own local disk storage, etc. The argument is that such personal computers are more expensive than is needed in a corporate environment as they are more highly specified than is strictly necessary and require more specialist support. The NC on the other hand, it is claimed, will be cheaper both to buy and to support. However there is considerable debate about the strength of the argument for the Network Computer. It will be interesting to see whether users will give up their local autonomy – the NC is dependent on the availability of the network and/or central computer.

Off-line reader or OLR Used to quickly download items of interest from an on-line service and allow them to be read and replies composed without being connected to the telephone system (off-line). This reduces costs compared with doing it all on-line.

OLAP On-line analytical processing. The rules for designing and using a data warehouse.

Operating system The program that manages the hardware and isolates the user from it. The best-known operating system is MS-DOS: this was used on most personal computers until *Windows 95* came along and, by incorporating MS-DOS functionality, became an operating system in its own right (rather than simply a **GUI** that used an operating system).

Optical disk A form of disk that reads and writes its data using an optical system and laser (similar to CD), but which is re-writeable. Data can be erased and rewritten many times. Traditionally, disks have used and continue to use magnetic storage.

Outsourcing Similar to facilities management. Using an outside agency to provide services previously provided in-house.

Packages Standard computer software that can usually be slightly personalised for individual companies. Can be any application such as accounting, word processing, graphics or whatever. If you can think of it, someone has probably written some form of package for a similar set of functions.

PCMCIA or PC Card A credit-card sized peripheral for computers. It can be used to increase memory, or to provide network links for modems or any other add-on that may be required. Usually used on portable computers.

Proprietary Specific to a particular manufacturer. For instance, an operating system that will only run on that manufacturer's equipment is said to be proprietary, as opposed to the more open operating system *Unix* which is available for many different manufacturers' computers.

Prototyping An approach to developing software. A quick and dirty version is written that looks something like the required solution (but without all the functionality), which is then revised with the end-user until the needs are clear. It is then rewritten properly for production use and the protype discarded.

RAM Random access memory. This is the memory that the computer uses while it is processing data. It is usually volatile in that it loses its contents when the power is removed.

Rapid application development – RAD A step on from prototyping that uses the protype as the final solution after further refinement. It relies on a tool that can quickly produce a prototype, but which is also a powerful development tool. Traditionally, the two did not exist in the same product – hence the throwaway prototype.

RDBMS Relational database management system.

Relational database Most data storage systems are now based on relational databases which allow different views of the same data to be created for different purposes. They usually use **SQL** for data manipulation.

RISC Reduced Instruction Set Computer. See **CISC**. These processors are optimised to handle a few basic instructions very efficiently. The more complex functions used by a CISC are built up from many of these small, fast operations. There is some evidence that this produces an overall faster solution.

It is practical now that most programming is in languages that are not tied to a particular computer: a program (compiler) converts the high-level instructions into the many more instructions specific to the target computer.

ROM Read only memory. **ROM** is memory that cannot be over-written (except sometimes with special equipment) and usually retains its contents when power is removed. ROM tends to be used to store hardware-specific programs and data for use by operating systems and application programs. It is then used when the computer is switched on to load the main operating system.

Software house An organisation that specialises in writing software.

SQL Structured query language. The language used by many database management systems to write queries and to manipulate the data held in them.

SQL server See **RDBMS**.

SSADM Structured systems analysis and design method.

System software The operating systems, database management systems programming languages that support the hardware and the application software.

Systems integrator An organisation that pulls together the hardware, software and other elements required to fulfil a business need for customers.

Systems house Much the same as a **systems integrator**, but more of a software house element.

TLA Three-letter acronym. The IT industry is fond of acronyms: ROM, RAM, CPU, etc. It is a useful shorthand, but it has got to the stage that the same TLA can mean different things to different people depending on their particular specialisms within the IT field.

Unix A popular operating system for powerful workstations used for computer-aided design and other applications with heavy processing requirements. But it is better-known as a non-proprietary operating system for multi-user computers.

Utilities All the programs used for managing a computer system. They vary from those that check for viruses to programs that do complex reconfiguring of disk space to make it more efficient in use.

Vapourware IT products are often announced at an early stage of development or even at concept stage. They are often delivered late or even not at all. Products that are announced, but not available or even demonstrable are frequently referred to as 'Vapourware'. They are even more ethereal than software!

Virus A program that can replicate itself and do damage to the data on a computer. Can be transmitted on floppy disks or by downloading programs from networks. Good policies, strictly enforced and the use of virus checking utilities can practically eliminate the problem. Any utility has to be regularly updated as new viruses are being written all the time.

Windows NT A GUI operating system from Microsoft available on a range of computers. It can also be used for network file-servers – shared data storage.

Windows The leading graphical user interface for personal computers from Microsoft. Most personal computer applications now need a version of *Windows* to run.

World Wide Web or WWW The fastest-growing part of the Internet and increasingly being used on internal networks for sharing and publishing information. Many Web pages are multimedia, although the disadvantage is that they then become slow to download.

WORM disk Write-once, read-many disks are similar to CD-ROM: they can be written to once, but the data cannot be over-written. They can be read as often as necessary. Paper and pen is a better-known example of WORM storage.

X-Windows A Unix-based **GUI**.

SOME TECHNOLOGY ISSUES

Information management is not a technology issue, although there are many opportunities to exploit information technology. Most organisations are not making full use of the technology they already have. Simply adding more of the latest technology will do nothing for the performance of the business.

However if the business needs are fully understood, and the requirements for information support are recognised, then an appreciation of the technology will be useful. But – and it is a big but – technology should not lead the thinking. The question is not, 'How do we use this technology?', rather, 'Does any of this technology make our information system requirements easier or cheaper to achieve?'

Technology is not the answer. It might be the means if the role of information is fully understood in the context of your organisation's strategy.

Information Superhighway

Much hyped and far from being a superhighway. At best it is a busy trunk road, and often it is like the M25, slow and congested. So far, it consists of established on-line service providers such as CompuServe or Profile and the Internet, most particularly in the form of Usenet and the World Wide Web.

Some of the established providers such as Profile simply provide chargeable access to specialist databases in all manner of fields: finance and company data, materials science and Press reports as examples.

CompuServe and Usenet provide discussion groups of one sort or another. But there is a major difference between them. The Usenet news groups are largely a free-for-all, which means that the useful information is often buried in a huge volume of trivia and junk E-mail.

CompuServe and other forums and some Usenet groups are moderated – that is, they are managed by a sysop (system operator) who prevents abusive messages, advertising and anything else that is outside the rules. This makes them much more useful as the discussion is more focused, but there is still a lot of chit-chat. They can be very useful – for example, I now get most of my technical support and advice through appropriate CompuServe forums. I often post a message in the evening, and have a response by the following morning from the US or points west.

From that point of view, there is access to a lot of useful information if you know where to look. It is possible to establish business contacts in this way. I have received commissions for a couple of magazine articles and a book from contacts made on CompuServe. They will pay for my on-line usage for about five years! Bigger business has been done, and I am sure I will get more opportunities in this way.

All the services provide E-mail, which is a way of sending private messages and files directly to another correspondent. It is fast and effective, and I find I am using it more and more. There are caveats about security, and particularly with regard to sending credit card details on the Internet. There are moves afoot to make it safe to send payment via the net, but standards are not yet established.

The World Wide Web is a means of publishing and linking documents, and was originally established for researchers to do just that. It has now become rather more glossy, with more and more organisations having a presence. Much of it is essentially advertising, although it is often backed up by access to services such as brochures or software updates and the like.

As web pages get more glossy, with graphics, sound and video, they are becoming slow to download using normal dial-up services. It is not unusual to wait ten minutes or more for a glossier page to be fully downloaded. And that is all connect time – it is possible to pick up a lot of telephone call charges using the WWW.

It is not expensive to get on to the Information Superhighway, and it need not be too expensive to use if you are sensible and do not spend a lot of time just 'surfing' or browsing. I use an off-line reader which dials in, sends my outgoing messages, picks up the messages from the areas that interest me and then disconnects. It is usually less than two minutes. I then read the messages without being connected, prepare my replies which are uploaded when I next dial in. I usually go in twice a day – once first thing, and again late afternoon or early evening.

Multimedia

Multimedia was the fashionable thing before the Internet took off. Basically it is the merger of traditional computing with publishing, graphics, sound and video. It has also become part of many applications and is not a facility in its own right. Rather it is a set of tools for publishing or presenting information in new ways.

Most of the cover disks on computer magazines contain some element of multimedia. The other main uses are in publishing and training, although small elements are creeping into mainstream applications. Many traditional encyclopedia publishers have produced multimedia versions on

CD-ROM of their printed titles. And more reference works are appearing in this form, although it would seem that they are not turning out to be the goldmine that many expected.

So far it has nearly all been on CD-ROM, as it has the storage capacity and is now fast enough (on a fast computer) to support video at normal speeds (25 frames per second). Most other media including external network access is too slow for this purpose.

Client-server

When computer terminals were first introduced, they were all connected to an organisation's central multi-user computer. This remained the standard set-up until the arrival of the personal computer.

The personal computer put computer power on the desktop, but it was originally used for personal purposes, as its name implies. As they grew in sophistication and power, more and more functions were moved to the user's PC. Eventually they were linked together into networks, usually with shared data storage on a central fileserver. These local area networks have developed into complete enterprise-wide systems and often replaced the central computer.

Even where the central computer has been retained, that desktop personal computer has been utilised to handle some of the processing for applications. This is client-server: the personal computer is the client and the central computer or fileserver is the server. On a multi-user computer, all the processing traditionally took place at the centre, whilst on a network, all but the data access took place at the desktop.

Now the two approaches are merging and often run in parallel. As fileservers have become more powerful, they have become more than data stores, and have become data search machines. Instead of all the data being processed at a PC with client-server, only the result of the processing is passed to the PC, the fileserver does the rest. So more and more of the processing is being moved back to the central processing computer.

Conversely on a multi-user machine, the increased power of the PC has allowed that to take over much of the display processing and the data validation. An increasing amount of the business rules processing has been moved to the desktop from the centre.

Client-server gives greater flexibility as to where data is held and where processing power is needed. From the user's point of view, it should look little different, hopefully it will be faster or more reliable. There are essentially three processing elements:

- **data management** – searching and storage of the data;
- **business rules** – the application-specific processing;

- **presentation processing** – this is the presentation of data recovered from the centre or input by the user. It also includes validation-of-user input.

Thick clients do much of the processing at the desktop usually handling the business rules and the presentation. In a *thin* client, most of the processing is done centrally, usually just using the personal computer to handle the presentation functions.

Relational databases

Most client-server systems, and many other applications, are built around database management systems which take care of storing the applications data in a way that is efficient and in a form in which it can be recovered quickly.

There have been many approaches, but there is a strong trend to the relational database model. When first mooted, only the largest computers had the power to support the necessary processing.

These tables require the data to be broken down to a lower level than that usually required by the user. This reduces the need for duplication of data or wasted space, but it means that the data has to be reassembled to give views that are appropriate to the user. Hence the processing burden in the early days meant only the most powerful computer could use it. Technology and database techniques have moved on to make it generally viable. The other big advantage is that because the view the user sees is built from a collection of elements, different views can be created for different users or purposes.

It is this last flexibility that makes relational databases so useful. Coupled with the use of Structured Query Language (SQL), it has made it possible to separate the database from the application. So most application software that uses a relational database can usually use most of the common database management software from any of the main vendors. It does not tie the user in to a particular supplier in the way the old database management systems did.

Middleware and componentware

This separation of tasks into generic tools has created a new class of software often dubbed 'middleware' or 'componentware'. The two terms are all but interchangeable, but 'middleware' is usually applied to those parts that can be regarded as extensions of the operating system, such as database management systems. On the other hand, 'componentware' tends to be used for application elements such as spell-checkers. But the distinction can get blurred as different people use the terms in different ways.

In the past, if you were writing an application package such as an accounts system or a word-processor, you had to write it all and build it into one complete system. You had to write code that interfaced with the operating system at a low level, and was therefore highly specific to particular configurations. This made it difficult to convert it to other computers.

Also in recent years many applications have been getting bigger and bigger as more capability is built into them. Early word-processors would run from a floppy disk of less than 1Mbyte – now it is not unusual for a word-processor to occupy 30Mbyte of disk space. And this has happened for most applications. Yet much of that space is common functions, for example, more and more applications have their own spell-checker built in. So each user may have a spell-checker in their word-processor, spreadsheet, presentation graphics software, desktop publishing, even their database system and their E-mail programs.

The componentware approach recognises the problem, so that the spell-checker is written as a component that can be shared by each application – hence consistent dictionaries, no duplication, etc. But complete applications can be components.

Many applications such as accounts systems had their own usually fairly simple word-processor, built in to allow the production of standard letters using the names and addresses held in the customer and supplier accounts. Now it is not necessary, as it is possible to use your favoured word-processor as a component of your accounts system. And you can add more capability by adding your spreadsheet or E-mail or whatever as a component.

Middleware is slightly different. As its name implies, it sits in the middle and has separate applications from generic support elements, such as database managers. It may sit between the accounting package, say, and its data. This separation allows the data to be shared more readily with other applications. So instead of building a word-processor component into the accounts system, the word-processor reads the accounts data directly through a middleware element.

These techniques allow tailored information systems to be built from a collection of components that may be complete in themselves. In combination, they can be much more powerful. It is these kinds of techniques that make the Corporate Information System (see Chapter 12) possible.

Object orientation

But the idea of working with components goes much deeper, and is increasingly used as means of building applications from scratch. Very little programming of one-off systems is done by writing a lot of program instructions. It is much more likely to be built up by assembling built-up elements – a bit like using Lego or Meccano.

This allows much quicker software development, and hence the interest in Rapid Application Development (RAD) techniques. This enables a prototype to be quickly built and then refined. Unlike the older prototyping approach, the prototype is not thrown away, it becomes refined into the final product.

This has only been made possible by the use of object-oriented techniques. And it is now possible to buy libraries of objects for use in the various development tools. You need a charting facility, drop a charting object into the application, set a few parameters and the facility is there. As with most of the object-oriented development tools, it takes almost as long to describe as to do.

It must be noted that these techniques speed up the program writing stage. They need good design, especially of the data, and testing has to be as thorough as before. So the overall savings are not as great as might be imagined. But because the objects are prewritten and used widely, they get more testing and should prove more reliable, so the maintenance element due to 'bugs' may be reduced.

The object approach is being taken wider, and will be used in data structures and other aspects of an application. It will create new ways of doing things as the relatively young technology develops.

Data warehousing

Much is being made of data warehousing as a means of using information more effectively within an organisation. At its simplest it is not much more than a traditional management information system working on a separate set of data from the operational systems.

In its most powerful incarnation it uses specialised database systems optimised for the complex data structures needed. It allows a user to dig down ('drill down') into the detail and ask 'what-if' type questions. Many go further and have automated analysis tools that will identify patterns and relationships. This is usually called 'data mining' and can give useful insights into what is happening. It should be noted that even though the analysis might be automated the interpretation of the results must still use the human brain and people's knowledge.

Creating and maintaining such systems needs a good understanding of data, data analysis and information management and their role within the organisation. It is not a panacea or quick fix – data warehousing needs a good understanding of the data available to load into the warehouse and careful planning and design if it is to be fully effective.

Open systems

Open systems are those systems that are not tied to a particular manufacturer's systems. So OS/400 is a proprietary operating system that only runs on IBM computers (and then only one range). Unix is available to run on many manufacturers' computers including as an alternative to proprietary systems. It is usually applied to operating systems but applies to many other aspects.

It gives the customer flexibility and avoids being 'locked-in' to a particular supplier.

Open systems' products are not usually in the public domain and may be the product of particular suppliers. For Unix there are standards so that software that will run on one supplier's system will run on another that complies with the same standards.

It is not perfect but many of these trends are a step in the right direction. There is still a long way to go. But it will continue as inter-operability and inter-changeability grow in importance as we build more complex systems.

EXAMPLE, SPECIFICATION AND INVITATION TO TENDER

INTRODUCTION

This is an example of a typical invitation and supporting specification – it is based on a real project, but modified slightly to address a wider range of issues. The invitation to tender documents are fairly standard, but would need to be more extensive for a public sector procurement under EU/GATT regulations.

The specification in this case was deliberately high-level, because the requirement was basically simple, and the invited suppliers were all offering standard packages. It is also lighter in that the chosen software was to be made available for a trial implementation. But it covers the main points and gives a feel for what is required. Most specifications would be more substantial, perhaps less specific in some areas but with more explicit essential requirements and measurable targets.

INVITATION TO TENDER – LETTER

1 October 1996

Invited Bidder Co.

Dear . . .

Invitation to Bid: Information Systems Provision for Business Support

Attached is the specification against which we would like you to bid. You have confirmed your interest in submitting a proposal for this work, and we are happy to ask you to do so. If, for any reason, you are unable to submit a proposal, I would be grateful if you would let us know as soon as possible.

Please note that the deadline for receipt of proposals is 12 noon on Wednesday. . . (approximately three weeks hence). Please ensure that your proposal is sent in the enclosed package with no external marks that might identify the sender. These rules will be strictly enforced.

All questions relating to the specification and the bidding process should be through Jill Bloggs who is the project manager for this work. She will be available most days, but will ensure that she is available all day each Tuesday between now and the closing date.

I thank you for your interest and look forward to receiving your proposal.

Yours sincerely

M P Wilson

Director

INVITATION TO TENDER DOCUMENT

Introduction

Test Organisation plc reserves the right to not necessarily select the cheapest proposal or indeed any at all. No reason may be given.

Process

1. Proposals
2. Evaluation
3. Shortlist for presentations
4. Presentations
5. Evaluation or presentations
6. Final selection
7. Negotiation with selected supplier
8. Contract
9. Implementation

Timetable

Required format

Equal opportunities and other issues

1. Employment
2. Disabilities
3. Collusion

Rules

1. Packaging

SPECIFICATION

Introduction

Background

History

- The Test Organisation plc (TOP) had developed an information resource (Topline) for its members, clients and staff. This includes a database of all UK employers and is maintained by Third Party Marketing – a specialist information provider. Topline is written in DataEase.

- As part of its BS5750 accreditation TOP also developed procedures which included some information recorded on the Topline database and paper based reporting and filing managed through the Topline section.

- The systems were not operating as effectively as required and a review of the problems and the options for resolution was undertaken in conjunction with Solidus Limited, a firm of management consultants. It was found that:
  - Topline database was far too slow to be used as intended.
  - Paper-based systems were not being operated as envisaged, because of other pressures and the benefits to advisors, etc., were limited.
  - There were limited facilities for reporting or extracting data from the Topline databases or for analysis.
  - There was insufficient integration between various parts of the data with resulting problems for data quality and ease of use.
  - Lack of information meant that several TOP representatives could be visiting the same client without any cross-reference – this was felt to give a less professional image than TOP desired.

- As a result of these and other difficulties, the credibility of the systems declined and hence the procedures were not operated as intended.

- The resulting recommendation was to re-implement Topline and link the other sub-systems to a common UK employer database. At the same time visit reports and contracts were to be recorded on the system directly by advisers and their managers who were to have direct access to the system, so that they could be better informed about all business support activities with a client before visiting.

- This document provides a high-level specification and explanation of the proposed business support system. It sets out the key requirements in sufficient detail to allow the new system to be priced and implemented.

Information strategy

- *Hardware*

  Test Organisation plc has an IT strategy based around networked personal computers. The following specification takes that into consideration.

- *Software*

  The IT strategy requires that data should be accessible from mainstream products such as FoxPro. This requires that data should be held in an ODBC compliant database files or can be exported in a form acceptable to FoxPro.

- Other applications in common use include . . .

Future developments

- *Strategic alliances*
  - TOP and partners have put forward plans to the group board to create a separate training company. Presentation of the case is scheduled for January 199X. If the application is successful the training company plans to move ahead with its own IS/IT strategy as quickly as possible. A formal business plan will need to be presented in the Spring of 199X for approval by the group board which will need to incorporate detailed plans and costing for the IT infrastructure.
  - However it is intended that systems implementation will start early in 199X, and the key client and contact management system will be fully operational across all locations by the end of 199X. Generous contingency should be allowed because of the complexity of the technical and political issues around agreeing the systems approach across such a diverse group.
  - It would appear that the current thinking is to use PC-based systems linked by networks (both local and wide area). The applications software will run under *Windows*, and will use mainstream file systems such as *Oracle* or other SQL databases. The hardware proposed for business support is mainstream and will be reusable for the eventual training company system.
  - The proposed business support system reflects the proposed training company IS/IT strategy (as far as is currently known) and will use a similar approach. It is felt by the training company project manager that whilst they may use the data from the business support system it is likely, for a variety of reasons, to use different application software. This has been borne in mind in the proposed solution – the data will be readily available to the training company if it should require it.

- *Wider integration within TOP*
  - The initial system will be to provide client and contact management for business support. There are already other systems in use for finance and budgets, etc., which are accessed by the business support group, and it is envisaged that such information will be made available through the business support system in the future, in particular the ability to interrogate and report on data from other systems.
  - Similarly, there are other groups who may benefit from using the business support system to record their contacts. If the system is implemented more widely, this will enable all TOP consultants to be aware of TOP involvement with clients. This can only raise the professional image of Test Organisation plc.
  - There are many other data and information sources provided by third parties or generated internally. Where possible, it is envisaged that access to these will be provided through the business support system to give a consistent 'look and feel' for users.
  - These enhancements are not included in the initial project but should be considered in the design and choice of software tools.

Other considerations

Flexibility has been a key consideration in designing the business support system for TOP. Whilst it is clear what is required at this stage, there are external factors which may change the needs of the systems.

- *Political environment and changing role*
  - The environment in which TOP operates is heavily influenced by national and local government. This means that the future of TOP and its services are at the mercy of changing political priorities. A change of national government at the next election could have a significant impact on the scale and nature of the services provided by TOP.
  - Similarly, the success, or otherwise, of the training company will change the way in which TOP operates. The system would have to change to meet those new challenges.
  - The system, as detailed here, is intended to be the start of an evolutionary development with all the above considered. Although there is an overall vision, it is not 'set in stone', so that changing requirements can be accommodated as the business support system grows. It will meet tomorrow's needs, not yesterday's.

Information services section

General considerations

There are several problems with the existing Topline system that this specification seeks to address:

- *Speed of processing*
  The existing system is effectively unusable because of slow processing – it can take several minutes to find a single client. This is due to a combination of reasons including the software used, the data structures and the amount of traffic on the network. This results in the system only being partially used.

  Requirement: Response time to a company enquiry under normal load to be less than 5 seconds. Under heavy load from 25 users, it should not fall below 15 seconds on the recommended hardware configuration.

- *Lack of flexibility*
  The existing system has limited reporting facilities and requires the information department to produce ad-hoc reports. Because of other demands on their time such requests often take too long, which means that Topline and business support staff re-key data or analyse it manually. This is expensive in terms of time, and has an impact on the quality of data; re-keying generates errors and people use out-of-date information rather than re-key.

  Requirement: There should be integrated facilities for users to define their own reports and enquiries.

- *Duplication of data*
  Because of the way the data is currently structured, changes to data in one area, say, members, is not reflected in another, such as clients. This results in discrepancies. There should be a single master copy of the company data in particular that should be shared across all sub-systems; members, clients and eventually approved suppliers, etc.

  Requirement: There should be **NO** duplicated data entry. All data should need to be entered only once.

- *Proposed structure*
  As a result, the new business support system will be integral with a new Topline, thereby giving all users immediate access to the information held in Topline at the PC on their desk. It will also ensure that there is a single master copy for the core company and client data.

  Requirement: There should be single shared company and contact databases shared by all sub-systems.

- *Appropriate tools*
  It is proposed to re-implement Topline using a product designed for professional development rather than end-user development. However it should be supported by tools suitable for user definition of their own reporting and enquiry needs. This should result in:

- A more robust application
- A more powerful application
- Higher performance
- Greater flexibility in how and where the system is implemented
- Better facilities for end-user enquiry and reporting
- Less burden on the IT department

Main UK organisations database

- *Data requirements:*
  - Organisation name
  - Address and post code
  - Telephone number
  - FAX number
  - E-mail address
  - Local authority district
  - SIC code
  - Membership indicator
  - Director names
  - No: employees, male or female, full- or part-time
  - Turnover
  - Unique identifier – used for verification by Third Party Marketing
  - Description of business
  - Comment/notes
  - Maintenance and other internal system data

- *Processing – need the ability to:*
  - Load updates from Third Party Marketing
  - Amend employer record locally. Also require facility to confirm or undo change (changes to key data will be checked with Third Party Marketing)
  - Add narrative and comment

- *Reports*
  Client list optionally selected by various parameters such as: post code, local authority, SIC code, number of employees, etc. Ability to create extract file for word-processing mail merge.

Members

- *Data requirements*
  Employer record plus:
  - Date of original application
  - Date last renewed
  - Introduced by name
  - Member's name
  - Member's position
  - Note

- Payment history:
- Date of action
- Amount required
- Amount received
- Date received
- Date of certificate
- Certificate number
- Comment

- *Processing – ability to:*
  - Create
  - Amend
  - Enter renewals
  - Ability to create records for new members not on UK employers database. Subject to confirmation through Topline section and Third Party Marketing

- *Reports:*
  - Membership list selectable by various parameters
  - Members due for renewal, plus extract file for mail merge
  - New and renewed members needing certificate plus extract file for labels and acceptance letter
  - Members overdue plus extract file for mail merge letters

Clients

- *Data requirements*
  Employer details plus:
  - Case number
  - Creation date
  - Enquiry only indicator
  - Contact name
  - Business type (very broad, e.g. engineering)
  - Enquiry details
  - Enquiry date
  - Appointment date
  - Appointment time
  - Venue (client or TOP)
  - Publicity code
  - Counsellor or advisor
  - Enquiry code
  - Enquiry notes

- *Processing:*
  - Create client details
  - Amend client details
  - Create enquiry details

- – Amend enquiry details
- – Create new UK employer record if required for confirmation and/or completion by Topline section or Third Party Marketing

- *Reports:*
  - – Appointment list, full or by counsellor/adviser
  - – Extract file for appointment confirmation letter
  - – New client file labels

Salesmen and consultants

- *Data requirements:*
  - – Code (probably initials)
  - – Name
    - Surname
    - Initials
    - Title
    - Salutation
  - – Address and post code
  - – Telephone number – work
  - – Telephone number – home
  - – Telephone number – mobile
  - – Fax number – work
  - – Fax number – home
  - – E-mail address

- *Processing:*
  - – create
  - – amend
  - – mark for deletion (can be deleted only if no visit reports)

- *Reports:*
  - – List details
  - – Extract file for mail merge
  - – Appointment list
  - – Visits by salesman/consultant, summary or detail.

Other reference data

- Data will be needed for reference and validation purposes and will include:
  - – SIC codes
  - – Visit types, e.g., telephone, visit, letter
  - – Services and products, e.g., IT reviews, marketing reviews, training videos, etc.
  - – Accreditation/commitment codes, e.g., ISO9000, IIP, BS 7750 etc.
  - – Enquiry codes
  - – Local authority districts
  - – Other agencies

- *Processing:*
  - Create
  - Amend
  - Delete – where not referenced; otherwise mark, as not allowed

- *Reports:*
  - List (by range if necessary)

Business partners
- *Data requirements*

The data requirements for the business partners list will start with the same details as the employer database. In addition at company level it will require:
  - Performance status (typically, Excellent, Good, Satisfactory, Poor)
  - Approval level (viz.: Provisional, Full, Unsatisfactory)
  - Date approval level applied
  - List of other approvals/accreditation, etc.
  - Membership status and date renewed will be required if the business partners system is not linked to the Topline employers database

For each partner, there will need to be a list of associates/consultants with the following details:
  - Name and personal details
  - Performance status (as for suppliers (1) above)
  - Approval level (as for suppliers (2) above)
  - Principal contact marker
  - List of capabilities (against TOP code table)
  - List of professional memberships (ACA, etc.)

For each associate, there will be a project history covering, at least, the previous 12 months which will need to hold the following information:
  - Date of project
  - Description of work
  - Performance assessment – indicators:
      Quality of work
      Timeliness
      Co-operation with client/TOP
  - Adherence to specification/terms of reference
  - Overall performance status
  - Assessor's initials (link to consultants)

Performance assessment indicators will use the same codes as for performance status for both suppliers and associates as above, i.e., E, G, S, P.

There will also need to be a table of codes for capability (defined by TOP) for validation purposes, and this will consist of:

- Capability code (structured to allow appropriate grouping)
- Standard capability description
- SIC-code (optional), where expertise is tied to an industry sector

- Processing and reporting will be similar to that for members. If the approved supplier system is integrated with Topline, then the main company details will be maintained through the facilities already described for UK employers. There will need to be the ability to add and maintain supplier companies who are outside the UK

In the event that the approved supplier system is a stand alone system there will need to be the facility to maintain supplier company details. This will require the ability to:
- create
- amend
- delete where a supplier has not reached full approval and has not undertaken any work through TOP. Where they have undertaken work and reached Full approval, they will remain on the system even if their approval is reduced to Unsatisfactory to prevent their inadvertent use by business consultants and others. The only other situation allowing deletion is if the supplier ceases trading.

All the above processing will be managed by Topline and approved supplier staff only. All other users will have read-only access to the data.

There will need to be several ways in which the data can be searched and subsequently reported either on-screen or via a printed report.

- Search suppliers by short name. The most basic access will be as for other functions and will be through the use of the first few characters of the company name. The system should provide a pick list of all those that meet the requirement (or the pick list should start with such companies, but may continue to the end of the list). There should be the facility to show associates, with their capabilities and performance indicators, who work for the supplier.
- Search associates by short name. What supplier do they work for and what are their capabilities?
- A common enquiry will be: Who (associate) can provide consultancy in a particular field? Therefore there will be the need to search the associates for the appropriate (range of) capability codes (and SIC-code) and show the name, company and performance assessments for both the individual and the company. A supplementary question that will need to be answered is: Have we used them and how often in last year?
- How many times has TOP used the associate or company in the last period (usually the current year)? How well has the individual performed?
- What other accreditation or professional memberships does the associate hold?

- Is the supplier a TOP member?
- It will be necessary to extract all those suppliers who are still only provisionally approved. This will also mean extracting all their associates and their related project histories. This will allow both the individual and the company to be reviewed, and if appropriate have their approval status confirmed or denied.

- *Mail merge.* It is required that the users should have the capability to merge user-selected name and address details into standard letters for sending selected reports to members who are seeking assistance.

Business support management

Event recording
All significant contacts (visit, telephone conversation, letter) with clients must be logged on the new system as the system will replace the existing paper-based visit-report system.

- *Data requirements:*
  - Date of visit
  - Case number
  - Initials of lead TOP representative
  - Initials of lead client representative
  - Type of event
  - Purpose of event
  - Narrative – visit report etc.
  - Action required/outcome
  - Contract Number/outcome reference where known

- By recording activity in this way, it will be possible for a consultant or salesman to view these details before visiting a client or whilst talking to them on the telephone. In the later case, the system must allow the user to switch to the business support system, pull up the client details, and access the history during the initial 15 seconds or so of the conversation. To do this the user will need to use *Windows* for all their main work and the business system will need to be running, logged in, in the background all the time so that the user can switch to it with one or two keystrokes (Alt-tab).

Requirement: Be able to pull up the contact history for company and/or contact in less than 10 seconds under normal load.

- The enquiry process will broadly be (assuming the user already logged on):
  - Enter the case number (if known), client name (short name) or another key (e.g., telephone number)
  - *Display list of clients meeting criteria*
  - Pick required client from displayed list
  - *Display main client details (name, address, etc.)*

- Select other pages of information to view as needed including: event history, contract history, IIP details, membership details, client contact names, other support agencies perhaps
- *Display appropriate pages*
- Print any pages needed
- Enter contact report if necessary; it will be possible for the creator to amend the report for up to seven days from date created – it will then be read only
- Print contact report if needed
- Return to client selection screen

● Consultants will be able to make amendments to UK employer details but these will be held until confirmed through Topline and Third Party Marketing. The unconfirmed data will show as the main record with an indicator that it is unconfirmed; the original data will be available for viewing.

● Then the user will be able to switch back to whatever else they were using on their computer.

● There will be a range of standard reports to include:
- List of contacts, in detail or summary, selected by parameters such as advisor, date or client
- List of clients who have not received a visit in a given period;
- List of amended UK employers and an extract file for third party marketing

Diaries/scheduler
● With few exceptions, there was a general consensus that centralising diaries was not practical immediately. This is particularly true as many salesmen and consultants are freelance or part-time and rarely visit the office.

● However, it is acknowledged that they should be implemented as phase 2. Therefore an integrated diary and resource scheduling system will be required to be part of the proposed solution.

Requirement: The diary system should include the ability to arrange a meeting for teams and to confirm the availability of all people and any rooms or other resources that may be needed. It should be possible to reschedule such a meeting for all participants and resources in one step. It will *not* be acceptable to have to apply the change to, or by, each participant separately.

● As part of providing business support systems it is proposed that individuals continue to maintain their own diaries. They will have access to computerised organisers/schedulers such as Schedule+ which is provided with *Windows*. They will be able to use these if they wish but at this stage it is not intended to integrate these into the main business support system.

Schedules

Requirement: It must be possible to print a schedule in calendar form for each consultant and adviser for use by reception. Or to provide an equally rapid computer access to such information – bear in mind that reception have low specification personal computers as they are very much occasional users.

Sales team

- Appointments for salesmen to visit clients will continue to be made centrally by Topline, and will be recorded on the business support system. After a visit, most salesmen will produce a handwritten visit report which will be filed in the client master file held by Topline. A brief summary will be entered on to the business support system by the Topline staff to make colleagues aware of the visit and its importance. There will be a pointer to the paper-based file.

- If they wish, there is no technical reason why salesmen should not use the system directly and record their visits themselves, printing off a copy for the Topline file. However it is recognised that they spend little time in the office and their opportunities for using the business support system directly are limited.

- The business support system will have facilities to maintain salesmen's details for reporting and interrogation.

Consultants

- Unlike salesmen, business consultants spend more time in the office and have their own desks which gives them more opportunity to use the business support system. The level of computer competency amongst consultants is very varied, from none to extremely able, and as result the system has to accommodate that spread of ability.

- The basic functions, enquiring about client details and recording visits will be a simple as possible – it has been outlined elsewhere. The business support system and associated procedures will encourage consultants to use the system themselves, but recognises that there will be a need for some third-party data management.

- The more sophisticated computer users amongst the business consultants will require extensive enquiry and analysis facilities. Therefore it is proposed to provide a user enquiry and reporting tool that requires no programming and will allow users to:
  - create their own enquiries and allow them to produce reports that are directly usable in spreadsheets or word-processing without having to go through further processing on paper

- analyse the client and contact data in a flexible way; and eventually to link it to other data sources such as the XYZ finance system
- extract reports, charts and data directly into word-processor documents or spreadsheets

- There is also need for additional databases for Investors in People, Special Accounts and no doubt others in the future. The business support system should be able to accommodate these as the need arises, and where appropriate they should be linked to the main Topline database of UK employers. At this stage it only proposed to implement the Investors in People recording as this is a priority area for TOP.

- As with salesmen the system, through Topline, will maintain a list of business consultants.

Outcome recording and analysis

Contracts
- *Data requirements:*
  - Date
  - Adviser/Counsellor
  - Supply type (business line, product)
  - Supplier
  - Cost (to TOP)
  - Contract number
  - Cost code
  - Comment

Whilst it would be ideal if the system could be used to assist consultants in managing their contracts, claims, budgets, etc., there are many timing and other issues that need further investigation before it will be possible. This should be a next step in the evolution of the business support system.

- *Processing:*
  - From initial enquiries, it appears that much of the above information should be available from the existing accounts system. If it is possible to extract the key data from the accounts system into the business support system, then it will save the data having to be entered manually. Investigation will continue, and the final approach determined during development – in any case there will be a way of creating and maintaining the data.
  - Extract file by period for creating questionnaires, mailing labels, etc., via word-processing mail merge.

- *Reports:*
  - List of contracts selected by client, consultant, or other agreed parameters
  - Contracts that have had no follow-up visit within a given period

Other outcomes

- *Data requirements:*
  - As contracts, except replacing contract number with an outcome reference.

- *Processing:*
  - create
  - amend
  - extract file by period for mail merge purposes

- *Reports*
  - As contracts

Analysis

- This will be via user reporting tools and will be under individual control. There will be the ability to transfer an extract into a spreadsheet or other product for further manipulation there.

Management and user reporting

Enquiry and reporting

- Apart from the standard production reports already defined, routinely required management reports will be produced through a user enquiry and reporting tool. This will provide several benefits:
  - Easy modification for new requirements
  - No need for programming skills – all pick and point
  - The view of the data can be made appropriate for individuals or groups
  - Less need to produce paper-based reports – the question can be answered on-line
  - Ability to view the data from different angles
  - It minimises the need to start from scratch for a new requirement, as it can be based on the nearest equivalent
  - A basis for ad-hoc reports and enquiries
  - Creation and maintenance of new reports
  - Linkage to spreadsheets and other tools for more complex analysis
  - High-presentation quality, so that retyping is not needed before presentation in management or board meeting or inclusion in reports

- This approach recognises that management reports need to be flexible, as the same question is rarely asked in exactly the same way twice.

Links to word-processing, spreadsheets, etc.

- There will be the ability in the main system to produce extract files for mail-merge purposes for the more common requirements.

- The proposed enquiry tools should allow tables or charts to be lifted straight across into a *Windows* word-processing package, currently *Word*, as a picture. It can be done in such a way that subsequent changes at source can be reflected automatically in the document or where more appropriate fixed at time of transfer.

- Similar facilities for transferring data and diagrams straight into a Excel should also be available.

Future opportunities

It is anticipated in the design of the system and the choice of tools that data from other sources, the accounts system for example, can be made available to the user through the same route. This would allow linkage between data held in other TOP applications such as finance and activity or client information from the new business support system or Topline.

Information resources

There will be a need for the same workstations to provide users with access to other resources. Apart from basic office automation facilities (WP, spreadsheets, etc.) they will also need access to other information sources; some available in-house, others external.

Although not included in the initial project, these links should be considered and it should be possible (in most cases) to provide access from a single business support system menu.

Internal data

- Approved suppliers
- Budgets and finance

Third-party internal data

- TOP subscribes to several other data sources, many of which are available in computerised form. It is anticipated that future development of the business support system will either add their access programs into its menu or will integrate the data more closely with the business support systems data. In the latter case, the business support system will have to be extended to provide access to this new data source. Current third-party data held and used in-house (sometimes in the form of paper-based directories) include:
  - grants
  - property
  - resources (other agencies, grant-making bodies, sources of expertise, etc.)

External databases

- Some of the consultants use external, usually on-line, databases for a variety of purposes. It is expected that the use of such facilities and access to the others' experience and knowledge will grow – much is currently being made of the 'Information Superhighway'. In fact there are already many (millions, worldwide) people sharing ideas, expertise and knowledge across electronic networks and external databases will no doubt grow in importance for TOP.

- Some of this expertise is available for modest connection costs whilst other data appears relatively expensive until one considers the costs of finding it oneself through other routes (library searches, telephone, etc.).

- *Low-cost on-line sources* (all available through local BT calls to the service provider)
  - CompuServe, through its forums for general expertise, ideas, problem-solving. Worldwide but shows its US origins
  - CIX – as above but a UK service
  - Internet – in its Usenet form
  - and others

- *Commercial data sources*
  - Dun & Bradstreet
  - Profile
  - Pergamon Infoline – includes scientific and technical sources as well as business and financial data
  - CompuServe – better for US business data
  - and many others covering a variety of general and specialist topics such as health and safety, etc.

Security and access control

Security levels

It is anticipated that there will essentially be three levels of security:

- Application manager who will take responsibility for the maintenance of the system at a technical housekeeping level.

- Topline, who will have access to some, limited, additional facilities for the maintenance of UK employer and member databases.

- Other users who will have:
  - full access to the data in the business support system and Topline on at least a read-only basis. This overcomes some people's fear of deleting or damaging data – however facilities will be provided for local amendment
  - an ability to enter changes to UK employers but these will subsequently be confirmed by Topline in conjunction with the data supplier, Third Party Marketing

- an ability to create and maintain their own or team members' visit reports or contracts/outcomes. These will be frozen after a week to prevent inadvertent alteration, etc.
- access to user enquiry tools with the ability to save their own report formats

- In the initial phases it is not anticipated that the business support system will hold any data that is confidential within UK Training and Enterprise Council. However this may change as the system evolves, and it will be possible to accommodate revised access controls to accommodate future needs.

Technical requirements

Hardware
- As already indicated the hardware should be based on, or at least be compatible with, Intel-based PCs running MS-DOS and networked together using Ethernet and Novell Netware.

Software
- It is believed that the task-switching capability of *Windows* will be essential, as will the consistent application interface for occasional and sometimes reluctant users of the business support system. Other products such as OS/2 would also be suitable, but do not have the range of applications available, and so at this stage have been discounted.

- Current applications in use are:

  - *Word* – version 7
  - Excel for spreadsheets
  - FoxPro is being used for internal systems and is replacing DataEase
  - DataEase is used for Topline and some other, limited, purposes but no new development is being made
  - The XYZ accounts package for finance and budget control

- There are other products but they are not used widely within the business support group.

- It will therefore be necessary for the new system to be able to link to the above products, or more probably their *Windows* equivalents, and any other mainstream products that may be introduced in the future.

Performance
- As the system is to be used to support consultants whilst on the telephone, the response time of the system is of paramount importance. It is believed that it must be possible for the user to switch tasks, enter a client key, select client and display their first details screen in around five seconds. This will require users to log on to and

leave the business support system running in the background all the time they are at their desks.

- To maximise performance, it is proposed to move to client-server architecture for many applications. This will also give flexibility where data is held.

Sizing

It will be suppliers' responsibility to determine the specification of the required configuration. They should indicate the basis of their estimate.

TOP have estimated the record counts and anticipated growth for key data as follows:

Data table	Current count	Anticipated count in 3 years
Employers	570,000	920,000
Contacts – employer-related	690,000	1,565,000
Contacts – individual	0	39,000
Communication history	1,100 per month	5,200 per month
. . .		
Number of concurrent users	27	140
. . .		

(The above table is merely an example, and is incomplete. It should be expanded to give as much information as is practical.)

APPENDIX D

REFERENCES AND ADDITIONAL READING

Shorter Oxford Dictionary, Oxford University Press, 1983

R Burns, *To a Mouse*

T Cannon & F J W Taylor, *Management Development to the Millennium, The Cannon and Taylor Working Party Reports*, 1994

L Carroll, *Through the Looking Glass*

J Champy, *Re-engineering Management, The Mandate for New Leadership*, HarperCollins, 1995

M J Cronin (ed), *The Internet Strategy Handbook, Lessons from the New Frontier of Business*, Harvard Business School Press, 1996

G Cutts, *Structured Systems Analysis and Design Methodology*, Paradigm, 1987

N C Daniels, *Information Technology, The Management Challenge*, Economist Intelligence Unit/Addison-Wesley, 1994

T H Davenport, Process Innovation, *Re-engineering Work through Information Technology*, Harvard Business School Press, 1993

M Hammer & J Champy, *Re-engineering the Corporation, A Manifesto for Business Revolution*, Nicholas Brealey, 1993

M Hammer & S A Stanton, *The Re-engineering Revolution, The Handbook*, HarperBusiness, 1995

J Harvey-Jones, *Managing to Survive*, William Heinemann, 1993

D A Mankin, *Teams and Technology, Fulfilling the Promise of the New Organization*, Harvard Business School Press, 1996

J Martin & A R D Norman, *The Computerized Society*, Pelican Books, 1973

B Minto, *The Pyramid Principle, Logic in Writing and Thinking*, FT/Pitman, 1987

National Computing Centre, *Guidelines for Computer Managers*, NCC, 1981

R L Nolan & D C Croson, *Creative Destruction*, Harvard Business School Press, 1995

J S Oakland, *Total Quality Management*, Heinemann, 1989

E Obeng, *The Project Leaders Secret Handbook/All Change!*, FT/Pitman, 1994

PA Consulting Group/CBI Initiative 1992, *Information Technology: The Catalyst for Change*, Mercury/W H Allen, 1990

R Paton et al (ed), *The New Management Reader*, Routledge/The Open University, 1996

M E Porter, *Competitive Strategy, Techniques for Analyzing Industries and Competitors*, The Free Press, 1980

M E Porter, *Competitive Advantage, Creating and Sustaining Superior Advantage*, The Free Press, 1985

J E Rayport & J J Sviola, *Exploiting the Virtual Value Chain*, Harvard Business Review, November–December 1996

D J Silk, *Harnessing Technology to Manage Your International Business*, McGraw-Hill, 1995

A Toffler, *The Third Wave, The Revolution that will Change Our Lives*, Collins, 1980

M Tse-Tung, *Thoughts of Chairman Mao*

M Treacy & F Wiersema, *The Discipline of Market Leaders*, 1995

R Turner et al, *The Project Manager as Change Agent, Leadership, Influence and Negotiation*, McGraw-Hill, 1996

G Walsham, *Interpreting Information Systems in Organizations*, John Wiley, 1993

J Ward et al, *Strategic Planning for Information Systems*, John Wiley 1990

J Watson, *Management Development to the Millennium*, The New Priorities, Institute of Management, 1995

O Wilde, *Lady Windermere's Fan*

M P Wilson, *Getting the Most from Consultants*, Institute of Management/Pitman, 1996

E Yourdon, *When Good Enough is Best*, Byte, September 1996

FORMAL EVALUATION MODEL

Multiple-level weighted option assessment system

I have used this method for evaluating offerings from many suppliers, and found it very flexible and easy to set up and use. It will expand from a simple single-level model for a small project to five or six levels quite happily, and probably beyond. I would recommend using a computer spreadsheet both to develop the model and to score each proposal.

Building the model

First develop a list of the main headings under which you wish to evaluate the proposals (this will probably reflect the structure of the invitation to tender and the required format for proposals). Then spread 100 per cent across them on the basis of their relative importance, for example:

Company	10%
Understanding	15%
Software	20%
Hardware	15%
Support	20%
Timetable	10%
Costs	10%
Total	**100%**

These percentages are the weights or factors that will be applied to the scores for each heading.

The next step is to break each of the headings down into sub-headings, and repeat the exercise at the next level down. For example:

1   Company

    1.1 Attitude   50%

    1.2 Financial stability   30%

    1.3 ...   20%

As before, 100 per cent is spread across all the sub-headings under each heading, in this case 'Company'. The process is repeated for each heading and each level down, until the end of each leg consists of an independent item with no further elements. These final elements are the questions which are scored; all the others are calculated as intermediate values on the way to the overall score.

So we might have:

1 Company (100%)
    1.1 Attitude (50%)
        1.1.1 **Responsiveness** (30%)
        1.1.2 Cultural compatibility (70%)
            1.1.2.1 **Shared values** (25%)
            1.1.2.2 **Compatible with managers** (25%)
            1.1.2.3 **Compatible with staff** (30%)
            1.1.2.4 **Compatible with customers** (20%)
    1.2 **Financial stability** (30%)
    1.3 ... (20%)
        1.3.1 ... (50%)
        1.3.2 ... (50%)
2 Understanding (25%)
etc...

Note that at each level the weights add up to 100% for all the items within a higher category.

Create a score sheet consisting of just the scoreable elements with none of the other factors to cloud the issue. The lowest-level items, the scoreable items are in bold above; they can occur at any level in the model.

Scoring

The actual scoring of each proposal can be handled in two ways.

1. Each member of the assessment scores each proposal on a scoresheet. The scores are then averaged and applied to a final scoresheet which is used for input to the overall model.

2. The panel meet, and for each item to be scored, come to a consensus for the points to be awarded and recorded on the scoresheet. These are then applied to the model.

Scores should be consistent, and I would recommend using a range from 0 = totally unacceptable, no compliance, to 10 = perfect, full or exceptional compliance.

It is important, especially in 2 above, that the scores are only applied to the model after all proposals and all scores have been determined. This will help prevent bias being applied to an instinctively favoured choice. Such bias can not quite be eliminated by this process, but it comes close – I have seen some very surprising results, which turned out to be right, from this formalised approach.

Scoring in the evaluation model works from the bottom up. Each of the lowest level items within a heading are scored by applying the weight to the score awarded. This is then totalled for all the items within the heading to give that score for the heading. This is done for each heading.

As the scoring moves up the model, the input scores and those that have been calculated from a lower level have their weights applied. The new totals are the score for the next heading up. This is repeated until a final single score for the overall model is determined.

	Score	Weighted
Overall		
1 Company (100%)		
1.1 Attitude (50%)	6.94	3.47
1.1.1 Responsiveness (30%)	6	1.8
1.1.2 Cultural compatibility (70%)	7.35	5.145
1.1.2.1 Shared values (25%)	8	2.0
1.1.2.2 with managers (25%)	7	1.75
1.1.2.3 with staff (30%)	8	2.4
1.1.2.4 with customers (20%)	6	1.2
1.2 Financial stability (30%)	9	2.7
1.3 ... (20%)	...	
1.3.1 ... (50%)	...	
1.3.2 ... (50%)	...	
...1.n		
2 Understanding (25%)	...	
etc...		

The scores in bold are entered values from the scoresheet. The other scores are intermediate scores calculated from lower level entries. For instance the score for 1.1 Attitude would be made up of the entered score (6.0) for 1.1.1 Responsiveness multiplied by its weight of 30%, the calculated score for 1.1.2 Cultural compatibility (7.35, being the sum of the weighted scores 1.1.2.1 to 1.1.2.4) times its weight of 70%. In other words:

$$(6 \times 30\%) + (7.35 \times 70\%) = 5.945$$

The score for 1 Company would then be the total of the weighted scores from headings in the next level down, i.e. 1.1 to 1.n. This would be 1.1 Attitude (3.47) plus 1.2 Financial stability (2.7), plus all those to 1.n.

It should be noticed that if the scoring range for each item on the scoresheet is between 0 and 10, then all the calculated heading scores, before their weights are applied, will be in the same range. If they are not, then there is an error in the weights: they will not add up to 100% within a category. The final score, too, will be in the same range.

The best score, then, is the winner. If I use a spreadsheet, I would display scores to only one decimal place at most – there is no need for spurious accuracy. After all, you should be looking for significantly different scores; if the differences in scores are in the decimal places, then either the evaluation model is too crude, or it is possible that both proposals are equally good.

The model takes a little while to set up, but the speed with which it produces a definitive result makes it worthwhile. It is actually easier to do than to describe. I commend it to you.

Other uses

I have also used a variation of this sort of approach for assessing options when working on strategic or business planning projects.

Free offer

If you would like a copy of a (very) basic model for evaluating a proposal, then please send your business card or your business letterhead with a SAE to:

> *Managing with Information* – Disk Offer
> Solidus Limited
> 11 Sandringham Drive
> Beeston
> Nottingham
> NG9 3EA

Please note that this model is unsupported and unwarranted, and is only supplied on that understanding. It is intended simply to provide an example and starting point to allow you to develop your own version. It requires Excel version 5.0 or later.

INDEX